ONE DAY
SMARTER

ONE DAY SMARTER

Hilarious, Random Information to Uplift and Inspire

EMILY WINTER

A TarcherPerigee Book

tarcherperigee
an imprint of Penguin Random House LLC
penguinrandomhouse.com

Most TarcherPerigee books are available at special quantity discounts for bulk
purchase for sales promotions, premiums, fund-raising, and educational needs.
Special books or book excerpts also can be created to fit specific needs. For details,
write: SpecialMarkets@penguinrandomhouse.com.

Library of Congress Cataloging-in-Publication Data

Names: Winter, Emily, author.
Title: One day smarter: hilarious, random information to uplift and inspire / Emily Winter.
Description: [New York]: TarcherPerigee, an imprint of Penguin Random House LLC,
[2021] | Includes bibliographical references.
Identifiers: LCCN 2020057485 (print) | LCCN 2020057486 (ebook) |
ISBN 9780593329771 (paperback) | ISBN 9780593329788 (ebook)
Subjects: LCSH: Curiosities and wonders.
Classification: LCC AG244 .W558 2021 (print) | LCC AG244 (ebook) |
DDC 031.02—dc23
LC record available at https://lccn.loc.gov/2020057485
LC ebook record available at https://lccn.loc.gov/2020057486

Printed in the United States of America
1st Printing

Book design by Laura K. Corless

For Bob & Jan

CONTENTS

Introduction   xi

On Failure & Rejection   1
Music   7
Art   15
Sports   21
Animals   29
Celebs   45
Food & Drink   53
Writers & Books   67
Word Origins & Language   73
Morbid Facts for Know-It-All Goths   83
TV & Movies   91
The Human Body   101
History   107
Love the Lewk (On Beauty, Style & Fashion)   117
Technology   123

Human Nature	**129**
Love	**137**
Life Hacks from Science & Psychology	**143**
All Around the World	**155**
Crazy but True	**167**
Trivia Games	**175**
Acknowledgments	**203**
Notes	**205**

INTRODUCTION

N ever stop learning. Because when you stop learning, you stop growing."

Those were the words of the SCUBA dive master who certified me for the sport when I was twelve. That was a long time ago, but I remember his advice exactly. For years, I ruminated on it. I journaled about it. It stuck with me because it was so simple, yet so profound, and the dive master was hot.

Even though that dive master is now approximately one thousand years old and seemingly off social media (What? A good writer always does her ~~stalking~~ research!), I still keep his words in my mind. They've helped me often throughout my career as a writer and a comedian. There's always more to learn, more to discover, new metaphorical mountains to climb. Admittedly, sometimes thinking about the inexhaustible amount of information in the world stresses me out, but more often it makes me feel excited, determined, and energized. I'm lucky that I work in a field that encourages fresh ideas.

Stand-up comedy, in fact, demands it. And as a game and joke writer for the NPR trivia show *Ask Me Another*, I'm constantly going down encyclopedic rabbit holes in search of fascinating, oft-forgotten tidbits.

I'm very excited about this book, and grateful to be researching uplifting facts during turbulent times. So often, it seems as though all the news, all the history, all the *information*, is negative. And when it feels like I'm trapped in a tumble dryer with only bad news, I get depressed and panicked, stuck in an unproductive, unhealthy combination of anxious paralysis. In short, I become a Quivering Puddle Person. And I wonder if there's any good left in this world.

But today I'm happy to report: There is. In my research, I have discovered that there is kindness, beauty, empathy, humor, resilience, wonder, silliness, cuteness, strength, hope, and joy in our world. Thank friggin' goodness.

And thank *you*. Thank you for considering reading this book of my favorite trivia, as well as cherished facts from bona fide experts, and the smarty-pants who walk among us, former *Jeopardy!* contestants. My aims for this project are twofold: to make you one day smarter every time you read it, and to light up your brain in a positive way. While we can't—and shouldn't—ignore all the problems in our world, it's also helpful, calming, inspirational, and necessary to learn about the good stuff, too.

I think we all could use a little good stuff right now.

ONE DAY
SMARTER

ON FAILURE & REJECTION

I thought this was a book of *uplifting* trivia," you may be saying out loud to your cat, who is ignoring you. It is! Truly, what's more comforting than realizing even your heroes have been rejected? Literally all of us are failures, and internalizing that fact makes future rejections less scary and painful.

This chapter is particularly dear to my heart. A few years ago, after a stinging job rejection, I set out to collect one hundred professional failures as my New Year's resolution. Did I get one hundred? Nope. I got *107.* I wrote about my failure project for *The New York Times* and even got to appear on the *Today* show. Now I get to write this book for you, a task I consider a dream job. So even though I've collected more rejections than anyone I know, I'm not embarrassed, because my life and career are better off for them. I know I'll face heaps of noes in the future, but with all of those rejections come the odd, glorious acceptance. And every time I fail, I can think about one of these comforting facts:

Peanuts creator Charles Schulz's drawings were rejected by his high school yearbook.

Oprah Winfrey was fired from her first job as a news anchor in Baltimore for getting too emotionally invested in her work.

Gisele Bündchen was rejected by forty-two modeling agencies before her career finally took off. Tyra Banks was rejected by six.

It took Sir James Dyson fifteen years and 5,126 unsuccessful protypes before he nailed his Dyson vacuum. Today he's worth an estimated $9.7 billion.

Both HBO and Showtime passed on *Mad Men* before AMC scooped it up.

E. E. Cummings wrote a book of poetry titled *No Thanks*, dedicated to the fourteen publishers that rejected him.

Steven Spielberg was rejected from the University of Southern California (and its prestigious film school) three times.

Elvis failed high school music class.

In 2012, Uzo Aduba hit rock bottom, crying her way home from yet another audition and deciding it might be time for her plan B, law school. Forty-five minutes later, she was offered the role of Suzanne on *Orange Is the New Black*, for which she later won an Emmy.

Shakira was cut from her grade school choir, and peers made fun of her for sounding like a goat.

Einstein didn't speak until he was four and didn't speak fluently until he was nine.

Lady Gaga, Destiny's Child, Bruno Mars, and Katy Perry have all been dropped by a record label.

Of Emily Dickinson's more than 1,800 poems, only ten were published in her lifetime. Now there's an entire museum dedicated to her work.

Before getting cast as the star of *Homeland*, Claire Danes hadn't booked a role for two years. She almost gave up acting to become an interior designer.

When President Ulysses S. Grant was a kid, his father nicknamed him "Useless."

After an audition, a casting director told Sidney Poitier he should stop wasting people's time and become a dishwasher. Poitier later became the first Black man to win an Oscar for Best Actor.

Vera Wang didn't make the 1968 Olympic figure-skating team and later didn't get the job as *Vogue*'s editor in chief. It wasn't until she was in her forties that she began designing wedding gowns and became a world-renowned fashion designer.

"Can't act. Can't sing. Balding. Can dance a little." Those were notes about an early screen test of Fred Astaire, who's now regarded as one of the best dancers ever to appear on film.

Get rejected from Harvard? If you aren't a legacy, don't feel bad: 29 percent of 2019 Harvard freshmen were relatives of Harvard grads.

Get rejected from working at Walmart? Well, the superstore accepts even fewer applicants than Harvard. (Walmart takes 2.6 percent of applicants. Harvard accepts 4.5 percent.)

Before he was president, Thomas Jefferson anonymously submitted an architectural design for the White House. It was rejected.

In 1851, Herman Melville received a rejection letter for *Moby-Dick* that read: "First, we must ask, does it have to be a whale? While this is a rather delightful, if somewhat esoteric, plot device, we recommend an antagonist with a more popular visage among the younger readers. For instance, could not the Captain be struggling with a depravity towards young, perhaps voluptuous, maidens?"

If you've ever failed at a New Year's resolution, don't feel inferior to your fellow Earth mates. Only 8 percent of people achieve their resolution goals by the following year.

The Beatles were told that they had "no future in show business" when they auditioned for a major record label called Decca Records in 1962, just under two years before their breakout.

Before getting cast as Alexis Rose on *Schitt's Creek*, Annie Murphy hadn't landed a role in nearly two years, her apartment burned down, and she had $3.00 in her bank account.

Stephen King's *Carrie* was rejected by thirty publishers before King literally threw it in the garbage. His wife, Tabitha, fished it out and convinced him to resubmit it. Finally, it was accepted by Doubleday, and it went on to sell more than 4 million copies.

Successful people are better liked when they talk about their failures in addition to their achievements.

MUSIC

This chapter goes out to everyone who (like me) has tried but failed to unleash their inner musical goddess. As a kid, I disappointed several piano teachers and flubbed every recital. In college, my drum teacher told me it's impossible to teach percussion to a person who has no rhythm. That was harsh but true. Though I'm a musical potato, I still enjoy the stuff, so I checked in with an expert to give the genre its due. *Billboard* editor Joe Lynch enlightened me with several of his all-time favorite music facts:

"Little Richard fired Jimi Hendrix from his band because he upstaged him."

"*Purple Rain* was Prince's attempt to write a song in the Bob Seger style."

and

"Singing in a group maintains and even improves mental health."

. . . Unless, of course, you're singing with *me*, in which case you might become depressed. But that's beside the point.

The idea of the "song of summer" has been around since the early 1900s. Newspapers wrote about one-hit wonders like 1909's "My Wife's Gone to the Country! (Hooray! Hooray!)" and the 1923 warm-weather bop "Yes! We Have No Bananas."

The *Billboard* Hot 100 has existed since August 1958. The first song to ever top the chart was Ricky Nelson's "Poor Little Fool."

In 2013, Canadian astronaut Chris Hadfield recorded an album in space. It's called *Space Sessions: Songs from a Tin Can* and includes a cover of David Bowie's "Space Oddity."

Lil Wayne originally went by the name Shrimp Daddy to honor an artist he admired, Pimp Daddy, and give a nod to his own short stature. He changed it in the mid-'90s.

Beethoven's composing process always began with pouring ice water over his head.

Donald Glover got his stage name, Childish Gambino, from an online Wu-Tang Clan name generator.

Researchers from England's Museum of Science and Industry found that the Spice Girls' "Wannabe" is the catchiest song of all time. Lou Bega's "Mambo No. 5" came in at (Mambo) No. 2.

Billie Eilish was the first artist born in the twenty-first century to have an album hit #1 on the *Billboard* 200: 2019's *When We All Fall Asleep, Where Do We Go?*

Billy Joel got so tired of seeing bored rich people in the front row of his concerts that he stopped selling tickets to that area and instead gets his crew to find dedicated fans in the nosebleeds and bring them down to the best seats in the house.

Panic! At the Disco started their career as a Blink-182 cover band.

In 1989, Will Smith and DJ Jazzy Jeff boycotted the Grammys because the show refused to televise the Best Rap Performance. The pair won the Grammy for "Parents Just Don't Understand." The following year, the Grammys included the category during the television broadcast.

The piano has 7,500 working parts.

"Jingle Bells" was originally performed around Thanksgiving and not written for Christmas. The "bells" aren't Santa's sleigh bells, but bells jingling during sleigh races, a common nineteenth-century pastime.

Leo Fender, the guy who founded Fender Musical Instrument Manufacturing Company, could not play the guitar.

Two days before her death, Janis Joplin changed her will to allot $2,500 for a two-hundred-person pub party when she died, "so my friends can get blasted after I'm gone."

JEOPARDY! CONTESTANT FAVE FACT

The "city boy" who was "born and raised in south Detroit" in Journey's epic "Don't Stop Believin'" must have been Canadian: There really is no "south Detroit," as immediately south of downtown Detroit lies Windsor, Ontario, across the Detroit River.
—Jeff Spoeri

"The Star-Spangled Banner" was written to the tune of an eighteenth-century British drinking song, "The Anacreontic Song." All of the verses in the original version end in a line similar to the first: "I'll instruct ye, like me, to entwine, The myrtle of Venus with Bacchus's vine."

Lizzo's stage name comes from Jay-Z's "Izzo," a song she liked in middle school.

Meanwhile, Lady Gaga's name comes from the 1984 Queen song "Radio Ga Ga."

Mary did have a little lamb! The song was written about a young girl, Mary Sawyer, whose brother convinced her to bring her lamb to school.

Sister Rosetta Tharpe was the first gospel singer who became a recording star. She performed from the 1930s through the 1970s, and some of her hits include "Rock Me" and "This Train."

Taylor Swift has a framed picture from her infamous squabble with Kanye West at the 2009 MTV Video Music Awards that reads "Life is full of little interruptions."

While we're on the topic of Her Swiftness: In 2014, Swift accidentally released eight seconds of white noise on Canadian iTunes. It quickly became the No. 1 track on the iTunes charts before it was removed.

Carly Simon's dad cofounded the publishing company Simon & Schuster.

According to the *Oxford English Dictionary*, the Beastie Boys invented the word "mullet." Also, their 1986 hit "(You Gotta) Fight for Your Right (To Party!)" was intended to parody party anthems, not become one.

Many Japanese workers, including police officers, wear white gloves. For Japan's Imperial Guard, this tradition predates the 1960s, but the rest of the police joined in when the Beatles played in Tokyo in 1966. The head of security knew the arena would be packed with women and told his officers—who would need to restrain the unruly mobs—to wear white gloves for propriety. (Please respect my self-restraint in not making a glove/love lyric pun here.)

Also: There's a whistle in the Beatles' song "A Day in the Life" that's audible only to dogs.

Most toilets flush in E flat.

The first woman inducted into the Rock and Roll Hall of Fame was Aretha Franklin in 1987.

Before they were pop stars, Selena Gomez and Demi Lovato were child actors together on *Barney & Friends*.

Tupac Shakur said his lyrics were inspired by the raw storytelling of Shakespeare. After the genius rapper and songwriter died in 1996, his hip-hop group Outlawz smoked his ashes.

During a 2016 Carpool Karaoke taping for *The Late Show with James Corden*, the lead singer of the Red Hot Chili Peppers, Anthony Kiedis, was flagged down by a mother with a baby who wasn't breathing. Kiedis kept the baby alive with CPR and belly rubs until an ambulance arrived.

Big Mama Thornton was the first artist to record "Hound Dog" (before Elvis), and wrote and recorded "Ball and Chain" before Janis Joplin made it famous.

Johnny Cash had a brother named Tommy Cash who's also a singer/songwriter. He's good-natured about being related to one of the most famous singers of all time. Tommy Cash's songs include "I Didn't Walk the Line" and "My Mother's Other Son."

"Old Town Road" by Lil Nas X was No. 1 on the *Billboard* Hot 100 chart longer than any other song in history. It lasted nineteen weeks before it was ousted by Billie Eilish's "Bad Guy" and smashed the previous sixteen-week record held by "Despacito" by Luis Fonsi and Daddy Yankee featuring Justin Bieber, and Mariah Carey and Boyz II Men's '90s hit "One Sweet Day."

JEOPARDY! CONTESTANT FAVE FACT

Former president Jimmy Carter has won as many Grammy Awards as Elvis Presley (3). —Wes Hazard

Freddie Mercury's bed size? Queen. Also, Mercury had four extra teeth, which pushed forward his front chompers, but he didn't want to remove them because doing so could have affected his voice.

Hearing beloved music can help people with brain injuries recall memories.

Jay-Z went to high school in Brooklyn with the Notorious B.I.G. and Busta Rhymes. Jay-Z and Busta once had a rap battle in the cafeteria, and when Jay-Z talked about it on *Jimmy Kimmel Live*, the billion-dollar artist, recording exec, and entrepreneur implied that he won.

Attention, '90s kids: The theme song for the original TV show *All That* was performed by TLC.

Total number of gifts in the song "The Twelve Days of Christmas": 364.

Ida Cox (1894–1967) is considered the "Uncrowned Queen of the Blues" and wrote an early feminist anthem, "Wild Women Don't Have the Blues." She was inducted into the Blues Hall of Fame in 2019.

Bruce Springsteen's "Born in the U.S.A." was the first CD ever pressed in the United States in 1984.

ART

⊙ ⊙

What's more artistic than makeup? The Sistine Chapel? Okay, fair. But makeup *is* art, and Andy Warhol knew it. As the executive director of the Makeup Museum, Doreen Bloch explains:

"Pop artist Andy Warhol is famous all around the world, but less known is that he also had a drag queen identity, called Drella. He created a series of portraits of his alter ego in 1981. Drella is a portmanteau of Dracula and Cinderella, and was chosen to reflect the opposing sides of Warhol's personality."

Now I can't stop fantasizing about a drag adaptation of *A Streetcar Named Desire*. "Drella!!!"

On the topic: Frequent Warhol collaborator, neo-expressionist, and graffiti artist Jean-Michel Basquiat became, at the age of twenty-one, the youngest-ever artist to show works at the prestigious exhibition documenta in Kassel, Germany. Basquiat later appeared in the music video for Blondie's "Rapture."

In 2018, a painting by the elusive artist Banksy was auctioned at Sotheby's for $1.4 million, and it self-destructed the moment it was sold.

Da Vinci's *Mona Lisa* is so popular, she has her own mailbox at the Louvre. Not only that, Da Vinci's *Salvator Mundi* sold for $450 million at auction in 2017, making it the most expensive painting ever.

During the COVID-19 pandemic, a British woman named Sarah Lamarr decided to turn the bus stop across the street from her home into a children's art gallery. Kids from the community contributed colorful paintings and drawings, which she used to cover the walls of the bus stop.

Between 1912 and 1948, painting was an Olympic event.

Salvador Dalí would doodle on his checks so that recipients would save or sell them as art rather than cash them.

In 2016, the Art Institute of Chicago re-created Vincent van Gogh's iconic *Bedroom in Arles* as an actual bedroom. The life-size room matched the painting down to the brushstroke, and you could book it on Airbnb for $10 a night.

More on ol' Vinny van G: He painted *The Starry Night* when he was in a psychiatric ward.

Graffiti and street art are not the same. Graffiti is directed at other graffiti artists, which is why it often doesn't make sense to the public. Street art, on the other hand, is intended for the masses.

Modern graffiti began in the 1960s in Philadelphia, and it started with a love story. A teen named Darryl "Cornbread" McCray tagged "Cornbread loves Cynthia" around the northern part of the city to get his crush's attention. It worked. He and Cynthia dated until her disapproving family made her transfer schools. Later, Cornbread tagged the Jackson 5's private plane.

The mayor of Florence, Italy—and sponsor of Michelangelo's *David*—thought David's nose was too big. Legend has it that a young Michelangelo responded by climbing the statue and *pretending* to shave off some of David's nose while sprinkling marble dust beneath him. The sponsor was impressed with the "change."

The artist Kim Dong Yoo creates portraits of famous faces made up of other famous faces. For example, he created Marilyn Monroe portraits made of tiny John F. Kennedys, and a portrait of Donald Trump made of tiny Kim Jong-uns.

French artist Yves Klein worked primarily in blue and even created a new shade called International Klein Blue. In 1958, three thousand people showed up to his latest exhibit in Paris . . . and walked into an empty room, where they were promptly served gin cocktails. The confused guests would soon realize the drinks contained dye that turned their pee International Klein Blue for up to a week.

Georgia O'Keeffe once told a *New York Times* art critic: "I hate flowers—I paint them because they're cheaper than models and they don't move."

American art museums have a long way to go in terms of diversity, both in the artists they display and the people they hire. But their staffs are slowly starting to reflect the population at large: In 2015, 26 percent of employees were people of color. In 2019, that number was 36 percent.

Late in life, Claude Monet had cataracts and couldn't see blue or purple. His vision was also blurry, and not only did he never stop painting, these factors probably contributed to the iconic look of his work.

In the fifth century BCE, a Greek painter named Zeuxis supposedly died from laughter. The story goes that he was commissioned to paint a strange-looking old woman as the goddess Aphrodite. When he stepped back to gaze upon his finished work, he cracked up, couldn't stop, and his body gave out.

In 2016, someone defaced a Soviet-era star statue in Russia to make it look like Patrick from *SpongeBob SquarePants*.

In 2017, students at Robert Gordon University in Scotland put a pineapple in the center of a table in the school's art exhibit to see if they could pass it off as art. When they returned four days later, they realized it had worked: The pineapple was under a glass box.

Frida Kahlo got into an extremely prestigious school at age sixteen and planned to be a doctor. But she was in a horrible bus accident in which she was stabbed in the pelvis with an iron bar and nearly died. She then underwent more than thirty operations and began painting during her recovery.

This is the most British thing ever: In 2002, an artist named Andy Brown created a portrait of Queen Elizabeth II using one thousand stitched-together tea bags.

In 2011, the actor James Franco sold a "non-visible" "sculpture" made of air for $10,000.

The oldest known figurative painting in the world depicts cattle and is between forty thousand and fifty-two thousand years old. Scientists discovered it in 2018 in a jungle in Indonesia.

In the late eighteenth and into the nineteenth century, it was trendy in certain circles to commission an artist to paint a miniature portrait of your eye, set it in jewelry, and give it to your lover. The richer you were, the more "lover's eye" jewelry you owned.

Picasso often painted his dog, a dachshund named Lump. Picasso died just a week after Lump in 1973. (He was ninety-one years old; Lump was seventeen.)

SPORTS

ooooooooooooooooooooooooooooooooooo

S ports! So exciting, yet safe to discuss at family gatherings. For that, I am forever grateful. But my enthusiasm pales in comparison to basketball commentator Noah Savage, who works for ESPN and the Ivy League Network. Here's a sampling of his favorite Sports Facts™:

"[Basketball player] Jack Twyman took care of Maurice Stokes, who suffered a traumatic brain injury during a game [in 1958]. Stokes was an all-star who was going to be an all-time great, but was severely debilitated by the injury. This led to a series of charity games to raise money for Stokes's medical expenses at Kutsher's Hotel in the Catskills that became an annual event attended by all of the NBA's biggest stars. According to other teammates, Twyman and Stokes did not get along when they played together, but Twyman took him in, cared for him, and was even his legal guardian until he passed away in 1970."

"[One of the NBA's tallest-ever players at 7'7"] Manute Bol broke his teeth on the rim the first time he tried to dunk."

Even more amazing: He kept playing. I'm equally wowed by these tidbits:

Serena Williams has won twenty-three Grand Slam tennis titles, which is more than any other human in history, *and* she won the Australian Open while pregnant.

Tug-of-war was an Olympic sport from 1900 to 1920.

Babe Ruth was said to have put a cabbage leaf under his ball cap to keep his head cool during games. In 2005, South Korean baseball banned cabbage leaves under caps after one of its star pitchers revived Ruth's tradition.

Ice skates have existed almost as long as the wheel. A pair of skates were found in Finland that date back to 2000 BCE.

Sprinter Wilma Rudolph had polio, pneumonia, and scarlet fever as a child and had to wear braces on her legs. Despite this, in 1960 she became the first American woman to win three gold medals in track and field Olympic events.

Two-time Super Bowl champion Eli Manning's first name is Elisha.

The average, nearly three-hour-long Major League Baseball game has only eighteen minutes of action.

Two-time Olympic medalist Abby Wambach was the first soccer player to be named the Associated Press's Athlete of the Year, in 2011.

JEOPARDY! CONTESTANT FAVE FACT

Jim Brown, the great football player, and Michael Jordan HAVE THE SAME BIRTHDAY (February 17). Different years, of course, but they are each respectively among the VERY BEST EVER (maybe THE best ever) in their respective sports. —Kate Waits

"Bullet" Bob Hayes is the only person to have won an Olympic gold medal *and* an NFL Super Bowl. In 1964, Hayes won two sprinting gold medals, and in 1972, he was with the Dallas Cowboys when they beat the Miami Dolphins in the Super Bowl VI blowout.

Speaking of the Super Bowl, an estimated 17 million Americans take the day off, call in sick to work, or ghost their employers the day after the Big Game.

Colder air is denser than warmer air, which is why a golf ball won't travel as far in cold weather.

In 2002, Lisa Leslie became the first player to dunk a basketball in a WNBA game.

In Philadelphia, it is known among real estate developers not to erect any building higher than a statue of William Penn that rose from the top of City Hall, lest the city be cursed. But in 1987, a developer did just that. The city wouldn't see another No. 1 sports status until 2008, after ironworkers put a statue of Penn on the *new* tallest building, the Comcast Center. That year, the Phillies won the World Series. In 2018, an even *taller* Comcast building was built, complete with a Penn statue at the top. That's the year the Philadelphia Eagles won the Super Bowl.

Shin kicking is a real sport that was developed in sixteenth-century England and is still played today in the UK.

In 2017, the Switzerland-based Global Association of International Sports Federations gave "observer" status to three sports, the first step to potential inclusion in the Olympics: foosball, poker, and pole dancing.

American astronaut Sunita Williams was the first person to ever run a marathon—the 2007 Boston Marathon—in space.

Since ESPN's twenty-fifth anniversary in 2004, several American babies have been named ESPN (pronounced *Ess-pin*) every year.

In 2018, mixed martial artist and wrestler Ronda Rousey became the first woman to be inducted into the Ultimate Fighting Championship (UFC) Hall of Fame.

In Major League Baseball, batters have 150–250 milliseconds—about half the time it takes to blink—to decide whether they're hitting a pitch, as well as where and how to swing.

The confetti that rained down after the Kansas City Chiefs 2020 Super Bowl victory was printed with fans' tweets.

In 1971, astronaut Alan Shepard snuck a golf ball and club onto Apollo 14 and hit a golf ball on the moon.

Running a mile may not seem like a big deal, but one mile is 5,280 feet, which is nothing to sneeze at. (I will keep this in mind next time I start walking halfway through a 5K.)

In 1970, Pittsburgh Pirates pitcher Dock Ellis threw a no-hitter game while on acid.

Speaking of the Iron City, the Pittsburgh Penguins were named because their original arena looked like an igloo.

Nike took off as a brand only after cofounder Bill Bowerman revolutionized the running shoe. He got the inspiration for the sole from his wife's waffle maker, and the prototype was made from that very waffle iron.

Candace Parker was the first basketball player to win the WNBA's Rookie of the Year *and* MVP in the same year, 2008.

> ### JEOPARDY! CONTESTANT FAVE FACT
>
> **The official state sport of Maryland is jousting.**
> **—Rachel Shuman**

There's a basketball court on top of the Supreme Court Building called the Highest Court in the Land.

In 1984, one single point in a professional women's tennis match took twenty-nine minutes. That's one minute longer than the shortest-ever pro match in its entirety.

The fastest human who's ever lived is the aptly named Jamaican sprinter Usain Bolt. At his fastest, he hit 27.8 miles per hour. For comparison, most of us would be lucky to clock 17 miles per hour.

In 2007, golfer Lexi Thompson became the youngest-ever person to qualify for the U.S. Women's Open. She was twelve.

The longest-ever Major League Baseball game lasted eight hours and six minutes. It was played at Comiskey Park in Chicago on May 8, 1984, between the White Sox and the Milwaukee Brewers. The White Sox won. (Silly Author Note: I was born on this very date in Chicago. I'm a former softball pitcher and lifelong White Sox fan. I'm more into baseball than astrology, so this game is my version of the stars aligning.)

The average NFL career lasts just over three seasons.

In 1957, Philadelphia Phillies center fielder Richie Ashburn accidentally hit a fan named Alice Roth with a foul ball and broke her nose. While she was being carried out of the stadium on a stretcher, he hit her with a foul ball again, breaking a bone in her knee. Ashburn went to the hospital to visit her the next day, and later the team invited her grandkids to the clubhouse and gave them autographed baseballs.

When Air Jordans came out in 1984, the NBA fined Michael Jordan $5,000 per game for wearing them because they weren't white, per the uniform rules. Nike happily paid Jordan's fines, seeing the press coverage as an invaluable marketing opportunity.

JEOPARDY! CONTESTANT FAVE FACT

The 1956 Summer Olympics were the only Olympic Games held in multiple hemispheres, due to Australia's long horse quarantine at the time. The equestrian events were held in Stockholm, Sweden, while all other events were held in Melbourne, Australia. —Bryan Cothorn

Simone Biles is the most decorated gymnast in world history. She has nineteen gold medals, three silvers, and three bronzes for everything from floor exercises to uneven bars to best all-around individual performance, to name a few.

During World War II, rival football teams the Pittsburgh Steelers and Philadelphia Eagles combined due to lack of players. They were called the Steagles.

In 1919, a Cleveland Indians pitcher named Ray Caldwell was struck by lightning during the ninth inning—and finished pitching the game.

AMAZING AND HILARIOUS COLLEGE MASCOTS

Scottsdale Community College, Arizona: Artie the Fighting Artichoke

University of Louisiana: Cayenne, a giant hot pepper

Trinity Christian College, Illinois: the Trinity Troll

Delta State University, Mississippi: the Fighting Okra

University of California–Santa Cruz: Sammy the Banana Slug

North Carolina School of the Arts: the Fighting Pickle

Stanford: the Stanford Tree

Concordia College, Minnesota: Kernel Cobb, the angry ear of corn

ANIMALS

This section is dedicated to my dog Bingo. And my late dog Sparky. And my parents' late dogs Buddy and Cocoa. And their living, half-blind dog Mulligan. And my sister's dog Lenny. And my childhood rabbit Racer, guinea pig Shakespeare, and parakeet Carolyn. And my childhood fish, all of which I named after college and Olympic fast-pitch softball players (I had three spotted mollies named Jennie Finch). And . . . well, this is why I resist the temptation to get tattoos of my pets.

For this chapter, I consulted with the world's three most knowledgeable experts on the topic of animals: Connor, Matthew, and Thomas Mullany, my nephews. Sure, they may all be under the age of twelve, but every time I see them, they hit me with animal facts I somehow didn't discover while researching this book. Here are their favorites:

"Flamingos are actually white or gray, but the food that they eat turns them pink . . . And when the flamingos are pregnant or something, they lose some of the pinkness, because they give the pinkness to the babies." —Thomas Mullany, age seven

"Platypuses are one out of two species of mammals that can lay eggs. They have a beaver tail, a duck bill, and they can swim." —Matthew Mullany, age nine (The other mammal that lays eggs is the echidna.)

And

"Black-footed ferrets are the only the ferrets native to North America. There are only 370 remaining in the wild." —Connor Mullany, age eleven

If your heart is already flying open with unbridled wonder, love, and sympathy for the animals we share this planet with, let me offer a #lifehack: Quorn "chicken" and plant-based "meats" like Beyond and Impossible burgers have completely changed my eating habits, bringing me to near-vegetarianism and making me feel wayyyy less guilty when I'm staring into the eyes of a sweet, stinky, adorable animal. Enjoy—the food and the facts!

In a crowded underwater situation, alligators give manatees the right of way.

Baby elephants suck their trunk the way baby humans suck their thumb.

Cats have thirty-two muscles in each ear. Humans have only six.

What we call horse "hooves" are one big toe. Horses used to have more toes but were able to bear more stress and weight with a single giant one, so they evolved. You can still spot small vestigial toes above some horses' hooves.

The eyes of giant squids are as big as basketballs.

In 2019, California passed a law stating that pet stores can sell only cats, dogs, and rabbits that were obtained from shelters in order to reduce harmful puppy mill practices.

Snakes, spiders, bees, and other insects can see colors we can't.

Certain species of scallops have two hundred eyes.

Alaskan wood frogs can hold their pee for up to eight months. Their bodies recycle urea waste into nitrogen, which helps preserve their cells and tissue during hibernation.

At 116 decibels, the mating call of the male white bellbird is the world's loudest birdsong. For context, that's about twice as loud as human conversation. Their mating call is called a "bonk."

Swordfish are the fastest swimmers on the planet. They can reach 60 miles per hour.

Porcupines regularly impale themselves on their own quills but survive because those quills contain antibiotics. Also, porcupines float.

Elephants, dogs, and chimps can catch yawns from humans.

Rats are ticklish and can laugh.

In 2019, a newly discovered species of beetle was named after climate activist Greta Thunberg. It's called the *Nelloptodes gretae*.

Scientists are working on modifying spider venom to create a pain reliever that could replace opioids.

In Oregon, there's a therapy llama called Caesar the No Drama Llama who did window visits for nursing home patients during the COVID-19 pandemic and made appearances at Black Lives Matter protests in Portland.

A cow's weight can fluctuate up to seventy-five pounds from day to day.

Giraffe tongues are black for sun protection.

Butterflies drink the tears of crocodiles and turtles for sodium.

For more than two thousand years, queen bees were called king bees. Even Aristotle thought they were male.

JEOPARDY! CONTESTANT FAVE FACT

Armadillos always give birth to identical quadruplets, and their defense mechanism is to jump up in the air, about the height of a front car bumper. I do love the little weirdos; they remind me of Gonzo from *The Muppet Show*. —Heather Breslin

Boxer crabs are impervious to the sting of sea anemones, so they carry the anemones around like defensive pom-poms. When a fish sees the crab as prey, the, ahem, *boxer* crab punches the anemone out to sting the fish and protect itself.

The short-horned lizard, aka the horned toad, squirts blood from around its eyes as a defense mechanism. TBH, same.

Giraffes with darker spots tend to be more solitary, while giraffes with light-colored spots are of the more sociable variety.

Several species of wasps in Central and South America have the ability to make honey.

Approximately one million American dogs have been named the primary beneficiary in their owner's will.

Red sea urchins and bowhead whales can live more than two hundred years.

Goats love bonding with humans. Like dogs, they communicate with us through body language and staring. They're also known to nuzzle against humans, possibly to use us as a scratching post. But unlike dogs, goats *must* be around other goats to be happy.

Grizzly bears use barnacle-covered rocks as combs for their faces.

Ribbon-tailed astrapia male birds have relatively gigantic, white three-foot tail feathers that have no function besides looking attractive to female birds when they fly. To the human eye, though, it looks like they just have toilet paper stuck to their feet.

Pregnant alpacas avoid males at all costs during their eleven-and-a-half-month gestation and will even spit on them when they get near.

Bat poo is sparkly due to the insect exoskeletons in it.

Racehorses fly to the Kentucky Derby and other major races on a plane called Air Horse One.

An albatross can stay airborne without flapping its wings for up to six days.

Throwing rice at weddings does not result in birds eating the rice and then their stomachs exploding! That's false and never happened! Woo-hoo!

A blue whale can fit its weight in water in its mouth.

Bird bones are hollow because their lungs extend into their bones. Our feathered friends need lots of oxygen to fly, hence the creative pulmonary expansion.

JEOPARDY! CONTESTANT FAVE FACT

During the wildfires in Australia in 2020, the notoriously territorial wombat saved several species by allowing them safety in their underground burrows. The wombats didn't really *actively* do anything—just built giant burrows that other animals could live in—I still think it's cool that wombats A) are territorial and B) let other animals chill in their empty pads. —Raj Sivaraman

Ninety percent of trained pigeons can distinguish between a Picasso and a Monet, and Cubist vs. Impressionist paintings in general. Even when the paintings were blurred and shown in black and white, the pigeons could recognize the difference. This is why you've never seen a pigeon in an Art History 101 class. Honey, they already know.

When male ring-tailed lemurs square off, they waft nasty scents at each other until one backs down. It's called a stink fight.

Butterflies can taste with their feet.

The COVID-19 pandemic reduced noise pollution in cities, which led sparrows to hear one another better. The sparrows were able to lower their volume from a virtual scream to a more comfortable level, and *that* allowed them to sing more complex mating songs.

Cats can't taste sweets. Also, most cats are lactose intolerant and shouldn't be given milk, even if they look adorable lapping it up.

When a male bowerbird is ready to mate, he decorates his bower—which is basically a long hallway of a nest—in objects of the same color, often blue. The female then arrives, inspects his interior design work, and makes her decision.

Sloths poop only once a week.

More than sixty species—from beetles to tadpoles to leeches—live in *elephants' footprints*. The longer a footprint indentation has been around, the more species inhabit it.

One study has confirmed what dog people already know: Your pup would likely attempt to save you in the case of an emergency.

There's a type of wallaby that secretes purple dye through its neck. It's called—drumroll—the purple-necked rock-wallaby.

A lion will refrain from attacking a cow from behind if the cow has eyes painted on its butt.

In New York City, "uptown" and "downtown" rats are genetically different. (Downtown rats are more likely to go to art school.)

Frogs close their eyes while eating because their eyeballs drop to their esophagus to help push their food down.

Jellyfish are being studied because they're one of the few creatures that never develop cancer.

Male club-winged manakin birds woo females by rapidly shaking their wings, which creates a violin-like sound.

Don't believe the hype—goldfish are smart! You can train them to do tricks, and they appreciate it when you change up their aquarium. Just like us, they need to redecorate every once in a while.

When an osprey catches a fish, it turns the fish face-forward before flying away with it in order to be as aerodynamic as possible (and to show the fish a good time before it becomes a meal?).

The term for alpacas giving birth is "unpacking."

Many sea otters have a favorite rock, which they keep in their "pouch" of loose skin under their arms.

When male blue manakin birds are ready to mate, they sing in unison and take turns fluttering their feathers for a female. She compares them all and makes her choice.

There are 380,000 species of beetles.

Ostriches can run more than twice as fast as an athletic human (43 miles per hour vs. 17–20 miles per hour).

Octopuses and honeybees can recognize human faces.

Leeches have thirty-two brains and ten stomachs.

When lightning bugs light up, it's usually a mating call.

Cats spend 30 to 50 percent of their day grooming.

In Australia, the giant Gippsland earthworm can grow up to nine feet long.

But all is not terrifying in Australia. There's also an animal called the wallaroo, but it's not a kangaroo/wallaby hybrid. It is, however, extremely cute—it looks like a chubbier, friendlier kangaroo.

Most species of fish have taste buds all over their bodies.

Sloths are so slow that algae grows on them. But they can turn their heads almost 360 degrees.

Elephants can't jump.

Spiders who have been fed LSD make especially intricate designs in their webs.

Smaller dogs dream more often than bigger dogs.

Pigs are one of the cleanest domestic animals. They're associated with dirt because they can't sweat and they roll in mud to stay cool.

No one can figure out how eels reproduce, and they won't do it in captivity.

JEOPARDY! CONTESTANT FAVE FACT

Tama, a calico cat, served as the stationmaster of Kishi train station in Japan from 2007 until her death in 2015. She was such a popular mascot that she increased ridership by at least 10 percent and helped the railway stay in business. She was succeeded by her deputy Nitama, the current stationmaster, who is also a cat. —Liz Greenwood

With the legalization of marijuana in many states, weed-related dog names skyrocketed in 2019. Budder was up 600 percent, Dank 116 percent, Indica 93 percent, Herb 66 percent, and Kush 62 percent.

American lobsters and a species of jellyfish called *Turritopsis dohrnii* are "biologically immortal," meaning they could live forever if not for predators, disease, disasters, climate change, and accidents.

In 1996, a cat named Ketzel jumped onto a piano. Her owner, a retired composer, transcribed the notes she hit with her paws. Her "song" earned a special mention in a 1997 competition by *The Paris New Music Review*.

Because of their incredible sense of smell, bloodhounds can follow tracks that are up to twelve and a half days old.

Humpback whales sometimes protect other species from being attacked by killer whales.

Certain frogs can be frozen and then thawed back to life.

Female dolphins "sing" to their babies in the womb. The singing is a signature whistle, which is effectively the mother's name. The dolphin identifies with that whistle its whole life.

Three dogs survived the *Titanic* sinking.

A group of ravens are known as an unkindness. Maybe *we* shouldn't be so unkind about them, though: Ravens can make friends and recognize them later, and they are good at problem-solving and planning ahead.

Don't try this at home, but ants won't get hurt if they're microwaved.

It's estimated that 45 percent of Americans' dogs sleep in their owners' beds.

Pigs are smarter than cats and dogs. In fact, they can learn as quickly as chimpanzees.

Elephants recognize themselves in mirrors, help other species, play, and console family members.

Epaulette sharks can walk on the ocean floor using their fins.

When a flounder is a juvenile, one of its eyes migrates to the other side of its face so both eyes can look upward when it buries itself in the sand.

In 1995, a green cat was born in Denmark. Vets couldn't figure out why. The same thing happened to a puppy born on the island of Sardinia in 2020. The puppy's brothers and sisters were all normal-colored.

The average dog is as intelligent as a two-year-old human.

Welp, wombat poop is cube-shaped.

In 2017, scientists found an underwater city off the east coast of Australia that had been built by octopuses. The octopuses fought over the best "homes," which were dens made of shells.

Dolphins jump out of the water to conserve energy, since air is less dense than water.

Koala "bears" aren't bears; they're marsupials.

When puppies hit puberty, they tend to defy their caretakers, just like human adolescents. This usually starts around a pup's eighth month and ends a little after month twelve.

Ants have two stomachs: one for their food and one full of food to share with the group or eat later. Also, there's a species of ant that lives only in Manhattan. Its real name is the ManhattAnt.

Fish cough, yawn, and burp.

Red pandas use their tails as blankets, and IT. IS. ADORABLE.

In 1992, White House staffers received a memo that they were not to feed President George H. W. Bush's dog Ranger, because he "looks like a blimp." According to the note, at Camp David, "staff including the Marines, Naval personnel, All Civilians and Kids are specifically instructed to 'rat' on anyone seen feeding Ranger."

Dolphins can put one side of their brain to sleep at a time. The other stays awake to look out for predators.

How do fish populate new lakes? Their eggs are preserved in bird poop and dropped into bodies of water during flight, where they then hatch.

A sea lion once saved a man who tried to kill himself by jumping off the Golden Gate Bridge and broke his back. The sea lion kept him afloat until the Coast Guard arrived. The man, Kevin Hines, now dedicates his life to suicide prevention.

Koko was an incredibly smart, charismatic gorilla who got lots of media attention from the late 1970s until her death in 2018. When she met Mr. Rogers, she took his shoes off for him, since he began every episode of his show by removing his shoes.

The alpine bumblebee can fly higher than Mount Everest (30,000 feet).

A male penguin "proposes" by presenting a female with the smoothest pebble he can find. This is how he shows his intentions to build a high-quality pebble nest with her.

Contrary to popular belief, armadillo shells aren't bulletproof, but they are strong and flexible enough to serve as a model for human armor.

Herrings communicate by farting.

You can hear a lion's roar from five miles away.

There are way more male cuttlefish than female cuttlefish, and the fish usually mate all together, in one big party. The strongest male cuttlefish tend to push out the weaker, smaller ones to get the attention of the females. So smaller males evolved to disguise themselves as female, infiltrate groups of females, and then "woo" a partner from the inside. Female cuttlefish are more likely to choose a mate who has disguised himself as female.

There's a biker gang called Rescue Ink that rescues animals from abusive situations.

Cats spend up to 70 percent of their lives asleep.

A sloth can hold its breath up to forty minutes.

Houseflies hum in the key of F.

In 2004, a black bear descended on a Seattle area campsite. It tried a Busch beer and discarded it. Then it drank a full thirty-six cans of a local brand, Rainier Beer, and fell asleep.

Goats have rectangular pupils.

CELEBS

⊙ ⊙

Writing about celebrities is a little scary. The last thing an author wants is to publish a glowing profile or adorable fact about a famous person who, the next day, gets arrested for eating his neighbor.

As the entertainment editor of *Seventeen* magazine, Tamara Fuentes knows all about the risky business of covering Hollywood. Still, she confidently offered up a few of her favorite celebrity facts:

"Mindy Kaling's first name is actually Vera, while Mindy is her middle name, which comes from [the TV show] *Mork & Mindy*."

And

"Reese Witherspoon wrote into her contract for *Legally Blonde 2* that she would be able to keep all the clothes Elle wore after filming ended."

And that is why Reese is a national treasure. Yes, I said it. Now, Reese, please don't eat your neighbor. In fact, to all the celebrities mentioned in this section: Stay out of trouble. Be kind. Make great art. Help people. And above all, please stay relevant so this book can, too.

Despite being one of the most-followed people on Instagram, Selena Gomez doesn't have the app on her phone because she says it makes her feel bad about herself (celebrities: They're just like us). Instead, she logs on to someone else's phone when she feels like posting a photo.

Prince William's college nickname was P-Willy.

Dwayne "The Rock" Johnson eats ten pounds of food per day.

In 2018, an eighteen-year-old clenched her teeth so hard while watching a shirtless Michael B. Jordan in *Black Panther* that she broke her retainer. The woman's orthodontist posted about it on Tumblr, where it got back to Jordan, and he offered to buy her a new one.

Rebel Wilson pursued showbiz after getting malaria and hallucinating about winning an Oscar.

Samuel L. Jackson has it written into his contracts that he gets to golf twice a week while shooting movies.

Jennifer Aniston turned down an offer to be a *Saturday Night Live* cast member when she was in her early twenties. She cited the not-so-great treatment of women on the show as her reason for refusing.

Beyoncé had only one boyfriend before Jay-Z.

Julie Andrews (aka the original Mary Poppins) has a horrible potty mouth. Her children tried to convince her to quit swearing so much. It didn't work.

Ryan Gosling likes to knit.

Florence Pugh carries a specific tea brand—Yorkshire—everywhere she goes.

Tyra Banks has a phobia of dolphins. It's called "delfiniphobia."

Jennifer Lawrence has "H20" tattooed in light ink on her hand to remind her to drink water.

Bill Murray has a 1-800 number instead of an agent.

When Meghan Markle was eleven years old, she wrote a letter to Procter & Gamble asking them to change sexist language in a commercial for Ivory dishwashing soap. They did.

Harry Styles has four nipples. Also, he and Ed Sheeran have matching tattoos of a British cartoon penguin named Pingu, whom they both loved as kids.

Emma Roberts is Julia Roberts's niece. (No word on whether she has also insured a body part, unlike Aunt Julia, whose smile has been insured for $30 million.)

Speaking of insuring body parts: Rihanna's legs have been insured for $1 million; Heidi Klum's for $2 million; Tina Turner's for $3.2 million; and Taylor Swift's for

$40 million. But none compare to Mariah Carey's legs, which have been insured for $1 billion.

Snoop Dogg and Brandy are cousins. So are Al Roker and Lenny Kravitz.

And Lenny Kravitz and his actress/singer/model daughter Zoë Kravitz have matching tattoos. The tattoos, which say "Free at Last," are a nod to Lenny overcoming a difficult time in his life.

When he was in high school, Adam Driver loved the movie *Fight Club* so much that he started his own fight club.

Eighty-five percent of American four-year-olds know that the OG celeb Santa Claus is real.

Emily Blunt had a debilitating stutter as a child. Therapists and speech coaches didn't fix it, but acting in her school play did.

Danny DeVito trained as a hairdresser before making it big.

Betty White refused a role in the movie *As Good as It Gets* because the movie includes a scene with animal cruelty.

Eminem's Alcoholics Anonymous sponsor is Elton John.

Leonardo DiCaprio's mother felt her in utero son kick for the first time while looking at a Da Vinci painting at the Uffizi Gallery in Florence, Italy. That's how the actor got his name.

Music legend Billie Holiday was Billy Crystal's babysitter.

Lizzo dropped out of college, panicked, and stopped speaking for three months. She now calls that period "a metamorphosis" because it made her realize her true calling of being a singer.

Michael J. Fox's middle name is Andrew. He thought Michael A. Fox sounded like "Michael, a fox," and there was already an actor named Michael Fox, so he chose J in honor of actor Michael J. Pollard.

Here are the real names of a few asteroids: Asteroid 12818 Tomhanks, Asteroid 8353 Megryan, Asteroid 214476 Stephencolbert.

Madonna was fired from a job at Dunkin' Donuts for having too much fun with the jelly filler machine.

Katy Perry's song "I Kissed a Girl" is about Scarlett Johansson's lips. Though Perry and Johansson never kissed, Johansson said she was flattered to be the inspiration.

Will Smith's real first name is Willard.

PLAYING YOUNG

Ever watch a movie and think, *That actor is way too old to play that character*? Well, you were probably right. Casting fully grown adults as teenagers happens a lot. So, my dear younger readers, the next time you see a character who's "your age" with the five-o'clock shadow, relatively clear skin, and giant muscles of a grown-all-the-way-up person, remember: They are grown all the way up. If you've ever felt like an awkward potato person in comparison to the "young" people you see on-screen, this is why:

In *The Amazing Spider-Man* (2012), Andrew Garfield played seventeen-year-old Peter Parker when he was twenty-seven. When Garfield filmed the sequel, in which Peter Parker is eighteen, he was thirty.

In *Breakfast at Tiffany's* (1961), Audrey Hepburn's Holly Golightly was supposed to be eighteen. Hepburn was thirty-two.

Shirley Henderson was thirty-seven when she played the fourteen-year-old ghost Moaning Myrtle in *Harry Potter and the Chamber of Secrets*, and forty in *Harry Potter and the Goblet of Fire*.

In the 2009 *Star Trek* reboot, John Cho played a twenty-one-year-old Sulu. He was thirty-six at the time.

Olivia Newton-John was twenty-nine when she starred as the innocent high school senior Sandy in *Grease* (1978). Stockard Channing was thirty-three when she played seventeen-year-old Rizzo.

Paul Wesley was thirty-five when the CW show *The Vampire Diaries* ended its eight-year run. His character, Stefan Salvatore, was supposed to be a one-hundred-seventy-one-year-old vampire in an eighteen-year-old's body.

In *Clueless* (1995)—a spectacular movie based on Jane Austen's *Emma*—Stacey Dash played a high school student learning to drive, Dionne Davenport, when she was twenty-eight.

In *Save the Last Dance* (2001), heartthrob Sean Patrick Thomas was in his early thirties when he played high school senior Derek, opposite then-nineteen-year-old Julia Stiles.

Jennifer Grey was twenty-seven when she starred as seventeen-year-old Baby in *Dirty Dancing* (1987).

When the first episode of *Hannah Montana* aired in 2006, Miley Cyrus's "sixteen-year-old" brother, Jackson, was played by twenty-nine-year-old Jason Earles.

FOOD & DRINK

◦ ◦

When life feels bleak, empty, and hopeless, remember: Your next meal could turn it all around.

I always need something to look forward to, and during the inevitable lulls of life, I sometimes pick a date on my calendar and schedule an exciting food day: I buy a semi-fancy bottle of wine and order something delicious, like fried cheese curds, buttery spaetzle, or a hefty grandma pie from my favorite pizzeria.

Former chef and food historian Michael Albanese also knows a lot about pizza. (I, too, consider myself a food historian—my credentials being that I just ate leftovers from nine days ago.) Some of his favorite related facts include:

"Sicilian pizza was invented in New York City. In an attempt to attract more business, bakeries in the Sicilian part of Little Italy started adding cheese and sauce to their traditional *sfincione* bread and calling it pizza due to its rise in popularity in New York City in the early 1900s."

"Tomatoes were thought to be poisonous until the late 1800s. It was because rich people ate them with pewter utensils [which were high in lead content]."

"Tomatoes *aren't Italian*! They first grew in Central America and eventually made it to Europe on trading ships."

And, unrelatedly: "Every kernel of corn has its own strand of hair."

Gregorio Pedroza, a chef with Restaurant Associates, added a dairy fact to the list (and, yes, now my stomach is fully rumbling):

"Philadelphia Cream Cheese isn't from Philadelphia. In 1800, Philly was known as *the* spot for quality dairy, so the creator slapped Philly on the name."

I hope these, ahem, morsels will make your mouth water, too:

German chocolate cake has nothing to do with the Vaterland. The chocolate, pecan, and coconut dessert was created by an American named Samuel German in 1852.

Ice cream is solid, liquid, and gas.

Ripe bananas glow blue in UV light.

"Cat pee aroma" is a real wine term used to compliment sauvignon blanc.

In September 2019, Chef Mariya Russell became the first Black woman to earn a Michelin star for her work at Kumiko and Kikko in Chicago.

Food scientists in China have figured out the best way to cook broccoli for maximum nutritious value: Chop it into very small pieces, let it sit out for ninety minutes, then lightly stir fry it.

Beer cans used to be 40 percent thicker, which is why crushing one was a way to show off strength.

A chef's hat has one hundred pleats, symbolizing all the ways you can cook an egg.

American cheese was invented by an immigrant, Canadian-born James L. Kraft.

Here's why you love those spicy peppers: Consuming hot sauce and chilis irritates your stomach, nose, and mouth. To battle the "pain," your body releases chemicals, dopamine and endorphins, that make you feel good.

Five percent of American adults are vegetarian.

Doritos is the most popular brand of chips in the United States, and they are most often consumed between 8 p.m. and 11 p.m.

The sweet potato has more nutrients per farmed acre than any other food.

If you're Catholic, maybe you've noticed that flying saucers, the candy, taste like communion wafers? Well, they basically are. The company that concocted the sweet, Belgica, was originally in the communion wafer business, but when church attendance began to decrease in the late 1940s, the company created a candy to make up for lost business. It debuted in 1951.

Even though only about 24 percent of professional chefs are women, more than half the students at the Culinary Institute of America are now women.

In 2010, Americans drank an average of 45.5 gallons of soda each year. That number is on a steady decline. In 2019, it was down to 39 gallons per year.

Contrary to popular belief, mayonnaise isn't a common carrier of foodborne illness. It contains substantial acidic elements like lemon juice and vinegar, enough to kill harmful bacteria.

Watermelons are both fruits and vegetables, and they are 92 percent water.

Here's one for the Chicagoans: The regional alcohol Malört was sold medicinally during Prohibition because law enforcement didn't believe anyone would choose to drink it for fun.

Almond milk was invented in the twelfth century, possibly earlier.

Brussels sprouts are bred to taste less bitter than they were twenty years ago, hence their rise in popularity (even if they still get a bad rap).

It takes approximately seven hundred grapes to make a bottle of wine.

Justice Elena Kagan had a fro-yo machine installed in the Supreme Court cafeteria in 2011.

In America, the most popular ice cream flavor is *drumroll* vanilla.

Lemons, limes, oranges, and grapefruits are all hybrid fruits.

Back in the 1880s when it was invented, what we now call candy corn was called "chicken feed" and was marketed to rural America.

If your grain alcohol is made in Scotland, Canada, or Japan, it's spelled "whisky." In the United States and Ireland, it's spelled "whiskey."

In 2018, a Girl Scout in San Diego sold more than three hundred boxes of Girl Scout Cookies in just six hours by setting up shop outside a marijuana dispensary.

Women are twice as likely as men to order soup for lunch.

Apple pie isn't American. The first known recipe for the dish is from England in 1381.

A Washington woman who was furloughed from her retail job during the COVID-19 pandemic spent eight hours a day, seven days a week, for months making lasagnas for anyone who asked for one. Michelle Brenner cooked more than 1,200 lasagnas, gave many to essential workers, and earned the nickname Lasagna Lady.

M&Ms are the most popular candy in the United States, followed by Reese's Peanut Butter Cups and Hershey's Kisses.

The word *mocha* comes from the Yemeni port city of Mocha, which was once a coffee epicenter and has always been known for its chocolatey coffee beans.

JEOPARDY! CONTESTANT FAVE FACT

From the introduction of the Hershey Bar in 1900 through 1969, there was a constant item called the nickel or five-cent Hershey Bar. The price was always a nickel, but the size of the bar would fluctuate, up or down, depending on changes in cocoa and sugar prices. I found it particularly interesting that it would increase in size when cocoa prices fell, as one assumes that stopped Hershey from increasing profits. In 1969, with the bar down to .75 ounce, they discontinued the bar (a ten-cent bar had been introduced a few years earlier and it also fluctuated; if you looked carefully on shelves you could find nickel bars more than half the size of the dime bar—I remember doing this at our local Ben Franklin store as a kid in the '60s). Hershey did the same thing with the dime bar until the hyperinflation of the mid-'70s. In 1974, the bar went to 15 cents and by the end of that year was smaller than the dime bar had been at the beginning of the year. —Rick Goldfarb

Yes, there are Outback Steakhouses in Australia.

Plastic absorbs carbonation, so soft drinks really *do* taste different in cans versus bottles. Plus, plastic has its own taste, and so does aluminum.

If you drop a raisin in a flute of champagne, the raisin will bounce back and forth between the top and bottom of the glass. Why? Science! It has to do with carbon dioxide dissolving in the champagne, and CO_2 bubbles attaching to the raisin.

Some experts believe you get a better taste licking ice cream than you do eating it with a spoon. The flavors are released when it melts, and licking creates more tongue-to-ice-cream time, thus giving the ice cream more of a chance to warm up and release its chilly goodness.

Meanwhile, the nation that consumes the most ice cream per capita is New Zealand. On average, New Zealanders eat 7.5 gallons per year.

The thirty-seven Yeoman Warders who guard the Tower of London—and are also known as Beefeaters—receive a free bottle of gin on their birthdays from the unaffiliated gin brand Beefeater.

Collectively, Americans eat one hundred acres of pizza per day.

In the eighteenth-century United States, caviar was a *free bar snack* because it was salty and would make patrons thirsty. It was also cheap. By the early twentieth century, sturgeon was overfished, caviar became a delicacy mostly imported from Russia, and prices skyrocketed.

From 1795 to 1858, manufacturers suggested opening cans with a hammer and chisel. Primitive can openers came after that, and significant improvements were made around 1870. Still, until about 1900, Americans would get their canned food opened by clerks at the grocery store.

The namesake of Granny Smith apples was an Australian grandmother named Maria Ann Smith.

Burger King was the first fast food chain to sell veggie burgers, in 2002.

In 2003, Red Lobster lost $3 million when they underestimated how much people would eat when offered Endless Crabs for $22.99. They almost went bankrupt.

People will rate a wine better when they believe it's expensive.

According to the Bible, specifically Genesis 1:20–22, the chicken came before the egg.

The number-one-selling beer in the United States is Bud Light.

The tradition of saving a slice of wedding cake to eat it on your first anniversary comes from the assumption that you'll have a baby around then, and this would be your (stale) celebratory cake for that event.

Some experts believe Guinness beer isn't originally Irish, it's Welsh.

Putting sprinkles at the *bottom* of a cone can stop ice cream leakage. Brilliant!

Hawaiian pizza was invented by a Greek guy in Canada.

Every year, one in six Americans get sick from food. However, food poisoning is probably not from the last meal you ate. It usually takes at least six hours to hit. This isn't the happiest fact, but it may help you identify the culprit next time your tummy feels off.

The indentation on the underside of a wine bottle is called a "punt."

Ben and Jerry originally intended to open a bagel shop, but the machinery was too expensive. Now the company does so well that employees of Ben & Jerry's headquarters in South Burlington, Vermont, are entitled to three free pints of ice cream a day.

Okay, I simply can*not* stop with the ice cream facts: Ice cream is filled with teeny tiny air bubbles that help make it smooth and light. When it melts, the air bubbles escape, which is why refrozen ice cream feels denser.

The Pillsbury Doughboy's actual name is Poppin' Fresh.

Here's a helpful fact if you're on a diet: The average chocolate bar has eight insect parts in it. (If you're not on a diet, I'm so sorry.)

The oldest cake that still exists is Queen Victoria and Prince Albert's wedding cake from the year 1840.

Danishes are from Austria, not Denmark.

Chock Full o'Nuts coffee has no nuts in it. The company started as a nut outfit, then added coffee, then stopped selling nuts.

Carrots! Do not! Improve! Your eyesight! And they don't help you see at night. During World War II, the British had just developed radar technology and were striking down enemy planes with unprecedented accuracy. In an attempt to obfuscate their invention, they spread the rumor that the pilots were successful because they ate so many carrots. This lie also helped sell carrots, which were plentiful at the time, in England. That said, even though carrots won't improve your vision, beta-carotene is slightly beneficial for eye health.

Drinking coffee can lower your risk of dying from heart disease, respiratory disease, and diabetes.

In Japan, farmers have started growing square watermelons because they stack better.

The Bloody Mary brunch cocktail was originally called a Bucket of Blood, named after a West Side Chicago nightclub. It was later called the Red Snapper. Then finally, the Bloody Mary. (It's unclear to which Mary the *Mary* refers.) (Silly Author Note: This is one of my favorite facts, as I host a Bloody Mary bar crawl every year called the Bloody Mary–thon. Bucket of Blood–a–thon doesn't exactly have the same ring.)

Popcorn was discovered by Aztecs about four thousand years ago. They had a word for the sound popping kernels make: *totopoca*.

If you put a can of Diet Coke in water, it floats, but regular Coke sinks. Coke contains a larger amount of sugar than Diet Coke has of its sweetener, aspartame—thus Coke is slightly denser.

Pound cake got its name because the original recipe called for an entire pound of each of its four ingredients: eggs, flour, sugar, and, mmm, mmm, *butter*, baby.

Starting in the 1850s, sausages were referred to as Bags O Mystery in the UK.

Ninety-six percent of American kids recognize Ronald McDonald.

There's a Starbucks at the CIA . . . but employees don't write your name on your drink, for obvious reasons.

During Prohibition, grape growers sold grape juice accompanied by detailed instructions "warning" buyers how, exactly, *not* to turn the grapes into wine.

The brand Pez comes from the German word for peppermint (*pfefferminz*), which was the original flavor of the candy.

Soup has been around for approximately twenty thousand years. The oldest soup remnants that have been discovered by archeologists date back to 6000 BCE. It was hippopotamus soup.

Pineapple is named such because early American explorers thought it looked like a pinecone.

Refried beans are fried only once.

Consuming chia seeds is a great idea before a workout because they absorb thirty times their weight in water and release it back into your system slowly over time.

In the mid-1980s, there was such a thing as Nerds breakfast cereal with different flavors separated by a partition in the box, just like the candy. It didn't last long: It was discontinued by the end of the decade.

Even though they're more expensive and many people believe they're "more natural," brown eggs are no better for you than white eggs. Egg color has nothing to do with how a hen was fed or treated; it reflects only the breed of chicken it came from. The two colors (or blue- or cream-colored!) are equally healthy.

How many licks does it take to get to the center of a Tootsie Pop? Researchers/heroes at Purdue University and the University of Michigan made a licking machine to find out. The Michigan licking machine counted 411, the Purdue licking machine found 364, and human Purdue "volunteers" took 252 licks. So the jury's still out. (And that's a good excuse to experiment.)

Discontinued Jell-O flavors include bubble gum, mixed vegetable, celery, seasoned tomatoes, and Italian salad, which was supposed to taste like pasta and Italian dressing.

Until 2013, Russia classified beer, and all spirits containing less than 10 percent alcohol, as food.

Flamin' Hot Cheetos were invented by a janitor.

Milk Duds got their name because, in 1928, the chocolate machine at F. Hoffman & Co. in Chicago couldn't produce perfectly round chocolate-covered caramels. Now the candies are owned by Hershey, but they still look like "duds."

In a 1907 ad, Kellogg's offered free cornflakes to women who winked at their grocers.

It's a myth that monosodium glutamate (MSG), a flavor additive in a lot of Chinese food, is worse for your health than table salt. It's not. The racist belief in MSG-induced sickness called "Chinese Restaurant Syndrome" was debunked in studies in the 1990s.

Mountain Dew was originally slang for moonshine.

Avocados are berries.

Froot Loops are all the same flavor.

In 1924, popsicles were accidentally invented by an eleven-year-old who left a mixture of sugary soda powder and water outside over an icy night.

Ripe cranberries bounce.

WRITERS & BOOKS

○ ○

As a lifelong writer and good student, it pains me to confess that I once got a *double* F on a college Shakespeare midterm. I remember staring at my blue book in confusion: two F's scribbled in thick, red marker. I turned to my friend Peter and asked with tears in my eyes, "What does a double F mean?"

"You Friggin Failed it," he said.

He was right. I had done so poorly that one F just wasn't enough.

Shockingly, I wound up with a B in the class. And while I grew to appreciate, even love, Shakespeare's works, I'll always associate him with the most terrifying moment in my academic life. Still, it won't stop me from including ol' Billy Shakes in this chapter.

But before we cross the pond, let's learn some Yankee trivia. Allison Sansone is the program director of the American Writers Museum. When I asked for her favorite literature fact, she hit me with a Hemingway, and I was happy she did. I'd always heard that the author was, frankly, a professional drunk, and wondered how he managed to find the time to write. Allison cleared that up:

"We remember Ernest Hemingway as much for the cult of Hemingway—the hard-partying, bad-husbanding stereotype of the twentieth-century male writer—as we do for his work, but, all wife jokes aside, he's immortal in no small part because he had the unshakable work ethic of a former journalist. He often wrote standing up, his typewriter atop a dresser or chest, because his wounds in World War I and later adventures left him in permanent chronic pain. However, he didn't let that stop him from doing three to five hours of work every morning."

Turns out Papa was the inventor of the standing desk!

Dr. Seuss's editor bet him that he couldn't write a book using fifty unique words or fewer. Dr. Seuss (real name Theodor Seuss Geisel) turned in *Green Eggs and Ham*. Also, Dr. Seuss's license plate read GRINCH.

Mark Twain was born in a year of Halley's Comet (1835) and predicted he'd die when it came back. He did, the day after it shone its brightest, in 1910. Also, despite writing dozens of books, Twain didn't have an education beyond elementary school.

Sophia Tolstoy, Leo's wife, transcribed seven drafts of *War and Peace*—by hand. Can you imagine? Apparently, Leo had horrible handwriting that couldn't be discerned by nearly anyone but her, so she did this during every writing, reading, and editing process. And while we're thinking about Leo: His real name was Lev Tolstoy. We call him Leo because that's the Anglo-Latin word for "Lion." In Russia, the word for "lion" is *Lev*.

In 1950, Gwendolyn Brooks became the first Black author to win a Pulitzer for her work *Annie Allen*.

The story of *Beauty and the Beast* was penned in France in 1740 by Gabrielle-Suzanne Barbot de Villeneuve to help women learn to accept arranged marriages. The beast was a combo of an elephant and a fish.

Mary Shelley finished writing *Frankenstein* by age nineteen, and it was published when she was twenty. It's a story about motherhood and mother figures and is widely regarded as the first science-fiction novel. Also, Frankenstein's monster was a vegetarian.

In the original story published in 1634, Sleeping Beauty slept for one hundred years.

Ancient Greek writing had no spaces between words.

Toni Morrison didn't start writing until her thirties and didn't publish her first book, *The Bluest Eye*, until age thirty-nine. Yay for late bloomers!

Cormac McCarthy wrote works including *Blood Meridian* and *No Country for Old Men* on the same used, $50 typewriter for more than fifty years. When it finally broke, he auctioned it off for $254,500 and gave the proceeds to the nonprofit Santa Fe Institute, a scientific research foundation.

Shakespeare created the name Jessica, who was Shylock's daughter in *The Merchant of Venice*.

To pay for college, and before she was the blockbuster author of *White Teeth*, *On Beauty*, and *NW*, to name a few, Zadie Smith worked as a cabaret singer in England.

Stuart Little wasn't a mouse. He was a human boy who looked "very much like a mouse in every way."

Pride and Prejudice was originally titled *First Impressions* when Jane Austen first, and unsuccessfully, submitted it for publication.

Reading is a proven stress-reducer.

Many women authors have written under male or androgynous pen names at some point in their careers so that their work would be taken more seriously: the Brontë sisters (who wrote under Currer Bell, Acton Bell, and Ellis Bell), Mary Ann Evans (aka George Eliot), Nelle Harper Lee (aka Harper Lee), Joan Cooper (aka J. California Cooper), and Louisa May Alcott (aka A. M. Barnard).

Chuck Palahniuk said the movie version of *Fight Club* was better than his novel.

The most expensive book ever was purchased by Bill Gates for $30.8 million. It was *Codex Leicester*, the sixteenth-century journal of Leonardo da Vinci.

Voltaire was said to drink forty to fifty cups of coffee every day.

You know those little notebooks reporters use? They were "invented" when journalist Claude Sitton cut his steno pads in half while reporting on the civil rights movement to avoid attracting attention. In fact, when he put one smaller notebook in each coat pocket, some assumed he was wearing a shoulder holster and treated him as an FBI agent.

Alice's Adventures in Wonderland was based on a real ten-year-old girl, Alice Liddell, a little sister of Lewis Carroll's good friend Harry.

Sherlock Holmes never says "Elementary, my dear Watson" in the works of Sir Arthur Conan Doyle. Holmes says "elementary" often, but the specific phrase seems to have arisen organically from the public sometime around 1902. Doyle wrote Holmes's stories between 1887 and 1927.

The longest book in the world is Marcel Proust's *À la recherche du temps perdu* (aka *Remembrance of Things Past*). It's 9,609,000 characters long and was published in 1913.

The longest-ever book title was written by Vityala Yethindra in 2019 and is 3777 words long. It starts: "The historical development of the Heart i.e. from its formation from Annelida . . ."

In 1773, Phillis Wheatley became the first published Black author in the United States. She was only twelve when her first poem was published.

The city of Warsaw, Poland, has the most libraries per capita of anywhere in the world, 11.5 per 100,000 people. Lisbon, Portugal, has more bookstores than anyplace else in the world: 42 per 100,000 residents.

In the entirety of R. L. Stine's fifty-eight-book horror series *Goosebumps*, nobody dies. Also, before he wrote scary books, R. L. Stine wrote the jokes on Bazooka Joe gum wrappers.

John Steinbeck's dog ate part of an early draft of *Of Mice and Men*.

WORD ORIGINS & LANGUAGE

As a stand-up comedian, I can tell you definitively: Soup is always funny. For example, the sentence "I was crying" is sad. But "I was crying into my soup"? The tragedy factor goes down, the comedy factor goes up.

But Greg Nedved, president of the National Museum of Language, taught me that soup could be even funnier than I previously knew. He said:

"Noah Webster's original spelling of *soup*, 'soop,' did not catch on."

"Soop" is amazing. It's somehow even sadder than "soup," but in a funny way, maybe because the double *o* looks like ghost eyes. I'm not sure. In any case, I'm all in on "soop." Let's start a revolution. But not before this literal word trivia, which the team at Planet Word, an interactive museum of language arts, sent me:

"*Trivia* comes from Latin and refers to the intersection of three roads. This is where people met and traded gossip and information, thus *trivia* came to mean just such tidbits of information."

So there's your trivia trivia. Now, more trivia:

The original meaning for the word *nimrod* was "hunter"—that's why Bugs Bunny called Elmer Fudd a "nimrod." But Elmer was also a moron, so the meaning evolved.

The first recorded use of OMG was in 1917. It was from a Lord "Jacky" Fisher to Winston Churchill.

Some identical twins make up a language that no one else can understand. This phenomenon is called cryptophasia.

Crossword puzzles were called "word-cross puzzles" when they were invented by *New York World* newspaper editor Arthur Wynne in 1913. A few weeks later, a printer transposed the typesets, and the mistake stuck as "crossword." In 1924, an opinion column in *The New York Times*—now the gold standard of crosswords—called the game a "sinful waste."

In Thai, the word for "five" is pronounced "ha," which is why Thai Internet slang for "hahaha," is "55555."

The word *forte*, meaning something you're good at, comes from fencing. The forte is the strongest part of the sword.

In 1973, Norman Mailer coined the word *factoid* to mean information that was only semifactual and used to manipulate the masses. The word evolved until it became synonymous with "fun facts." Like this one!

The term *honeymoon* may have come from the ancient Babylonian practice of sending newlyweds off to enjoy themselves and imbibe the honey-based alcohol mead for an entire lunar month after their wedding.

In 2019, *stan*, meaning "an extremely or excessively enthusiastic and devoted fan," was added to the Merriam-Webster dictionary. The term originated with Eminem's 2000 hit "Stan."

At the height of their popularity in the 1950s and '60s, drive-in movie theaters were colloquially referred to as "passion pits" because young couples would often go there to hook up.

In 1837, the Irish Marquis of Waterford got very drunk with friends in an English town called Melton Mowbray and painted all the doors—and a swan statue—red. That's where "Let's paint the town red" comes from. (He had to pay the town back.)

A Victorian-era term for a best friend was *chuckaboo*.

Hipster is almost a hundred years old. In the early 1930s, it referred to "a dancer" (aka one who uses their hips), and later that decade it came to mean "someone who is knowledgeable about jazz." At the time, *hip* and *hep* meant "in-the-know," and *hipster* and *hepster* were interchangeable. No one knows exactly how the definition evolved to its current meaning.

JEOPARDY! CONTESTANT FAVE FACT

When life hands you lemons—make lemonade! Fifteen-year-old Louis Braille, an avid reader who yearned to read more books, invented his alphabet to help blind people read more easily.
—Raj Sivaraman

The phrase *long in the tooth* comes from the fact that horses' teeth never stop growing. So if a horse is "long in the tooth," it's pretty old. Though other animals have teeth that never stop growing, it particularly matters with horses because people buy and sell them all the time, and checking a horse's teeth tells a potential buyer if the seller was truthful about the animal's age.

There's a word for the fear of misplacing your phone or being out of reach of cell service: *nomophobia*. It's a shortened version of "no mobile phone phobia."

One of the first recorded uses of *sneakers* was in England in 1862. Inmates of a women's prison called their wardens "sneaks" because their rubber-soled shoes allowed them to sneak up on unsuspecting prisoners.

The smell of rain is called "petrichor."

The technical word for the hashtag symbol is *octothorpe*.

Backlog refers to the biggest log in a fire—the back log can burn the longest without needing to be replaced.

JEOPARDY! CONTESTANT FAVE FACT

The sentence "I never said she stole my money" has seven different meanings depending on which of its seven words you emphasize when you say it aloud.
—Wes Hazard

There's a Japanese word for "death by overwork": *karoshi*. Even so, Japan has the second-longest life expectancy in the world.

In 2011, Merriam-Webster declared that *literally* also means "figuratively."

In Late Middle English, *fizzle* meant "to fart quietly."

The term *by and large*, meaning "pretty much all" or "all things considered," comes from nautical terminology. As early as the sixteenth century, *by* referred to ships sailing into the wind and *large* referred to ships sailing with the wind at their back. So *by and large* literally meant "in almost any situation."

In the nineteenth century, a "twitter" was an abscess on a horse's hoof.

When it's your turn in a game, and it hits you that any move you make will be to your disadvantage, that situation is called a "zugzwang."

When an Irish person says "Top of the mornin' to ya," you're supposed to say "And the rest of the day to yourself."

Goodbye originated from *God bye*, which is derived from the sixteenth-century phrase *God be with you*.

Thanks to Destiny's Child, *bootylicious* was added to the *Oxford English Dictionary* in 2004.

Pushing the envelope means "testing the limits," and has nothing to do with mail. The word also has a complex mathematical definition, and in the U.S. space program, it has long been common to discuss whether aircrafts could "push the outside of the envelope" in reference to their turn capabilities and speed. The term became colloquially popular when a book about the program called *The Right Stuff* hit shelves in 1979.

The fear of long words is called hippopotomonstrosesquippedaliophobia.

Griffonage is the word for very sloppy handwriting.

There are two verbs for eating in Germany: one for animals (*fressen*) and one for people (*essen*). Using *fressen* on a person implies they're gorging themselves like an animal.

When people started installing home phones around 1878, no one answered by saying "Hello." They said "Ahoy."

The word *karaoke* means "empty orchestra" in Japanese.

The German insult *Arschgeige* translates to "butt violin."

Competitive racehorses sometimes have a goat companion, which is said to have a calming effect, so to "get someone's goat" means to rile up and upset someone's Zen little universe. (In fact, many horses mourn if their goat doesn't travel with them!)

Jim Henson invented *muppet*. It's a combo of *marionette* and *puppet*.

The dot on the top of an *i* is called a tittle.

The word *espresso* translates to "pressed out" in Italian.

AC/DC was 1960s slang for bisexual.

FOMO has been in the *Oxford English Dictionary* since 2013.

The term *happy as a clam* comes from a longer expression, *Happy as a clam at high tide*, since clams are safe from being harvested at high tide.

The term *computer bug* was popularized by from a 1947 logbook entry by programmer Grace Hopper at Harvard. Hopper's team had found an actual bug, a moth, stuck between relay contacts in the computer. Hopper taped the moth to the notebook and wrote, "First actual case of bug being found."

A Victorian term for "mouth" was *sauce-box*.

There's a punctuation mark to denote irony, but most of us don't use it. It looks like this: ⸮

They're called "boxing rings" and not "boxing squares" because in early boxing, there were no boundaries besides the crowd, who would form a circle around the fighters.

When KFC was marketed in China, its slogan *Finger-lickin' good* was mistranslated to "Eat your fingers off!"

The word *testify* comes from ancient Rome, when men would swear on their testicles in court.

Some hors d'oeuvres are called "canapés" because in French, *canapé* means "sofa," and these snacks consist of a spread that sits atop toasted bread like a person sitting on a couch. I know, it's a stretch. But also? Delicious.

Archeologists use the initialism *B.P.* for radiocarbon dating. *B.P.* stands for Before Present, and "present" is the year 1950. Radiocarbon dating was invented in the late 1940s, so 1950 was selected as the "present" even though it was actually the "future." Archeologists are wild, man.

The Bible has been translated into Elvish and Klingon.

When we hold up our glasses at a celebration, we call it a "toast" because in ancient Rome, toast was dropped in the wineglass to temper the wine, which had sometimes gone bad.

In 1920s American diners, french fries were called "frog sticks," and *burn the British* meant "toasted English muffin."

Wait, there's more. In classic diner lingo, *dog soup* meant "water," *breath* meant "onion," and *drown the kids* meant "boiled eggs." *Chicks on a raft* was eggs on toast. And *cluck and grunt* meant "ham and eggs."

The word *karate* is both Japanese and Chinese. It's a combination of two Chinese characters that are used in the Japanese writing system called kanji. The character called *kara* means "empty," and the character called *te* means "hand."

That glob of toothpaste on your toothbrush is called a "nurdle."

It took Webster twenty-eight years to write his dictionary.

In France, a hangover is often referred to as a "hair ache." In Denmark, they call it "carpenters in the forehead," and in Poland, it's "a howling of kittens."

Bow wow mutton was a Victorian naval term for meat that tasted so bad it might as well be dog meat.

Muscle comes from the Latin word for "little mouse" because in the fourteenth century it was thought that muscles looked like little mice under the skin.

In the mid-twentieth century, *in the ketchup* meant "in the red," aka when someone is in debt.

The United States has no official language.

MORBID FACTS FOR KNOW-IT-ALL GOTHS

Y ou may think it's strange to include a chapter of morbid facts in an uplifting book of trivia. To that I say: Why must they be mutually exclusive? Death is as inevitable as bad selfies and misplaced socks, so we might as well embrace it.

I'm not alone here. The Order of the Good Death is an organization of funeral industry professionals, academics, and artists who dedicate themselves to preparing our death-phobic culture for mortality. They preach death positivity, and their executive director, Sarah Chavez, is full of fascinating information surrounding the topic:

"During the Victorian era, cemeteries were such a popular leisure destination that some cemeteries had to sell admission tickets to prevent overcrowding."

"Some cities once had dedicated transportation lines just to transport the dead and mourners. In the United States, cities like Los Angeles and Chicago had special funeral streetcars, while London had an entire railroad line, called the Necropolis railway, to ferry the dead to their final resting place."

"Ancient Greeks and Romans once believed that the souls of the dead resided in fava beans. Beans were eaten by the bride and groom at weddings to attract male ancestors."

Eat your beans, people! Nobody wants to leave Pop-Pop alone on a plate. (Sorry, *too* morbid?)

The ashes of the inventor of the Pringles can are kept in a Pringles can.

When Ford began advertising in Belgium in the 1970s, one of its ads was supposed to say "Every car has a high-quality body," but it was mistranslated to "Every car has a high-quality corpse."

A cat named Oscar who lives at a Rhode Island nursing home can predict which resident is next to die. The cat curls up with those who are soon to pass and was the subject of the book *Making Rounds with Oscar: The Extraordinary Gift of an Ordinary Cat*.

Austrian American composer Arnold Schoenberg suffered from the fear of the number *13*, aka triskaidekaphobia. When he turned seventy-six, a coworker told him it'd be an unlucky year to die, since seven plus six equals thirteen. He died later that year, on Friday the thirteenth.

There's an island in Mexico called La Isla de las Muñecas covered in dolls that are said to be haunted or possessed. Most of the dolls were placed, strewn, and hung by the island's caretaker, Don Julian Santana Barrera, who collected and displayed the toys to honor a young girl who'd drowned just off the island. In 2001, he was found drowned in the same place her corpse had been discovered fifty years earlier. Now, La Isla de las Muñecas is an offbeat tourist attraction.

According to a poll by *Who Wants to Be a Millionaire*, 4 percent of respondents answered "yes" to the question "Have you been decapitated?"

A few milligrams of the Belcher's sea snake's venom is enough to kill a thousand humans. (That's one of Bob's Burgers I'll pass on.)

Approximately 107 billion people have ever lived on Earth. Just 7 billion of them are alive today.

In Nederland, Colorado, there's a festival every March called Frozen Dead Guy Days, which honors two men who were found frozen in a shed in the 1990s: "Grandpa" Bredo Morstoel and Al Campbell from Chicago. The town tried to have the bodies buried, but after a flurry of media attention, the local government changed its mind. The bodies get re-iced once a month, and the festival includes coffin races, ice sculpting, and a dead guy look-alike contest.

It's a myth that women found guilty of being a witch were burned at the stake during the Salem Witch Trials. They were hanged.

In the 1940s, a chicken named Mike lived for eighteen months with its head chopped off.

Mortgage comes from French words that mean "death pledge."

There was spooky stuff going on during the filming of the iconic horror movie *The Exorcist*: Nine cast and crew members died surrounding the shooting and premiere; the set burned down except for Regan's possessed bedroom, which was left pristine; a priest was called to bless the set; the woman who played Regan's mom got a permanent spinal injury when she was thrown from Regan's bed for a scene in the film; and during the movie's premiere in Rome, lightning struck a four-hundred-year-old cross on top of a nearby sixteenth-century church.

The Great Fire of London burned down half the city in 1666, but only six people were killed. More people have died falling off the Great Fire of London monument.

Turnips and beets, not pumpkins, were originally used as jack-o'-lanterns.

The female black widow spider eats the male while or after they mate.

Your fingernails don't continue to grow when you die. It only appears that way because your skin recedes.

In 2019, a seven-year-old boy went to the hospital with a swollen jaw. Surgeons found that the boy had grown a mass filled with *526 miniature teeth*.

Forty-five percent of American adults believe demons and ghosts probably exist. Only 13 percent believe in vampires.

It is said that Peter the Great had his wife Catherine's lover decapitated, his head stored in a jar of alcohol and kept in her bedroom.

The band Kiss made a line of coffins called Kiss Kaskets.

Owls eat other owls. In fact, in 1927 an owl was found with an owl in its stomach, and that owl had an owl in *its* stomach. Talk about a *Russian Nesting D-owl*. (Am I fired from comedy? Probably yes.)

Thanatology is the scientific study of death and grief.

The number *4* is unlucky in China because the word for "four" is pronounced the same as the word for "death."

The number *9* is unlucky in Japan because the word for "nine" sounds like the word for "suffering."

Bedbugs have been around for 100 million years.

George Washington was terrified of being buried alive, so he demanded to be laid out for three days after he passed, just to make sure he was *really* dead.

A cockroach can live several weeks with its head cut off.

John and Yoko: A Love Story was a 1985 made-for-TV movie. The man who was cast as John Lennon had the same name as the man who murdered Lennon in 1980, Mark Chapman. Once executives realized this, they recast the role.

JFK's brain went missing from the National Archives in 1966 and has never been found.

In 2019, after a woman in Utah died, her husband's body was discovered in her freezer. It had been there for ten years, along with a notarized letter from him stating she didn't kill him. She didn't report his death so she could continue collecting his veteran's benefits, with his consent.

Russian prisoners used to tattoo one another with pictures of Lenin and Stalin because guards weren't allowed to shoot pictures of their national leaders, which meant the prisoners could not be shot.

The average human sheds about seventy-seven pounds of skin in their lifetime.

In July 1518, a "dancing plague" swept Strasbourg, Alsace, which is now in northern France. People danced uncontrollably, some to their death. The cause remains a mystery.

"Twelve plus one" is an anagram of "eleven plus two," and both equal thirteen.

The corpse of a wealthy woman called Xin Zhui (Lady Dai in the West) was discovered in a tomb in a hill in China in 1971. Her body was more than two thousand years old, but she had hair, eyelashes, and Type A blood in her veins. She was preserved in a mysterious liquid that still puzzles scientists.

Being scared releases dopamine, endorphins, and adrenaline. Watching horror movies causes us to get a hit of all those naturally occurring "happy" chemicals from the safety of our couch.

The fantastic book *Confederacy of Dunces*, whose author, John Kennedy Toole, died by suicide at age thirty-one, may never be adapted to film because every actor who gets cast in the starring role dies: John Belushi, John Candy, and Chris Farley. Also, the book's set in New Orleans, and the head of the Louisiana Film Commission was murdered by her husband soon after trying to get the movie off the ground.

It's unknown exactly how long a human brain remains conscious after decapitation, but it's at least several seconds.

In 2013, a man named Harrison Okene survived in a pitch-dark capsized tugboat for three days while listening to fish eat the corpses of his shipmates. He spent his time praying and says his rescue and survival were a miracle.

People with a morbid sense of humor tend to have higher IQs.

SUPERLATIVES FOR YOUR LIFE

You're ten times more likely to win an Oscar than you are to be struck by lightning.

You're eighteen times more likely to bowl a perfect game as a casual player than you are to be involved in an airplane crash.

You're two times more likely to be killed by a champagne cork than you are by a shark.

You're three times more likely to be killed by ants than you are by a shark.

You're fifteen times more likely to be killed by a falling coconut than you are by a shark.

You're ten times more likely to be killed by a freshwater snail than you are by sharks, wolves, and lions combined.

You're twenty times more likely to die at a dance party than you are to be killed by a black bear.

You're thirty-eight times more likely to become famous than you are to be killed by an alligator.

In America, you're forty-one thousand times more likely to die by an accidental firearm discharge than you are by a shark.

In a given year, there are ten times as many human-to-human bites in New York than there are shark bites in the entire world.

Doesn't that put "scary" things into perspective? (I'm probably going to be eaten by a shark and a black bear while on a crashing plane now.)

TV & MOVIES

Jennifer Keishin Armstrong is the *New York Times* bestselling author of *Seinfeldia: How a Show about Nothing Changed Everything*; a history of *The Mary Tyler Moore Show, Mary and Lou and Rhoda and Ted: And All the Brilliant Minds Who Made* The Mary Tyler Moore Show *a Classic;* and *Sex and the City and Us: How Four Single Women Changed the Way We Think, Live, and Love*. She knows everything there is to know about TV history, including:

"Lucille Ball and Desi Arnaz wanted to shoot *I Love Lucy* in Los Angeles, where they were living in the early 1950s. But most shows were live at the time and originated from New York City. To solve this problem, they agreed to take a pay cut to shoot on film, which was much more expensive. This turned out to be key to the show's enduring renown; because it was shot on film, it was preserved in syndicated reruns for decades to come, while other shows from the same time were not."

And

"In 1949, the coaxial cable that linked New York City—the main hub of TV production—to other parts of the country reached only as far west as St. Louis. So cities in that network, which included Chicago, Milwaukee, Detroit, and Cleveland, could get the live broadcasts coming from there. But the western United States could only get the "national" shows via kinescope, which was a bad copy of a show made by filming a monitor, kind of like a bootleg copy of a movie shown in theaters."

Just the idea of not being able to watch *The Great British Baking Show* on demand at 2 a.m. is giving me heart palpitations. *breathes deeply, counts to ten* I'm okay. We're okay.

In 2020, twenty-four-year-old Zendaya became the youngest-ever person to win an Emmy for Lead Actress for the show *Euphoria*.

The set for the impoverished, flooded neighborhood in 2020 Best Picture *Parasite* was built on a water tank and included items from actual abandoned homes to make it feel as realistic as possible.

The woman who played Phyllis Vance on the American version of *The Office*, Phyllis Smith, was an assistant casting director who did so well reading with actors that the director wrote her into the show.

Also in Dunder Mifflin news, John Krasinski shot the footage for the show's title sequence himself on a research trip to Scranton, Pennsylvania.

The original director of *Jaws* was replaced (with Steven Spielberg) because he kept referring to the shark as a whale. Also, on set, the three animatronic sharks that created Jaws were collectively nicknamed Bruce.

In *Dazed and Confused*, you never actually *see* Matthew McConaughey say, "All right, all right, all right." You just hear it.

When a Pixar movie comes out, head lice breaks out like crazy because kids flock to movie theaters. Lice prefer kids' heads because they're less acidic.

Frank Sinatra was offered the role of John McClane in 1988's *Die Hard*, when he was in his seventies. The movie is technically a sequel to a 1968 film called *The Detective*, in which Sinatra starred. Contractually, the studios were obligated to offer him the part. He turned it down.

Joaquin Phoenix shed fifty-two pounds to play Arthur Fleck in *Joker*, for which he won an Oscar. He said the weight loss highlighted the character's fragility.

James Cameron sold rights to his script for *The Terminator* to producer Gale Anne Hurd for $1 on the condition that he could direct it.

In 2019, *Black-ish* star Marsai Martin became the youngest executive producer in history at age fourteen.

Since 1996, Queen Latifah has had a clause in her movie contracts saying her characters cannot die.

Bill Murray was bitten by the groundhog twice while filming *Groundhog Day*.

JEOPARDY! CONTESTANT FAVE FACT

One year after the Supreme Court made interracial marriage legal, *Star Trek* had the first televised interracial kiss between Captain Kirk and Lieutenant Uhura, a significant moment for the civil rights movement. Ironically, this moment might not have been possible if not for the intervention of Dr. Martin Luther King Jr., a self-described "Trekkie," who urged Nichelle Nichols (the actress who portrayed Lieutenant Uhura) to not leave the show for Broadway.
—Raj Sivaraman

The Powerpuff Girls were originally called the Whoopass Girls, and their first short film was called *Whoopass Stew!*

The Owl House, which premiered in 2020, is the first-ever Disney show to feature a bisexual lead character, Luz Noceda.

Boyz n the Hood director John Singleton was both the youngest-ever director to be nominated for an Oscar and the first Black director to be nominated back in 1991. He was twenty-four.

That green code at the beginning of *The Matrix*? It's sushi recipes that the production designer pulled from his wife's cookbook.

The Cookie Monster has a name: Sid.

There were women gladiators in ancient Rome.

Harriet Tubman was a naturalist who could mimic birdcalls, and she used that ability to help her guide enslaved people to freedom.

The Nobel Prize was created as part of Alfred Nobel's will, and the first one was given out in 1901. He didn't want to be known only for inventing dynamite and all its destructive capabilities.

The words *I have a dream* were not part of Martin Luther King Jr.'s original, iconic speech at the Lincoln Memorial in 1963. Dr. King spoke those words extemporaneously after a friend, gospel singer Mahalia Jackson, shouted, "Tell 'em about the dream, Martin."

Winston Churchill came to the United States during Prohibition carrying a prescription for alcohol. Also, the reason he looks grumpy on the British five-pound bank note is because the photographer had just taken away his cigar.

Starting in 1913, the U.S. Postal Service increased the weight limit for mail to eleven pounds. The result was that several small children were mailed for 15 cents apiece.

President George W. Bush and Senator John Kerry, who ran for president against each other in 2004, are distant cousins.

From 1776 through 1807, all citizens of New Jersey who were twenty-one or older could vote, regardless of race or gender.

Ancient Egyptians shaved off their eyebrows when their cats died as a sign of mourning. Cats were so respected that they were mummified after death.

Bradley Cooper cast his own dog, Charlie, in *A Star Is Born*.

Contrary to what you'll see in your average Western, 25 percent of American cowboys were Black.

Apple will not allow villains to use iPhones in movies. So if you see a character with an iPhone, you know they're a good guy.

In *The Empire Strikes Back*, some of the asteroids are potatoes.

Martin Scorsese said Joe Pesci turned down his role in the 2019 Oscar nominee *The Irishman* at least fifty times before finally giving in.

When Paul McCartney voiced himself on the 1995 episode of *The Simpsons* "Lisa the Vegetarian," he did it on the condition that she would stay a vegetarian, and she has. Also, *The Simpsons* is the oldest prime-time scripted show on television. It began in 1989 and at the time of this writing is still going strong.

In 2003, Jay Leno ate a bite of a 125-year-old fruitcake on *The Tonight Show*. After one long chew he said, "It needs more time."

In the amazing* TV show *The Golden Girls*, Estelle Getty plays Bea Arthur's mother, even though she was younger than Arthur in real life.

---

* I'm serious, it's really funny. Watch some reruns!

Harrison Ford had dysentery while making *Raiders of the Lost Ark*.

Following the 2009 debut of the MTV show *16 and Pregnant*, teen pregnancy rates dropped by 5.7 percent.

The website for the movie *Space Jam* has been up, unchanged, since 1996.

An actor named Henry Hull played three different characters in the 1939 movie *Miracles for Sale* and was the first person to use contact lenses to change his eye color in a film. He had brown eyes, but for one role, he wore blue contact lenses. The movie was in black-and-white.

According to Greta Gerwig, the *Little Women* (2019) costume designer Jacqueline Durran had Jo and Laurie continually swap vests to symbolize that they were each other's "androgynous other half."

Actress Laverne Cox was the first trans person to play a trans series regular on television, the first trans person to appear on the cover of *Time* magazine, *and* the first Emmy-nominated trans actress.

The Jack Russell terrier Eddie from *Frasier* got more fan mail than any of the other actors. His real name was Moose.

Robin Williams's contracts included a clause stipulating that a certain number of homeless people must be hired to work on each of his films.

The inventor of the television wouldn't let his kids watch TV because he said there was nothing useful on it.

At the 1968 premiere of *2001: A Space Odyssey*, about 250 people walked out of the theater.

In every episode of *Friends*, someone says the word *friends*; the original title of the show was *Insomnia Café*; and Ellen DeGeneres turned down the role of Phoebe.

In the original story from the early 1700s, Aladdin was Chinese. His name was Aladdin because the storyteller, Hanna Diyab, was Syrian and decided to use Syrian names, despite his characters living in China. Also, Aladdin had infinite wishes.

On the set of the 1967 film *Doctor Dolittle*, the parrot learned how to say "cut" from the director, and its constant interjections stalled filming.

At the time of this writing, *The Witcher* is the most-viewed show on Netflix, beating *Bridgerton* and *Tiger King*.

Michael Myers's mask in *Halloween* was a *Star Trek* Captain Kirk mask painted white.

Leonardo DiCaprio's pet lizard was run over by a truck on the set of *Titanic*, but it survived.

Miss Piggy and Yoda were voiced by the same person, Frank Oz.

More than half of the TV episodes in the 2018–2019 season were directed by women. This is the first time that's ever happened.

In 1952, *I Love Lucy* was the first TV show to feature a pregnant person. But the network thought the word *pregnant* was too vulgar, so Lucille Ball had to use euphemisms, such as *expecting*.

Saturday Night Live has won more Emmys than any other show.

In *Back to the Future*, Doc Brown's first name is Emmett, *time* spelled backward (and then spelled correctly). His middle name is Lathrop, which is *portal* backward (plus an *h* to make it sound like a real, common name).

George Lucas modeled the Ewoks in *Star Wars* on his family dog.

The *T. rex* roars in *Jurassic Park* were created by slowing down the sound of a Jack Russell terrier playing with a rope. The Jack Russell was named Buster, and he belonged to the sound designer.

For more than half a century, film and TV directors who don't want to attach their names to a project because they're unhappy with the final product have been using the name Alan Smithee as a pseudonym. There's a 1997 film about a director whose name is actually Alan Smithee called *An Alan Smithee Film: Burn Hollywood Burn*. Possibly because he had a legitimate tiff with the film's writer and co-producer, or possibly as a way to drum up attention for the project, the *Alan Smithee Film* director, Arthur Hiller, was credited as Alan Smithee.

Fred Astaire loved to skateboard. He took it up in his seventies.

A British subway car driver named Redd Pepper was discovered as a voiceover actor when a Hollywood exec heard him giving updates on the tube. He later became the trailer voice for big movies such as *Amistad*, *Armageddon*, *Saw*, and *Men in Black*.

Nobody says "Play it again, Sam" in *Casablanca*.

Scooby's real name is Scoobert Doo.

The most common line in movies is "Let's get out of here."

THE HUMAN BODY

B odies are beyond weird. Isn't it crazy that we live in constantly
evolving, squishy, smelly, beautiful, confusing flesh jackets?
Everything they're capable of astounds me—especially what
goes on when we sleep.

Dr. Janet Kennedy is a clinical psychologist, an author, and the
founder of NYC Sleep Doctor, a psychotherapy and consulting
practice dedicated to treating insomnia and other sleep problems.
When I asked her for something we should all know about sleep,
she said:

"Memory is consolidated during sleep: What we learn during the day isn't really
ours to keep until we sleep on it."

Basically, night pics or it didn't happen. Ponder these other fascinating facts about our bodies the next time you're sick of counting
sheep:

Most people have four to six dreams per night.

Good news for busy bees: It's okay to work out only on weekends. Those of us who get at least 150 minutes of exercise on weekends lower our risk of dying from health reasons almost as much as those who exercise throughout the week.

Déjà vu, the feeling that you've already experienced something that's happening in real time, occurs most often in people between the ages of fifteen and twenty-five.

A healthy person has 1 trillion bacteria living on their skin.

Your body contains 0.2 milligrams of gold. Most of it's in your blood.

Human pregnancy uses the same amount of energy as running a forty-week marathon.

Eating carbs releases the hormone insulin, which removes most amino acids from your blood except tryptophan. When that tryptophan-heavy blood hits your brain, serotonin is released, followed by melatonin, aka the sleepy hormone. And that is why eating carbs makes you happy and then tired.

Human thigh bones, aka femurs, are stronger than concrete.

One to three percent of your body weight consists of bacteria, microbes, and fungi.

A parent loses approximately 350 hours of sleep at night over their baby's first year.

You can't tickle yourself.

Goose bumps are a vestigial trait (meaning "something we don't need anymore") from our hairier ancestors. Goose bumps make animals' body hair stand up and out, trapping body heat when it's cold and making the animal appear bigger and more threatening in dangerous situations.

There's a rare condition that turns food into alcohol, making sufferers drunk all the time.

Everyone who has blue eyes has a common ancestor. The feature is due to a genetic mutation that occurred between six thousand and ten thousand years ago.

You shed about 1.5 pounds of skin per year.

When you blush, your stomach lining also turns red.

More than two-thirds of cancer patients treated in the United States are cured.

Two people have been cured of HIV using cell transplants.

It's just as beneficial to do the same exercises over and over instead of constantly changing them to create "muscle confusion." Muscles don't work harder when they have new tasks to learn (but your *brain* will be more stimulated with new workouts).

No one who is born blind has ever been diagnosed with schizophrenia. No one knows why.

You are one centimeter taller in the morning because the cartilage in your spine stretches when you sleep.

Donating one pint of blood can save up to three people's lives.

If you swallow gum, it'll be there for a day or two, not seven years.

We blink so often that we spend 10 percent of our waking lives with our eyes closed.

Every person, regardless of gender, has about 2 million sweat glands, but men sweat more than women.

On average, people spend more time sleeping on their side than on their back and stomach combined.

Fist bumps spread only one-twentieth the bacteria that high fives do.

The tooth is the only body part that can't repair itself.

It takes up to two weeks after getting a flu shot for it to work. Schedule it for September or October and save yourself some barfs.

You lose a pound every night while sleeping.

Shaving does *not*, I repeat *not*, cause hair to grow back thicker. It just feels that way because shaved hairs lose their tapered ends, so they feel stubbly. But in reality, they aren't wider, fatter, or bigger in any way.

Seven percent of your body weight is your blood.

Dimples are caused by skin attaching itself to muscle.

A sneeze travels about 100 miles per hour.

Starvation causes some men to lactate.

No one knows why, but humans are the only animals with chins—that is, we're the only species with a small protrusion at the tip of our lower jawbone.

When you look up at a bright sky and see white dots, you're looking at your own blood—white blood cells, to be specific.

If you've ever completed a tough workout and felt demoralized because you look and feel bloated afterward, it doesn't mean all those torturous mountain-climber floor jumps were in vain. When we exercise hard, we gulp down air, which gets caught in our stomachs. Also, if we have food in our bodies, it goes undigested as our blood gets diverted from our stomachs to our extremities, causing more bloat. The more your body gets used to a type of workout, the less bloating will occur.

We've got a lot of eyelashes. Specifically, 90 to 160 on our upper eyelids and 75 to 80 on our lower lids.

You cannot snore and dream at the same time.

Thumbs have their own pulse.

HISTORY

ike any good nerd, I stay in touch with my favorite history teacher, Mr. Bob Rodey, formerly of Marian Catholic High School in Illinois. I asked Mr. Rodey for one of his most beloved facts, and he reminded me that there have always been misguided political superfans attempting to discredit candidates with petty lies:

"In the bitterly partisan presidential election of 1800, a Jefferson supporter said that his opponent, John Adams, was a hermaphrodite."

Today, of course, the term is "intersex," and it's not a bad thing. Now it's my turn to school Mr. History. Rodey, I hope there's something new in here for you:

Former president James Garfield could write in Greek with one hand and Latin with the other—at the same time.

Despite what we call the "Napoleon Complex," Napoleon was a little over 5'5", not short for his time. But in 1807, he *was* attacked by bunnies!

During Russian president Boris Yeltsin's first Washington, D.C., meeting with then-president Bill Clinton, Yeltsin got so drunk that he ran onto Pennsylvania Avenue in only his underwear, looking for pizza.

In 1912, President Theodore Roosevelt was shot on his way to give a speech in Milwaukee. The bullet lodged inside his chest but was slowed down by the fifty-page speech in his breast pocket. The speech was riddled with bullet holes, but Roosevelt gave it—all ninety minutes of it—and then went to the hospital.

The Roman emperor Caligula is said to have made one of his horses a senator.

During World War II, Dutch teenage sisters Freddie and Truus Oversteegen, along with their friend Hannie Schaft, seduced and killed Nazi soldiers occupying their country. They would also fire on Nazis while riding their bikes.

The oldest known horoscope is from 410 BCE. It reveals the placement of planets in relation to the constellations and pronounces, in Babylonian, "Things will be good for you."

The "she" from "She sells seashells by the seashore" was a real lady named Mary Anning. Mary was a nineteenth-century self-taught paleontologist who unearthed hundreds of fossils, including the first-ever ancient reptile ichthyosaur, but she wasn't accepted into the scientific community because of her gender. Instead, she sold her fossils (and some shells) by the seashore in West Dorset, England.

President Ronald Reagan saved seventy-seven people from drowning over his seven-summer career as a lifeguard.

In 1984, Berkeley, California, was the first city to allow city employees and their domestic partners—which included LGBTQ couples—to partake in one another's employment benefits.

America has used fireworks to celebrate Independence Day since 1777, and fireworks have been around since 200 BCE.

Archeologists and anthropologists discovered that ancient Mayans most likely used dried, fermented cacao beans (the basis for chocolate) as currency.

In 1997, David Wolf became the first astronaut to vote from space. When astronauts vote from space, they list their address as "low Earth orbit."

In 1860, an eleven-year-old girl named Grace Bedell wrote a letter to Abraham Lincoln stating she hoped he'd become president. The letter also urged him to grow a beard because his face was thin. Less than a month later, Lincoln had grown his signature beard.

Employment-based healthcare wasn't part of American life until World War II, when there were so many Americans fighting overseas that there was a labor shortage. President Roosevelt froze wages so businesses wouldn't compete to attract workers but allowed them to offer other benefits, such as health insurance.

Until 1969, there was such a thing as a $10,000 bill. They were discontinued because so few people used them.

Infamous mobster Al Capone ran a soup kitchen during the Great Depression that fed more than two thousand Chicagoans every day.

Around 1600, the kings of a playing card deck were standardized to be four important rulers: Charlemagne (Hearts), Alexander the Great (Clubs), King David (Spades), and Julius Caesar (Diamonds).

After the Boston Tea Party, tea was associated with Great Britain, so Americans turned to coffee for their caffeine fix. Soon the beverage became a symbol of patriotism in the colonies.

While Jimmy Carter was president, it is said that he once accidentally left nuclear launch codes in his dry cleaning.

There was about a five-billion-year period when the Milky Way stopped forming stars.

JEOPARDY! CONTESTANT FAVE FACT

Anne Frank, Martin Luther King Jr., and Barbara Walters were all born in the same year.
—Alistair Bell

There's a statue of John Harvard in Harvard Yard. It's not John Harvard. No one knew what he looked like, so a student sat in.

You shouldn't launch a rocket in the rain because it acts as a giant lightning rod. In 1969, Apollo 12 was struck by lightning twice, which caused temporary power outages on the rocket.

In 1953, the United States officially decided to name all hurricanes after women. This continued amid petitions from feminist groups to stop associating females with disaster. Finally, in 1979, a campaign by a Florida woman, Roxcy Bolton, worked. The first male hurricane was named Plato. Just kidding, it was Bob.

Plato's name wasn't Plato. It was Bob. Just kidding, it was Aristocles. Plato was his wrestling nickname. *Platon* meant "broad-shouldered."

Cleopatra was so rich that if she were alive today, her net worth would be an estimated $95.8 billion.

President Andrew Jackson had a parrot who wouldn't stop swearing.

"Uncle Sam" refers to a guy named Sam Wilson who helped get food to the U.S. Army in the War of 1812.

A "knocker upper" was a pre-alarm-clock job in England and Ireland. People would hit windows with giant sticks and peashooters to wake up their clients.

The game of chess dates back to the sixth century AD but originally didn't have a queen. When the piece was finally added, it was a weaker game piece until the end of the fifteenth century, when Queen Isabella of Castile took on Spanish military duties and arguably became more powerful than her husband, King Ferdinand. New rules for the chess queen piece were written, and modern chess was born.

The first woman in space was a Russian named Valentina Tereshkova, and she went in 1963. The Soviets forgot to put a toothbrush in her kit, and she had to brush with her finger.

An American woman wouldn't get to space until 1983. Sally Ride was that woman, and for her week-long trip, the men at NASA asked Ride if one hundred tampons would be enough. She explained that that was way too many tampons.

During World War II, Allied forces conjured a plan to sneak estrogen into Hitler's food to "feminize" him. The idea was that it would make him more like his unassuming secretary sister, Paula. The plan was not put into action.

Pirates wore earrings because they believed it improved their eyesight. That wasn't the case (obviously), but silver or gold earrings did often cover a dead pirate's burial or body-shipping costs.

Incoming freshmen at Ivy League schools used to be required to take a nude photo for their official academic records. These "posture photos" started at Harvard in 1880 and spread to other schools in the 1940s. The tradition didn't end until the 1970s! So if you ever get busted for sending NSFW pics, say you were just following in the Ivy League's prestigious footsteps.

Vikings didn't have horns on their helmets.

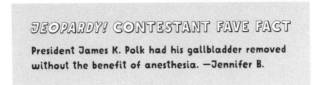

The handshake was created so both parties would reveal they didn't have a weapon in their right hand.

President William Howard Taft had a cow named Pauline Wayne who grazed on the White House lawn, was considered more of a beloved family pet than livestock, and was written about in *The Washington Post* more than twenty times.

The Leaning Tower of Pisa has always been like that. It began to tilt when workers were building the second floor.

Founding fathers John Adams and Thomas Jefferson died on the same day, July 4, 1826, the fiftieth anniversary of Congress adopting the official Declaration of Independence.

Related: The United States voted to declare independence on July 2, 1776. July 4 was the day the declaration was formally agreed upon after some small revisions.

The Hundred Years' War lasted 116 years (1337–1453).

Vikings gave kittens as wedding gifts to honor the goddess of love, Freyja, whose chariot was led by cats.

In ancient Persia, government officials debated laws twice: once sober and once drunk.

Julius Caesar was once captured by pirates who demanded a ransom for his safe return. Caesar laughed at the low ransom and told his captors to raise it. They received the higher ransom. (Although, upon release, Caesar organized fleets to capture the pirates. Then he had them killed.)

Napoleon Bonaparte penned a romance novel about a soldier called *Clisson et Eugénie*.

Theodore Roosevelt's daughter Alice Roosevelt Longworth was a rebel and a party animal. As a teen in the White House, she kept in her purse a dagger, a copy of the Constitution, and a pet snake named Emily Spinach. When she married, she cut her wedding cake with a sword, and she had a needlepointed pillow that read: "If you haven't got anything nice to say about anyone, come and sit here by me."

The Roman goddess of sorcery, hounds, and crossroads is named Trivia. ☺

LOVE THE LEWK

(On Beauty, Style & Fashion)

When I was twenty-three, I awoke for the first time in my life in the English countryside. My *Vogue* contributing editor boss (I'd gotten the job on a fluke, very *The Devil Wears Prada*–style) and I had arrived to her country house late at night. The house was dark; outside was dark. I didn't have a chance to take in my surroundings. So in the morning, my eyes almost popped out of my head when I realized my bedroom window overlooked the biggest expanse of lush rolling hills I'd ever seen. And then I peered around the room and realized I'd been sleeping in a bed covered in diamonds.

Lounging in a diamond bed in rural England was, and still is, the most fashionable snapshot of my life. And even though I worry about consumerism and try to be a frugal, practical writer, I must admit, waking up in what felt like a real-life music video was completely intoxicating. There's just something to be said for the particular way style can uplift the human spirit.

While some might think them frivolous, I see beauty and

fashion as extremely powerful forces. They're everyday art. So I was delighted to see that, in 2020, an institution called the Makeup Museum opened in New York.

The executive director of the museum, Doreen Bloch, is, as you would expect, bursting with fascinating style and beauty facts. Here are a few:

"William Dorsey Swann—also known as 'The Queen'—is the first known person to identify as a drag queen. Swann was enslaved in Maryland in the mid-1800s, and [once freed] he organized a series of drag balls in the Washington, D.C., area. It was at one of these galas that Swann was first arrested for 'female impersonation.'"

And

"Kevyn Aucoin, who is considered to be the world's first celebrity makeup artist, regularly applied makeup on models and celebrities while they were lying down on the ground. Several other makeup artists throughout history have been said to try this type of makeup technique . . . including Perc Westmore, who was the personal makeup artist for renowned Hollywood actress Bette Davis throughout her time at Warner Bros. Studios. It has been reported that Davis preferred to have her makeup applied while she was lying on a couch totally naked!"

Don't we all, Bette. Don't. We. All.

"Beauty sleep" is real. We have two types of collagen, one of which replenishes as we snooze.

In the early 1950s, fewer than 7 percent of women colored their hair. Today, it's 70 percent.

For most of us, the left side of our face is more attractive than the right. One theory behind this phenomenon is that our left side is controlled by the right side of our brains, which is better for processing emotion and may be superior at communicating how our face should appear to others.

"Black Friday" gets its name not from retailers going from "in the red" to "in the black" on this heavy shopping day, but from something else entirely. In 1950s Philadelphia, police called it "Black Friday" because so many suburban shoppers swarmed city stores that they had to work overtime on a day they'd rather take off.

In the early years of the Roman Empire, sex workers were required to dye their hair blond so everyone would know who they were.

Ancient Phoenicians used to "dye" their hair in the most fabulous way: by sprinkling gold dust on it.

Mark Twain invented the bra clasp. It was intended to replace snaps, buttons, and belts on all types of clothing, and he invented it because he hated suspenders.

Pink and blue weren't gendered before the twentieth century. In the early twentieth century, *blue* became the color for little girls, probably because it's associated with the Virgin Mary, and pink was the color for boys. This flipped in the 1940s.

When the bikini was first marketed in 1946, the Vatican called it a sin.

Ancient Romans believed there was a vein that ran directly from your heart to your fourth finger on your left hand. They called it the "vein of love," and that's why we wear wedding and engagement rings on this "ring finger."

The color purple wasn't accessible to the masses until 1856, when a young chemist named William Henry Perkin accidentally made a synthetic purple dye. Before that, you could get the color only from leaving mollusks in the sun and then squeezing out their glands. It took more than nine thousand mollusks to create one gram of purple. This is why purple-colored garments were so expensive and mostly reserved for royalty.

Male-pattern baldness does not come from your mom. That's a myth! It's from both your parents.

Yoko Ono married John Lennon in a pair of Keds.

Before they became an American staple, jeans were called "jean," designed in southern France, and manufactured in Italy. The term *jeans* is an adaptation of the city that produced them, Genoa.

The oldest evidence of human tattoos dates back to 3000 BCE.

The first people to wear high heels were men.

In fourteenth-century France, it was illegal to wear stripes. Striped garments were considered the Devil's clothing, and people were even executed for going out in them. (Fourteenth-century France would *hate* Old Navy.)

Before it was a nursery rhyme, "Pop Goes the Weasel" was a popular dance among the most stylish people in 1850s London.

When there was a nylon shortage during World War II, American women had "liquid stockings" professionally applied to their legs. The look was topped off with a "seam" up the back of the leg drawn in eyeliner pencil.

Both Russia's Peter the Great and England's Henry VIII imposed a beard tax during their reigns—the latter despite having a beard himself.

Marc Jacobs has a SpongeBob SquarePants tattoo, a red M&M's tattoo, a *South Park* tattoo, and a *Simpsons* tattoo, among many others.

Ancient Greek dramatic actors wore platform shoes to denote their higher status than the comedic actors.

People of Asian descent have the fastest-growing hair.

The average American owns seven pairs of jeans.

Men really do prefer ladies in red. They engage women in deeper conversations when their interlocutors are wearing crimson. The "why" is a mystery.

Elizabeth Taylor's last wishes were to arrive fashionably late to her own funeral. Her body was brought in fifteen minutes after the official start time.

Dyed socks used to contain arsenic and other toxic chemicals. Only white ones didn't. So white socks became popular simply because they wouldn't kill or maim you.

"Casual Friday" started in Hawaii in the 1960s as "Aloha Friday," when workers would wear their more breathable Hawaiian shirts to work on Fridays (and often all summer long).

That tiny pocket within your jeans' front pocket? It's for your pocket watch.

TECHNOLOGY

○ ○

W hy haven't you updated your phone since 2019?"
"Where's the charger for this?"
"Did you spill creamed corn on your computer?"
These are questions my husband asks almost daily. They're also questions I cannot answer. Though I'm a millennial, I feel fundamentally at odds with the mind-blowing technology around me. I can't help but destroy it. It is just my clunky, blundering nature. You know how they say, "If it ain't broke, don't fix it"? I say: "If it ain't broke, don't invite me over."

Thankfully, there are people much savvier and wiser than me. Nancy Colier, a psychotherapist and author of *The Power of Off: The Mindful Way to Stay Sane in a Virtual World*, is a guru when it comes to the intersection of humanity and technology. Her favorite fact is not the most uplifting one, but it *is* funny:

"In 2000, we humans had an attention span of twelve seconds. Now, with our digitalized lifestyle, we have an attention span of eight seconds . . . which might not be terribly interesting except for the fact that we can now hold our concentration for one second less than a goldfish, whose attention span is actually nine seconds."

Lesson? We must respect the goldfish, for it hath abilities beyond our own.

The world's smallest commercial camera is the size of a grain of sand.

That Twitter mascot? His name is Larry. As in Larry Bird, the basketball legend.

Facebook's brand is blue because Mark Zuckerberg is red-green colorblind.

In 1998, Sony came out with a camera specifically for photographing and taping the natural world at night. But it was recalled because with one particular lens, this NightShot camera could see through clothes.

Surgeons who, at some point in their lives, played video games three or more hours per week make 37 percent fewer surgical errors and perform 27 percent faster than surgeons who never played video games.

Steve Jobs (intentionally) dropped the first iPod into an aquarium, and it sank to the bottom while air bubbles floated to the top. This is how he proved the prototype should be redesigned even smaller—if there's room for air, it's possible to make it more compact.

Microsoft threatened to sue a teen named Mike Rowe when he made a website in 2003 called MikeRoweSoft.com. They settled out of court.

Your exact fingerprints can be pulled from flashing a peace sign in a photo if you're within nine feet of the camera.

Every time a product gains another star on its Amazon rating, its sales increase by 26 percent, on average.

That gust of air you feel when you enter a mall or a big retail store is not the air-conditioning. It's an "air curtain" that blasts downward over the door and serves as a barrier to keep hot air out and cool air in. Air curtains save energy and money.

The last-ever VCR was produced in July 2016.

Pokémon is short for *poketto* and *monsut* in Japanese. Those words mean "pocket monster."

In the 2010s, baby names based on Instagram filters became popular. Ludwig and Lux saw the biggest rise.

Google's original name was Backrub.

Nintendo character Mario wasn't always a Super Mario Bro. He was originally part of the 1981 arcade game *Donkey Kong* as Jumpman. He was renamed after the Nintendo of America office landlord Mario Segale.

Six thousand tweets are tweeted every second.

You can reopen an Internet browser tab you accidentally closed by hitting Command + Shift + T on a Mac and Ctrl + Shift + T on a PC.

Ninety percent of texts are read within three minutes of when they're sent.

In the 1960s, before they sold *the* phone of the early 2000s, Nokia made everything from tires to toilet paper. Microsoft bought the company in 2014.

That singing birthday card from Walgreens holds more computing power than all the Allied forces had at their disposal in 1945.

If you Google the word *askew*, your screen will appear slanted. CUTE, Google.

An early version of the fax machine was invented in 1843, more than thirty years before the telephone.

Robots seem more trustworthy when they're programmed to be a bit sarcastic.

In 1997, Bill Gates invested $150 million in Apple to save it from bankruptcy.

New crash test dummies were introduced in 2017 to reflect the aging, heavier U.S. population.

One study found we touch our phones, on average, 2,617 times every day.

The speed at which a computer mouse rolls is measured in a unit called Mickeys.

There's a robot that can solve a Rubik's Cube in under twenty moves and less than one second.

Playing *Tetris* after a traumatic incident can help prevent flashbacks.

Up until 2017, it was impossible to block Mark Zuckerberg on Facebook.

Instagram's original name was Burbn.

Our average phone-typing speed is getting faster all the time. The latest data shows it's at thirty-eight words per minute.

More than half of the elements in the periodic table are in an iPhone.

The CIA reads 5 million of our tweets every day. Hey, at least *somebody's* reading our bad jokes.

The Nintendo game *Castlevania* had a custom, high-processing music chip, which is why its music is still memorable (to us nerds) today.

In 2016, the United Nations declared Internet access a basic human right.

HUMAN NATURE

○ ○

When was the last time someone hurt your feelings? When did you last mess up and hurt someone else? These are the events we often dwell on, but that doesn't mean they're what make up the bulk of who we are or what we do. This chapter in particular should remind us that humanity isn't a completely failed experiment. There's good in us, too.

I talked to Margaret J. King, Ph.D., who researches human biology, brain, and behavior as the director of the think tank the Center for Cultural Studies and Analysis, and she gave me a 101 lecture on one of her favorite topics. King says:

"We speak at 120 words per minute. We read at 250 to 400 words per minute. We recognize situations and environments at 250 to 450/1000th of a second. We *think* at over 600 words per minute."

So the next time you get frustrated while processing or communicating information, remember, that's normal. Everything's happening at a different pace inside that spaghetti pile in your head. Take a deep breath, and give it a minute to sort itself out. It's just doing its thing. Now let's learn some more about ourselves:

Compassion is instinctive.

When people already have the basics to survive, they feel more satisfied spending money on experiences over things.

Americans are making more eco-friendly choices every year.

Adults laugh somewhere between four and twenty times a day. Four-to-six-year-olds laugh three hundred times a day.

On average, people change their sheets once every 24.4 days. Five percent of people change their sheets only once or twice a year! Nastified!

People who volunteer report being happier with their work/life balance than people who don't, even when both parties have the same amount of free time to begin with.

Most people become less narcissistic after their teen years.

Smiling is not learned; it's innate.

Ninety-six percent of candles are bought by women.

Only 1 percent of people are "short sleepers" who do fine with six hours a night, but one-third of Americans are sleeping that little. This is a *wake-up call* to SLEEP MORE, my friends.

The average American spends eight minutes in the shower.

Seven percent of people who pray have prayed for a good parking spot. The same percentage have prayed that they won't get caught speeding.

The average age at which people meet their best friend is twenty-one.

Acts of altruism stimulate the same parts of the brain as eating and sex.

More babies are born in the summer than in any other season. Especially in August.

Despite that, the most common birthday in the United States is September 9.

Only 46 percent of cultures partake in romantic kissing.

Good news if you've ever felt guilty about sleeping past your alarm: A British study showed that people who hit snooze are more intelligent than people who don't. The idea is that snoozers have evolved with the relatively recent invention of the snooze button, a sign of intelligence. Other studies have shown that people who go to bed late and wake up late are happier and more creative than those who don't.

Eighty-four percent of millennials donate to charity. That's a higher percentage than any previous generation. See, we're not so bad.

Heterosexual men tend to view their exes more favorably than heterosexual women do.

Every year, fewer and fewer workers are taking their full vacation days. In 2018, there were 768 million unused days. Please use your days!

Teenage laziness is innate. Your brain wants to take a lot of breaks while enduring puberty. According to science, you'll most likely grow out of it.

Being superstitious relieves anxiety by making us believe we have control over our world. Might as well carry a good-luck charm—it works.

Humans are hardwired for empathy, not fighting.

People who use curse words are more honest than people who don't.

Teens type ten words per minute faster on their phones than people in their forties do.

If you've ever eaten junk food when you're exhausted and felt bad about it, don't. Your body craves these items when you're really tired. But eating healthy foods when you're sleep-deprived will be more helpful when it comes to your energy levels.

Ever notice that your baby nephew's giggle sounds different from kids' and adults' laughter? That's because babies laugh on their exhales *and* inhales. The rest of us just laugh on the exhale.

Left-handed people win fights more than right-handed people. The reason is that right-handers aren't used to battling left-handed fighters and are caught off guard.

The number of Americans who meditate has been steadily rising. In 2012, it was just 4.1 percent, but five years later, that number had jumped to 14.2 percent.

Blind people may "see" in their dreams.

When "collective narcissism" happens, a person will believe unrealistic ideas about a group they belong to and inflate that group's importance. Acknowledging the existence of collective narcissism might help us avoid it.

If you fail at multitasking, you're not alone. Only 2 percent of people can effectively bounce back and forth between tasks.

If you think the world is going paperless, think again: 82 percent of millennials enjoy receiving paper greeting cards.

People rate jokes as funnier when there's a laugh track behind them, even when the jokes are bad.

Humans used to sleep twice per night instead of just one long sleep. We'd hit the sack right after dusk; wake up for a few hours late at night to relax, sew, chop wood by moonlight, or read; then go back to sleep until dawn.

Birth order does not determine your personality traits.

Drunk driving is still a big problem, but fatalities have dropped by 50 percent over the last forty years.

There's a personality type between extrovert and introvert, and it's called ambivert.

People stopped complaining about elevator wait times when buildings added mirrors next to them. Turns out we just wanted something to look at while we waited: ourselves!

The act of smiling releases endorphins, dopamine, and serotonin and improves your mood.

Women remember their dreams more often than men do.

Who says women are bad at math? Seventy-five percent of women under the age of forty-five manage their household's finances.

It's not just you: Rainy days make us sleepier.

People who feel excluded or lonely are more likely to believe in conspiracy theories. In the wise words of my aunt Peg, "Inclusion, people!" Being friendly to outsiders could ultimately stop them from believing the moon is a hologram.

Many of us humans (and some animals) have an "optimism bias" that makes us believe the future will be better than the present.

Hate speaking in front of crowds? You're not alone. About 25 percent of people have an acute fear of public speaking called glossophobia.

Millionaires who've earned their money are happier than those who inherited it.

One study showed the happiest age is eighty-two.

LOVE

ove is gross! Just kidding. It rules. When my husband proposed, I was so overcome with feelings of love that I couldn't stop crying and eating the fried cheese curds he'd ordered to our restaurant table. I didn't even answer him. I just cried and ate. Finally he asked me if I intended to say yes, and I nodded, blubbered, and asked for another basket of cheese.

I'd make a terrible romance writer.

For the vegan or lactose intolerant, please note that not all love is entangled with dairy. Psychotherapist Nancy Colier reminded me of one of the cutest, sweetest, tear-jerkingest, non-cheese-related love stories of all time, out of Japan:

"Hachiko, a dog of the Akita breed, met his master every day at the train station in the same spot at the same time. On the day his master died, Hachiko went to the station and waited for his master to come. His master never showed up, but for nine years, every day until his own death, the dog went to that same spot at that same time and waited."

You might want to keep those tissues nearby.

People who marry their best friend are less likely to get divorced.

When romantic partners hold hands, their breathing syncs up.

Comedian Jack Benny put in his will that his wife would have a single rose delivered to her every day after his death.

Couples who post photos with their partner and other tidbits about their relationships on social media are happier in those relationships than people who don't. Also, followers who saw photos of the couple rated them as more likable . . . unless the couple went overboard with constant postings (in that case, their followers got annoyed, which feels reasonable).

Opposites don't attract. You're more likely to be attracted to someone who has your own ideal qualities.

In 2001, an American couple got married in a tiny submersible on the bow of the *Titanic*.

Get dumped? Here's a silver lining if you're trying to lose some of that breakup weight: Crying for an hour burns seventy-eight calories.

American divorce rates have been declining for more than ten years.

In ancient Greece, men proposed by throwing an apple at a woman. If she caught it, that was her way of saying yes.

There's evidence of same-sex relationships in every documented culture.

Being married doesn't necessarily guarantee you'll be happier than you would be staying single or drifting in and out of relationships.

If you thought modern Valentine's Day was scarring, guess what: In mid-nineteenth-century America and England, sending "Vinegar Valentines," which were anonymous and contained cruel poems, became as popular as earnest love notes. Often, the recipient would be forced to pay for the postage, too. Those cheesy, flowery cards at Walgreens don't seem so bad now, do they?

Fathers-to-be sometimes go through hormonal changes that prepare them to be caregivers along with their pregnant partners. This can start as early as twenty weeks into a pregnancy.

One study showed that men who kiss their wives in the morning live five years longer than those who don't.

Nearly 25 percent of American married couples sleep in separate beds.

Cuffing season is real! People crave more human contact in colder weather.

People in early stages of romantic love have higher levels of cortisol, a hormone associated with stress. They also experience a spike in dopamine, which makes early love feel like a drug, albeit a stressful one. If you've ever felt out of control in the beginning of a relationship, it's because of these hormones: One's telling you your budding love is a crisis, the other's telling you to hold on to it at all costs.

Sex can alleviate headaches and migraines.

Our romantic partners tend to rate us as more attractive than we rate ourselves.

In Elizabethan England and nineteenth-century rural Austria, single women would put an apple slice in their armpit before a dance. The apple would absorb their sweat, and then they'd offer it to a "bloke" they "fancied." If the dude liked her back, he would smell or even *eat the sweaty apple.*

A study by the Smell and Taste Treatment and Research Foundation showed that the scent women find most arousing is the candy Good & Plenty mixed with cucumber. For men, it's the smell of pumpkin pie and lavender. (For me specifically, it's cheese.)

The people who voiced Mickey and Minnie were married in real life.

People who frequently use emojis while flirting via texts/messages have more success at getting dates than people who don't.

In 2001, the Netherlands became the first country to legalize same-sex marriage.

Here's a weird one: Dating app users who have the same initials as each other are 11.3 percent more likely to exchange numbers than users who don't.

The oldest illustrations of a heart as the symbol of love are from a 1250 French allegory that translates to "The Romance of the Pear." But in these illustrations, the "heart" looks more like an eggplant, pine cone, or pear than the symbol we use today.

It's predicted that by 2025, 53.3 million Americans will use online dating services.

Every year, thousands of people send love letters to a simple mailing address: "Juliet, Verona." Members of the Juliet Club in Verona, Italy, read the letters and select the most touching to be honored on Valentine's Day. Though this tradition began in the 1930s, it refers to Shakespeare's 1597 romantic tragedy *Romeo and Juliet*, which was set in (fair) Verona.

LIFE HACKS FROM SCIENCE & PSYCHOLOGY

ife hacks are helpful tips that we often know innately but forget because no one's ever told us that, scientifically, our intuition was spot-on. When I find out that a productivity tool is backed by research, it sticks in my brain, and I can put it to use on a daily basis. I hope you, too, find this chapter practical and valuable.

Naomi Arbit is basically a professional life hacker. She's a behavioral scientist who helps people find greater meaning in their existence. And she made me feel better about avoiding the wellness trend du jour when she told me:

"Diets don't work and are more likely to cause harm than they are to help you. As many as two-thirds of people who attempt to lose weight end up gaining more weight than they lost. And when people do lose weight, their metabolism drops and they have to eat less in order to keep that weight off. For example, someone that weighs 125 pounds after losing weight will have a much lower metabolism than someone who weighs 125 pounds but never went on a diet and lost weight in the first place."

But what if I want to fit back into my prom dress? Is there any safe, healthy way? Actually, yes:

"A better strategy for weight loss is to add up to ten servings of fruits and vegetables per day to your diet; eat whole, nonprocessed fresh foods; and make small, sustainable reductions to your intake of processed carbohydrates and sugar—all changes small enough that you'll be able to follow through over time. Another strategy is to aim to always keep your hunger level between a 4 and 6 on a scale of 1 to 10 (10 being super-full and 1 being feeling so hungry you don't feel well)—that is, don't let yourself get too hungry or too full."

Who doesn't love a commonsense approach?

People who make time for art—such as museums, opera, and concerts—tend to live longer.

Writing tomorrow's to-do list before you go to bed can help you fall asleep nine minutes faster.

Making eye contact with a person makes them less likely to lie to you.

Got gum stuck in your hair? Rub peanut butter on it, and the gum will dissolve.

Busy people are happier.

Putting ice cubes in a hot dryer with wrinkly clothes will create steam and get those wrinkles out.

Rinsing out your recyclables is great, but unless they're paper, you don't have to make them spotless. Recycling plants are equipped to handle slightly dirty plastics and cans. Isn't that a relief?! But don't put half-full bottles in the recycling—the food will spoil, attract rats, and generally be gross.

Coffee gets bitter if left out, and even more bitter when you microwave it. The best way to reheat is slowly on a burner. Chemical breakdowns will still occur, but fewer than would occur in the microwave.

But if it's too late and your coffee has come out bitter, try adding a pinch of salt. Some people can't stand the taste, but for others, adding a small amount doesn't change the brew—except to reduce bitterness.

Sharing a goal with someone you consider higher status will make you more likely to achieve that goal.

One Norwegian experiment showed that painting wind turbine blades black decreases the number of related bird deaths by 70 percent.

At a restaurant, patrons will spend more money when the menu includes prices but no dollar sign. The $ reminds people they're spending their hard-earned bucks.

When working toward a goal, it's more effective to build in planned "cheat days," aka days you take a break. Studies show that people with cheat days have more self-control the rest of the time than do people who have no breaks to look forward to.

Because of where your organs are located inside your body, it's better to sleep on your left side than on your right. Sleeping on your left side can help with digestion, heartburn, and even snoring.

Creating a Plan B makes Plan A more likely to fail.

Want to be a good listener? Engaging in "backchannel" feedback, which means responding to a story with short phrases like "yep," "mmm," and "uh-huh," effectively gives the storyteller a green light to keep going and increases their confidence.

Putting a humidifier in your room reduces static shock in the winter.

Getting multiple tattoos can strengthen your immune system.

People perform better at jobs or personal projects when they view themselves as part of a bigger picture. For example, hospital janitors who see themselves as a crucial part of keeping people healthy did better work than janitors who didn't see themselves as part of a larger contribution.

Changing up your routine can make you much happier. Unless your routine is reading this book, in which case, carry on.

Let's say a mosquito lands on you, and you slap at it, but you miss. That particular mosquito now associates your scent with the dangerous vibrations and is most likely to leave you alone after that. Good news for people who have a yard with . . . one mosquito.

You know how when you pull a sticker off a product, there's that sticky residue? Rub cooking oil on it to get rid of it.

High-impact workouts, such as hiking, tennis, and running, build and strengthen your bones.

You have more trouble realizing you're full if you eat while doing other things, such as working or watching a movie. It's easier to listen to your body when the meal is your central focus.

According to one French study, it's better to ask people out on a sunny day. The researchers sent an attractive man to ask strangers on a date, and 22.4 percent said yes on sunny days, compared to only 13.9 percent on cloudy days.

Reducing your consumption is more environmentally (and psychologically) beneficial than "buying green" or recycling.

Being in nature makes us happier and less stressed. But if hanging out in the great outdoors isn't an option, watching nature documentaries also achieves this effect.

Rubbing mayonnaise into a wood surface will remove water stains. If a few minutes of rubbing doesn't work, leave it on for a few hours and then rub it in.

The phrase *hair of the dog that bit you* goes back to 400 BCE. The advice is meant as a hangover remedy—the idea being that imbibing the drink that gave you the hangover can cure it—and was prescribed by the ancient Greek comedic poet Antiphanes, who wrote (in Greek, of course):

Take the hair, it is well written,
Of the dog by which you're bitten,
Work off one wine by his brother,
One labor with another.

No one knows exactly why, but it works.

Speaking of alcohol: Ever heard the adage "Beer before liquor, never been sicker. Liquor before beer, you're in the clear"? Well, that one doesn't hold up. It doesn't matter if you stick to one alcohol or drink different types of alcohol in various orders, your hangover will be the same. So imbibe in whatever order you like. The only real hangover-prevention tricks are water, pacing your drinks out, and, of course, moderation.

Being able to see the ocean from your home makes you calmer and more creative.

Calling someone on the phone creates stronger social bonds than emailing or texting. FaceTime or Zoom calls work, too; voice is the key element.

Pain tolerance increases immediately after laughing.

Hugging lowers stress, helps our immune systems, and may reduce blood pressure.

When reading a menu, people associate rounded fonts with sweet taste and edgier fonts with savory flavors.

You can save your bathroom from "toilet plume," aka fecal matter flying all over the place (sorry), by closing the lid before you flush. Even if it's just pee, *close the lid*. Old germs can erupt with every flush. If you haven't been closing the lid, get a new toothbrush.

Students who take notes by hand understand their lessons more comprehensively than those who type them.

Looking at a photo of a loved one can relieve pain.

Turns out debate and constructive critiques lead to better brainstorming sessions than positive feedback alone.

Want to make your jack-o'-lantern last longer? Choose a pumpkin with a green stem, which indicates freshness, and when transporting it, cradle it rather than carrying it by its stem. The stem provides nutrients to the pumpkin, so keep it attached and untampered with as long as possible. When carving the pumpkin, you can even cut open the back to remove the seeds instead of the top to keep the stem intact, and it'll last you the season.

Walking at least two thousand steps per day can improve your sleep. Also, it's easier to fall asleep when you wake up at the same time each day.

People give a wine a higher rating if the label has a difficult-to-read font versus a simple one.

Predicting obstacles to your goals and writing them down can help you avoid succumbing to them when they arise.

When you get in your car on a summer day, selecting the button that pulls air from outside will air-condition your car quicker than trying to recycle the hot air already trapped inside. Once the air is cool, you should switch to recycling the interior air. In the winter, recycling heated air in your car can lead to window fog, so it's best to always pull air from outside.

One more car fact: Do not idle your car to warm it up in the winter. All cars made after the early 1990s will warm up faster when you start driving.

We like seeing people's hands. When their hands are in their pockets or otherwise obscured, we trust them less.

Taking work breaks by playing a quick computer game or shopping online increases overall productivity. (Feel free to take a photo of this and send it to your boss.)

The cleanest and most efficient way to wipe with toilet paper is to fold it into squares for maximum coverage, then crumple the top square for texture.

Assuming you got enough sleep last night and aren't in serious need of REM, resting with your eyes closed (or "quiet wakefulness") can be as refreshing and stress-reducing as a nap.

Keeping a gratitude journal can improve your sleeping and relationships, *and* make you less materialistic and less stressed.

Drinking pickle juice during or after workouts will help muscle cramps go away 37 percent faster than drinking water, and 45 percent faster than doing nothing.

If you lie on your back and raise your legs slowly, you cannot sink in quicksand.

That life hack going around about freezing your jeans to kill germs is a myth. Sorry, putting your jeans in the freezer won't rid them of bacteria or stink. On the other hand, washing them works.

We sleep better when we have an article of our partner's worn clothing in bed with us.

Statistically, the strongest word to play against an opponent in the word-guess game of Spaceman (formerly known as Hangman) is *jazz*. Other tough ones to guess include rarely used letters, especially when they are used twice, like *fizz*, *buzz*, *jinx*, *puff*, *fuzzy*, and *vex*.

We tend to get sad after achieving a large goal. One way to deal with this is to schedule something smaller to achieve or look forward to after the goal's completion.

People who have multiple strong friendships live longer.

The most efficient way to work may be to take twenty-minute breaks every ninety minutes. This lines up with humans' natural ultradian rhythms.

Some of the easiest passwords to crack are *iloveyou*, *test1*, *12345*, and the top row of the keyboard: *qwertyuiop*.

Typically, serif fonts subconsciously convey conservative leanings while sans serif fonts have liberal connotations. Exceptions include the serif headlines of newspapers like *The New York Times*, since viewers associate that typeface with the newspaper's more liberal leanings. Whatever your politics, can we all please agree that Helvetica is over?

Writing about a traumatic event can reduce anxiety about it.

Wrapping your headphones in a figure eight will result in fewer tangles than wrapping them in a circle.

Five-cent fees for plastic bags work by making people feel that they are not doing the "norm" (bringing their own bags). In fact, they're more effective than giving people a discount for bringing a tote, since the real punishment is feeling bad about not fitting in with the changing times.

Napping is good for your heart.

Checking updates, messages, and emails in a batch makes you more efficient than reading or hearing them as soon as they arrive. This means—eeps!—turning off push notifications can lead to a smoother workday.

Forgiving others can reduce your stress levels.

When decluttering, it's easier to let go of an object you don't need anymore if you take a photo of it first.

Singing can reduce anxiety.

Ten to twenty minutes of direct sunlight a day will give you enough vitamin D to help stabilize your mood.

Studies show that positive goal-setting (e.g., cooking healthier meals) is more effective than negative or avoidance goal-setting (e.g., eating less pizza).

People's biggest regrets tend to be about things they didn't do, not things they did that turned out poorly.

ALL AROUND
THE WORLD

M y college boyfriend always told me traveling was a waste of money. Why trek all over the world when you can read books? Books, he said, would take you anywhere. That sounded really wise to me . . . until I started traveling. I quickly learned that vacationing, studying, or working in new environments offered the opportunity to analyze myself and my little universe from a fresh perspective. It lit up my brain in unprecedented ways. And guess what? When we travel, we're allowed to bring books with us. That's right: We can have the best of both worlds. Take that, Brian.

Anyway, I couldn't think of a better expert to introduce these fascinating, funny, wild, weird, and adorable facts from around the world than CNN travel editor Lilit Marcus. From her current home in Hong Kong, Lilit told me:

"Wilbur and Orville Wright are famous for flying the first heavier-than-air plane in 1903 near Kitty Hawk, North Carolina. However, the brothers were natives of

Dayton, Ohio, where they ran a bike shop. As a result, a small but committed feud exists between aviation fans in the two U.S. states: Ohio's license plates read 'birthplace of aviation,' while North Carolina's are printed with 'first in flight.' The famous plane, though, is in the Smithsonian National Air and Space Museum in Washington, D.C."

And:

"Before there was Lonely Planet, there was 1486's *Peregrinatio in Terram Sanctam* (*Pilgrimage to the Holy Land*), considered to be the world's first-ever travel guidebook. Bernhard von Breydenbach, a German politician, wrote the text, which was about his experiences visiting holy sites in Jerusalem. The illustrations, done by Erhard Reuwich, include the first known illustrated map of the city. What's unclear is if this book was the origin of FOMO."

Personally, I believe FOMO was invented when the first Neanderthal had a cave-warming party and failed to invite her entire rock-chiseling class. It's a tale as old as time.

Every August in the nine-thousand-population Spanish town of Buñol, twenty thousand people participate in the world's biggest food fight, a tomato battle called La Tomatina. There's also a greased-up wooden pole people try to climb to reach the prize on top: a ham.

New York City's Central Park is bigger than the country of Monaco.

In 2020, scientists studying penguins in Antarctica accidentally became high on nitrous oxide, aka laughing gas. Turns out that fermented penguin poo contains loads of the chemical compound.

JEOPARDY! CONTESTANT FAVE FACT

Melbourne, Australia, created email addresses for [approximately] seventy thousand trees so that people could report any issues with these trees. Instead, people have been writing love letters to them. —Raj Sivaraman

Alabama is the only state that has an alcoholic beverage as its official drink: Conecuh Ridge Whiskey.

In Japan, it's considered good luck if a sumo wrestler makes your baby cry.

Hooray! A recent NASA study shows that our planet is 5 percent greener than it was twenty years ago. This is mostly due to environmentalist programs in China and India that conserve and expand forests.

Bolts of lightning can shoot out of an erupting volcano.

Experts predict that the remains of the *Titanic* will disintegrate completely in the next thirty years.

In Igbo-Ora, Nigeria, the rate of twin births is four times higher than it is in the rest of the world, and no one has figured out why.

There are more than 1,200 plants in Hawaii that don't grow anywhere else in the world. One such plant is the Haleakalā silversword plant, which can live up to ninety years and blooms with six hundred flowers.

The exact geographic center of the United States is Butte County, South Dakota.

There are two adult ball-pit bars in London. All of the plastic balls are constantly cycled through a cleaner called the Ball Gobbler.

The auto racing competition 24 Hours of Lemons features exclusively old junkers. The lemon races happen across the United States, and drivers are penalized if their car is worth more than $500.

Well, this thrills me: Every spring in Gloucestershire, England, dozens of people enter the Cooper's Hill Cheese-Rolling competition, during which an artificial cheese wheel rolls 650 feet down a hill and everyone chases it. The cheese wheel can reach up to 70 miles per hour. The first person to run, roll, or slide over the finish line wins, guess what, a real wheel of cheese.

Seventy-five percent of women in China were illiterate in 1949. Now, only 5 percent of women in China cannot read.

In New Zealand, birth certificate registration officials can tell parents to rename their children if they think the name is offensive or will cause the kid to be ridiculed. Rejected names have included: Yeah Detroit, Fish and Chips, Stallion, and Twisty Poi. Somehow, the name Number 16 Bus Shelter slipped through the cracks and is now the name of a real New Zealander.

Most trees in Berlin are numbered. There are more than 386,000.

A man on the once-barren Indian island of Majuli planted a tree every day for thirty-five years, creating a thriving forest spanning 1,360 acres, twice the size of New York City's Central Park.

In 2019, Holland rebuilt 316 bus stops to have "green roofs," roofs covered in flowers for bumblebees and honeybees.

Minnesota is called the Land of 10,000 Lakes. Actually, it has 11,482.

The most common American street name is *drumroll* Second Street. Third Street is the second most popular street name, and First Street is the third most popular street name. (In some places, Main Street counts as the first street, which is why First Street is not the most common.)

When you donate blood in Sweden, you get a text message every time your blood saves a life.

The world's longest cave is Mammoth Cave in Kentucky. Four hundred miles of it have been explored, but scientists guess there are still six hundred miles that haven't been touched.

At 85.29 years, the people of Hong Kong have the longest life expectancy of anywhere in the world.

There's a sprawling, deserted housing development of Disney-style mini-castles in central Turkey called Burj Al Babas.

JEOPARDY! CONTESTANT FAVE FACT

Lake Baikal in Siberia, which is 5,315 feet deep, contains one-fifth of the fresh water on Earth.
—Dan Adkison

Since 2018, an underwater robot called LarvalBot has delivered hundreds of thousands of baby corals to Australia's Great Barrier Reef to revive it.

In Catalonia, Spain, there's a tradition in which, before bedtime on the nights leading up to Christmas, kids leave snacks for Tió de Nadal, a log with a red hat and a happy face, and on Christmas it "poops" out their presents. Tió's other common name is Caga Tió, which translates to the NSFW version of "Poop Log."

The cardinal is the most popular state bird in the United States. It's the bird of Illinois, Indiana, Ohio, North Carolina, Kentucky, Virginia, and West Virginia.

Two hundred fifty million Brazilians speak Portuguese compared to only 10 million people in Portugal.

The world's oldest living tree is in Sweden and is approximately 9,550 years old.

During the days leading up to Fat Tuesday, residents of Ivrea, Italy, restage an uprising against a twelfth-century tyrannical lord . . . by throwing five hundred thousand pounds of oranges at one another. The Battle of the Oranges is the biggest annual food fight in Italy.

With approximately 24.5 million people, the population of Shanghai, China, is roughly equivalent to the population of Australia.

The world's longest zipline is 1.7 miles long, takes zipliners up to 93 miles per hour, and is in the United Arab Emirates, starting atop Jebel Jais Mountain.

In 2019, the Michigan town of Hell was hit by a polar vortex and literally froze over.

When Los Angeles was colonized by the Spanish in 1781, it was named El Pueblo de Nuestra Señora la Reina de los Ángeles de Porciúncula, or "the Town of Our Lady the Queen of the Angels of Porciúncula." Now, we just call it L.A.

Japan has eleven "Cat Islands" where there are far more cats than people, and no dogs are allowed.

The Statue of Liberty attracts lightning and gets struck approximately six hundred times a year.

In Denmark, if you're unmarried at twenty-five, your friends and family cover you in cinnamon. If you're unmarried at thirty, it gets upgraded to pepper. This spicy tradition dates back several hundred years to a time when spice vendors had to travel a lot and thus were more likely to stay single. Now it's a silly way to celebrate birthdays.

It's suspected that New York City is called "the Big Apple" because to bet "a big apple" was a popular nineteenth-century phrase. Horse racing was popular at the time, and New York City was the nexus of the sport.

In 1959, a three-ton ice block was driven from the Arctic Circle to the equator in Africa so that a Norwegian company could prove the efficacy of its new insulating glass wool product. The journey took four weeks, and only 11 percent of the ice melted. Some of the remaining ice was shipped back to Oslo and used in cocktails at a media celebration of the trip.

There's one place in America where mail is still delivered by mule, to the Havasupai people, an American Indian tribe that lives at the bottom of the Grand Canyon.

Since 1963, the last Saturday in April marks Eeyore's birthday party in Austin, Texas. The daylong festival celebrating the depressed donkey from *Winnie-the-Pooh* raises money for nonprofits.

With more than 37 million people, Tokyo is the most populous city in the world.

Kentucky has more barrels of bourbon than people.

More than one thousand streets around the world are named after Martin Luther King Jr.

Sixty-two countries have independence days to honor their liberation from Great Britain.

There's a store in Alabama called Unclaimed Baggage that sells . . . unclaimed baggage. It's the only store of this kind in the country.

The Chicago River is the only one in the world that flows backward.

In 2012, a man wore sixty shirts and nine pairs of a jeans on a flight from China to Kenya to avoid paying baggage fees.

The Ethiopian calendar has thirteen months.

Some real American city names include Boring, Maryland; Disco, Wisconsin; Boogertown, North Carolina; Satan's Kingdom, Massachusetts; Nothing, Arizona; Buttzville, New Jersey; and Bacon Level, Alabama.

There are more than 3 million shipwrecks on the ocean floor.

There's a London Bridge in Arizona. From the 1830s to 1967, it passed over the River Thames, as one would expect, but once the British realized it was falling apart, they sold it to pay for an updated version. An eccentric American businessman who'd recently purchased land near Lake Havasu in Arizona bought it for a total of more than $7 million, including shipping and assembly. It debuted in its new home in 1971.

On the Friday before Labor Day in Santa Fe, New Mexico, residents burn a fifty-foot-tall marionette named Zozobra, or Old Man Gloom. The annual blaze in front of more than fifty thousand people symbolizes the elimination of worries and anxieties from the previous year.

For more than thirty years, on the last Sunday of November in Lopburi, Thailand, humans throw monkeys a giant Monkey Buffet. During the celebration, a few thousand macaques climb towers of their favorite fruits and vegetables and pig out. In Thailand, monkeys are seen as bearers of luck and prosperity . . . and are also responsible for much of the area's tourism.

For nearly fifty years, the World Toe Wrestling Championship has been held in Derbyshire, England. It is exactly what it sounds like. The referee starts every round by announcing, "Toes away!"

If you've ever thought Mount Rushmore looks weird and unfinished, you're not wrong. The plan was to include bodies, too, but the project ran out of money.

Hawaii is moving toward Japan three to four inches per year.

There's one year-round, all-water mail route in the United States, and it's in Magnolia Springs, Alabama. Mail carriers deliver by boat on the thirty-one-mile route.

In Rome, you can cash in thirty plastic bottles for a train ticket instead of paying for one. This has led to hundreds of thousands of bottles being recycled.

Every summer at the Minnesota State Fair, a sculptor sits in a refrigerated revolving glass booth and creates busts out of ninety-pound blocks of butter. There are twelve butter sculpture subjects, one for each day of the festival. One is the winner of a dairy farmers' annual contest, and she is called Princess Kay of the Milky Way. The other eleven are Princess Kay finalists. Eligible entrants are dairy farmers and daughters of dairy farmers. This tradition has been going since 1965, and sculptor Linda Christensen has carved more than five hundred of the sculptures over the last forty years.

JEOPARDY! CONTESTANT FAVE FACT

It is illegal to shoot a sasquatch in Skamania City, Washington. The law's on the books. —Kristin Philips

Eastern Tennessee used to be called Franklin and Frankland.

The area code at the Kennedy Space Center in Florida is 3-2-1.

THE WILDEST LAWS AND LAWSUITS FROM AROUND THE COUNTRY

You learned earlier that tattooing is a super-old practice. But it was illegal to get a tattoo in Oklahoma until 2006.

Red Bull has paid out more than $13 million to people who've sued over the fact that the product does not actually give you wings.

You can't force a monkey to smoke cigarettes in South Bend, Indiana.

In 2009, a lady sued Cap'n Crunch because there were no berries in her cereal. The case was thrown out on account of there being no such thing as a Crunch Berry.

In Tennessee, sharing your Netflix password is illegal.

Ghosts and God cannot hold copyrights.

It's illegal to frown at a cop in New Jersey.

In Gainesville, Georgia, it's illegal to eat fried chicken with a fork.

In Alabama, it's illegal to play dominoes on Sundays (arguably the best day to sit outside and play dominoes).

In Kentucky, it's the law that everyone take a bath at least once a year.

CRAZY BUT TRUE

This chapter contains some of the strangest, most arbitrary and hard-to-believe facts and news stories I could dig up. They're too fascinating not to include but defy categorization, much like this chapter's delightful expert.

Jo Firestone is a comedian, board game creator, actress, writer, and cohost of *Dr. Gameshow*, a podcast in which listeners make up games and special guests to play. Her favorite, random fact?

"For breakfast every morning, Alex Trebek ate a Milky Way or Snickers and a Diet Coke or Diet Pepsi. May he rest in peace."

Now *that* is a breakfast of champions.

When there are twenty-three people in a room, there's a 50 percent chance two of them will have the same birthday. This phenomenon is called the Birthday Paradox.

It likely rains diamonds on Saturn and Jupiter.

In 2004, a Canadian woman lost her wedding ring while gardening in her yard. In 2017, she found it growing on a carrot.

If you count half-dollars, there are 293 ways to make change for a dollar.

Starting in the late 1970s, a group of Tennessee women who called themselves the 9 Nanas woke up at 4 a.m. to bake for low-income residents and anonymously leave sweet treats on their doorsteps with a note reading "Somebody loves you." After thirty years, one of their husbands finally found out what his wife and her friends had been up to—and the husbands offered to help, too.

Banana trees aren't trees, as there's no wood in them. They're giant herbs.

In 2020, a 107-year-old New Jersey woman named Anna Del Priore had survived both coronavirus and the Spanish Flu of 1918.

In Greek mythology, Pandora opens a jar, not a box.

No woman has ever walked on the moon—but NASA has plans to send one in 2024.

Myanmar, Liberia, and the United States are the only three countries that don't use the metric system.

On April 18, 1930, BBC Radio reported, "There is no news."

Stressing about your student loans? Maybe this will make you feel better: The Obamas didn't pay off their student loans until they were in their forties, just four years before Barack became president.

Ninety-eight percent of the universe was created in a three-minute span.

When Pepto-Bismol is blowtorched, it turns to metal.

Before bumper stickers were invented in the 1940s, people made placards out of cardboard, metal, and thick wire to express their opinions on the go.

John Wilkes Booth's brother once saved Abraham Lincoln's son's life.

You can fold American paper currency four thousand times before it rips.

Please don't try this at home (instead, watch it on YouTube!), but if you pulverize a sea sponge, its cells will reaggregate to form a new sea sponge.

In 1988, a germophobe with severe OCD attempted suicide by shooting himself in the head. He didn't kill himself, but his mental illness disappeared with no negative ramifications.

We still don't know much of what's inside the great pyramids of Giza.

In the late 1950s and early 1960s, you could buy life insurance from vending machines in airports.

The fidget spinner was patented not recently, but in 1993.

Metal is odorless. The odor you associate with metal is the smell of the metal coming into contact with skin and sweat.

Neil Armstrong didn't say, "That's one small step for man." He actually said, "That's one small step for _a_ man, one giant leap for mankind."

There's a man in Nepal who can lick his own forehead.

In 2013, an unsuspecting woman swallowed a $5,000 diamond placed at the bottom of her champagne flute at a charity event. The diamond was meant to be a prize for one lucky donor. It was retrieved during a colonoscopy the following day.

A "buttload" is a real weight unit, measuring 126 gallons. The term is usually used for measuring wine and sometimes beer. For context, a standard barrel is sixty gallons, so a buttload would be a little more than two barrels.

If you count how many times a cricket chirps in fifteen seconds and then add thirty-seven, you get a rough estimate of the Fahrenheit temperature in your current environment.

In 1954, an Alabama woman named Ann Hodges was struck by a meteorite and survived. She is the only person on record to be hit by a meteorite.

The Centers for Disease Control and Prevention has an extensive "zombie preparedness" section of its website.

Carl Sagan said marijuana inspired some of his scientific revelations, and he even wrote about the benefits of smoking pot under the pseudonym Mr. X.

On Mars, sunsets are blue and the daytime sky is red.

Mixing tiny bits of carrots into wet cement makes concrete stronger.

Play-Doh was originally produced as a wallpaper cleaner.

In 2008, a fifty-nine-year-old West Virginia woman named Velma Thomas was taken off life support after being brain dead for seventeen hours. Ten minutes later, her heart stopped and she was declared dead. She then came back to life with full brain function. No one can explain it.

Viruses can catch other viruses.

There's a French newspaper called *La Bougie du Sapeur* that comes out once every four years, on February 29. It was started in 1980.

Ten percent of European kids were conceived on an IKEA bed.

More than 550 people have traveled to space.

Related: Buzz Aldrin's mom's last name was Moon.

In 1940, two bomber planes collided in midair over Australia, and their wings became interlocked. The collision blew out the engines on the higher plane, but the lower plane's engines still worked. Conversely, the lower plane had no navigation controls, but the higher plane did. The pilot of the upper plane was able to land the pair of conjoined bombers safely, with zero casualties.

If you blow bubbles when it's below 32 degrees Fahrenheit, the bubbles turn to ice.

Mel Blanc voiced Bugs Bunny, Tweety, Porky Pig, and many other Looney Tunes characters. In 1961, a car accident put him in a coma, and he was completely unresponsive—until a neurologist asked him, "Hey, Bugs Bunny! How are you?" Blanc responded in Bugs's voice, "Eh . . . just fine, Doc. How are you?" He made a full recovery.

Raindrops aren't tear-shaped. They're hamburger-shaped.

We've explored only about 5 percent of the world's oceans.

According to a Moscow monastery's records, a woman in the eighteenth century gave birth to sixty-nine babies.

There's an opera house on the U.S.-Canada border where the stage is in one country and the audience is in another.

Teleportation exists—physicists can do it with single atoms.

UPS trucks don't make left-hand turns, which saves the company time and CO_2 emissions.

A guy named Charles Osborne had the hiccups for sixty-eight years.

The fire hydrant patent was lost in a fire.

The time it takes for any mammal to pee has nothing to do with how big or small it is. It takes us all approximately twenty-one seconds.

There's a family in Italy that doesn't feel pain.

Great news: We don't actually swallow eight spiders per year during sleep. That's a total myth.

Richard Nixon's signature is on a plaque on the moon because he was president during the first moon landing.

In 2018, a woman got married in a wedding veil that was more than sixty-three football fields long.

You're as old as the universe: Your body contains hydrogen atoms that were created during the Big Bang, 13.7 billion years ago.

If the sun exploded at this very moment, we wouldn't realize it or feel the effects for eight minutes and twenty seconds.

Aircrafts' black boxes are orange.

Identical twins do not have matching fingerprints.

There were originally thirteen astrological signs, but Ophiuchus was dropped with the Babylonians' adoption of a twelve-month calendar. If we used Ophiuchus today, it would be for people born from November 29 to December 18.

Astronauts are 3 percent taller in space.

The biggest snowflake ever was fifteen inches wide.

More Monopoly money is printed every year than actual American currency.

A Portuguese aristocrat who didn't have family randomly chose seventy people out of a Lisbon phone book to inherit his wealth when he died in 2007. Each received several thousand euros.

No one knows who named Earth.

TRIVIA GAMES

This section contains twelve trivia games to play alone or with pals. If you're making a group trivia night out of it, divide into teams, choose the particular number of games you want to play (I recommend four to six), and take turns reading the questions. For matchup games like 1, 5, and 10, you may want to pass the book around so everyone can see the options. The answer section comes after the twelfth game.

Turn the page to start playing!

GAME 1
MODERN MYTHOLOGY

How would Greek gods make a living if they existed in modern times? Match the Greek god with the profession they'd most likely choose if they walked among us today. Give yourself a point for every correct answer.

OPTIONS:

1. Couples counselor	A. Demeter
2. Influencer	B. Nike
3. Marine biologist	C. Hermes
4. Party planner	D. Dionysus
5. Creator, owner, CEO	E. Aphrodite
6. Interior designer	F. Hera
7. Pilot	G. Athena
8. Professor	H. Zeus
9. Vegan chef	I. Poseidon
10. Professional athlete	J. Hestia

GAME 2
MUSICAL SYNONYMS

I'll give you a synonym for a popular band, musical group, or artist, and you write down the name of the original. These musical acts span many decades, so there should be something for everyone. Give yourself a point for every answer you get right.

Example: If you read Frozen Water Square, *you'd write* Ice Cube.

1. The Seashore Male Youths
2. Fate's Kid
3. Sneaky and the Kinfolk Rock
4. The Crimson Sweltering Nightshade Fruits
5. Male Duck
6. Soil, Breeze, and Blaze
7. Singular Guidance
8. The Fakers
9. Most Powerful Chess Piece
10. Sodium Chloride 'n' the Flowering Vine Spice

GAME 3
STATE THE FACTS

Okay, smarties, this is a tricky one. I'll give you three facts about a U.S. state, and you write down which state I'm referring to. Please feel free to consult a map if you'd like to refresh your memory on the fifty states. Give yourself one point (and a pat on the back) for every question you get right.

1. Which U.S. state . . .
   - Has the longest boardwalk in the world?
   - And is the most densely populated state in the nation?
   - And was home to the first professional baseball game ever played in 1846?

2. Which U.S. state . . .
   - Produces more apples than any other state in the union?
   - And has the orca as the state mammal (for good reason)?
   - And is home to Bill Gates and the late Kurt Cobain?

3. Which U.S. state . . .
   - Is home to the nation's first subway system?
   - And has the mayflower as the state flower?
   - And is home to the first American lighthouse?

4. Which U.S. state . . .
   - Is home to seven times more pigs than people?
   - And means "beautiful" in the Siouan Indian language?
   - And is where the movie *Field of Dreams* takes place?

5. Which U.S. state . . .

> ⊳ Surprisingly has no state lottery?
> ⊳ And is named after the Spanish word for "snow-covered"?
> ⊳ And is the driest state in the country?

6. Which U.S. state . . .

> ⊳ Has the highest percentage of people who walk to work?
> ⊳ And is home to the nation's two largest forests?
> ⊳ And has a town called Unalaska?

7. Which U.S. state . . .

> ⊳ Is where Rosa Parks wouldn't give up her bus seat?
> ⊳ And was, surprisingly, the first state to celebrate Mardi Gras?
> ⊳ And has the unofficial nickname "The Heart of Dixie"?

8. Which U.S. state . . .

> ⊳ Has a professional sports team named after an Edgar Allan Poe-m?
> ⊳ And is known for blue crabs?
> ⊳ And was one of the original thirteen colonies?

9. Which U.S. state . . .

> ⊳ Is where the atomic bomb was tested?
> ⊳ And has the yucca as the state flower?
> ⊳ And has more Ph.D.s per capita than any other state (take that, East Coast!)?

10. Which U.S. state . . .

> ⊳ Is where residents consume approximately 21 million gallons of ice cream every year?
> ⊳ And is home to the "Bratwurst Capital of the World"?
> ⊳ And is where the satirical newspaper *The Onion* was founded?

GAME 4
MOVIE SYNONYMS

I'll give you a synonym for a popular movie from the last forty years, and you write down the name of the original. Give yourself a point for every answer you get correct.

Example: If you read **The Famine Tournaments,** *you'd write* **The Hunger Games.**

1. Intact Jewels
2. Dwelling Exclusively
3. Concealed Characters
4. Insomnia in the Emerald City
5. Skirmish Mallet
6. Nearly Prominent
7. Expire Solidly
8. Elegy for an Aspiration
9. Diminutive Gals
10. Complete Absorption of Light on a Cat Genus

GAME 5
WHO SAID IT?

This one's pretty self-explanatory. Match the memorable quote with the amazing woman who originally said or wrote it, and give yourself one point per correct answer.

1. "We realize the importance of our voices only when we are silenced."
2. "I would venture to guess that Anon, who wrote so many poems without signing them, was often a woman."
3. "There is no greater agony than bearing an untold story inside you."
4. "Fight for the things that you care about. But do it in a way that will lead others to join you."
5. "We've begun to raise daughters more like sons . . . but few have the courage to raise our sons more like our daughters."
6. "When she stopped conforming to the conventional picture of femininity she finally began to enjoy being a woman."
7. "When they go low, we go high."
8. "You don't make progress by standing on the sidelines, whimpering and complaining. You make progress by implementing ideas."
9. "It costs a lot of money to look this cheap."
10. "I knew even as a teenager that my femininity was more than just adornments; they were extensions of me, enabling me to express myself and my identity."

OPTIONS:

A. Dolly Parton
B. Shirley Chisholm
C. Virginia Woolf
D. Malala Yousafzai
E. Laverne Cox
F. Maya Angelou
G. Betty Friedan
H. Gloria Steinem
I. Michelle Obama
J. Ruth Bader Ginsburg

GAME 6
CELEBRITIES ARE ANIMALS

This is a tough one, Mighty Trivia Warriors. But IMHO, well worth it. I'm going to describe a celebrity and an animal whose names perfectly mash up. Your job is to guess them both for up to two points per mashup (one for the celeb, one for the animal). Don't worry about spelling: each mashup will *sound* perfect, and the celebrity name will always come first.

Example: This Chicago-born rapper, designer, and entrepreneur has a new trick up his sleeve. He's becoming . . . a little white Scottish dog with adorable, pointy ears.

ANSWER: Kanye WESTIE (Kanye West + WESTIE. Also acceptable: the breed's formal name, Kanye WEST HIGHLAND WHITE TERRIER.)

Ready? Just breathe. That's good. You'll be fine. Here we go.

1. He wrote *Hamilton* and *In the Heights*, but now this actor, singer, writer, and rapper is reaching even *higher*. His next musical is about birds—specifically birds that represent peace and love and are related to pigeons.
2. This lady has been starring in movies for her entire life, from *E.T.*, to *Scream*, to *Never Been Kissed*, to *50 First Dates*. Now this sweet and lovely actress is taking on the hardest role of all—a KILLER WHALE.
3. This Bronx-born talent won a Grammy for best rap album in 2019 and is the first woman to ever have five Top 10 singles on the *Billboard* Hot R&B/Hip-Hop chart at once. She may not be a queen, but she's ready to lead her swarm of black and bodak yellow workers to nectar.

4. This actor and martial artist from *Rush Hour* and *Rumble in the Bronx* is now "home on the range." In his next film, he plays a hoofed mammal with beautiful, hollow horns.

5. I hope you're "Confident" in your answer about this singer who's both "Stone Cold" and "Cool for the Summer." "Sorry Not Sorry," she's taken a turn in her career and become a warty amphibian.

6. The "she" in the music duo She and Him is also known for acting in *New Girl* and *500 Days of Summer*. Her next role is set in Africa, where she plays a kindhearted giant land mammal with a great memory.

7. The rapper, born Dwayne Michael Carter Jr., retired at thirty-five with five Grammys. Now he lives in a freshwater fish tank and is known for his triangular body, graceful swimming, and peaceful temperament.

8. This actress and humanitarian has appeared in *Maleficent*, *Lara Croft: Tomb Raider*, and *Mr. and Mrs. Smith*, to name a few. Now she'll play a tree-dwelling mammal in Madagascar with big eyes and a long striped tail.

9. This singer-songwriter's haunting voice was "Born to Die," even on tracks like "Video Games." Maybe she'd be more cheerful if she got to pull Santa's sleigh with the other majestic caribou.

10. He's one of the most influential hip-hop artists in history . . . and he's married to Beyoncé . . . *and* he's part owner of the music streaming platform Tidal. You could say he's earned his stripes, and that's why he's such a good-lookin' black-and-white equine.

GAME 7
GREATEST MOMENTS IN NFL HISTORY

Here's one for the football fans. Answer the questions, and give yourself a point for every correct answer. Many have multiple parts, so are worth more than one point.

1. "THE CATCH" was the winning touchdown reception in the 1981 NFC championship game. For up to three points:
   ▷ Who threw it?
   ▷ Who caught it?
   ▷ What team were they on / who won?

2. "THE MUSIC CITY MIRACLE" took place during a wild card playoff game in the year 2000 and featured a controversial lateral pass when there was sixteen seconds left in the game. For up to two points, which teams played in this game?

3. "WIDE RIGHT" was a missed forty-seven-yard field goal attempt at the end of Super Bowl XXV on January 27, 1991. For up to three points:
   ▷ Which two teams played in this Super Bowl?
   ▷ Who missed the field goal?

4. "THE IMMACULATE RECEPTION" is known as one of the greatest plays in NFL history. It took place on December 23, 1972. For up to three points:
   ▷ Which two teams played in this game?
   ▷ Who caught the Immaculate Reception?

5. "THE DRIVE" was an offensive series in the 4th quarter of the 1986 AFC Championship game. For up to three points:
   ▷ Which two teams played in this game?
   ▷ Who was the QB for the winning team?

6. "THE FUMBLE" was the sequel to "THE DRIVE," and featured the same two teams. This play occurred in the 1987 AFC Championship game.
   ▷ Which player fumbled the football?

7. "THE MIRACLE AT THE MEADOWLANDS" was a fumble recovery after a botched handoff at the end of a game on November 19, 1978. For up to three points:
   ▷ Which teams played in this game?
   ▷ Who recovered the fumble that led to the winning score?

8. "THE MONDAY NIGHT MIRACLE" happened at Giants Stadium on October 23, 2000, and was voted the Greatest Game Televised on ABC's *Monday Night Football*. For up to three points:
   ▷ Which teams played in this game?
   ▷ Who was the offensive lineman who caught a surprise touchdown pass?

9. "THE TACKLE" was the final play of Super Bowl XXXIV and secured a Super Bowl win. For up to three points:
   ▷ Which teams played in this game?
   ▷ Who made the tackle?

10. "THE COMEBACK" was an NFL playoff game on January 3, 1993, and featured the largest comeback in NFL history. For up to three points:
    ▷ Which team made the comeback?
    ▷ Who did they beat?
    ▷ What was the deficit at halftime?

GAME 8
THE RAT PACK

While scientists don't necessarily call a pack of porcupines a "prickle," fun names for animal collectives date all the way back to fifteenth-century England, when the writer Julia Berners published *The Book of Hawking, Hunting and Blasing of Arms*. We've used her names for groups of animals ever since. Select the correct name for each animal collective, and give yourself one point for each correct answer.

1. A group of ravens is called
   A. an unkindness
   B. a nevermore
   C. a boop
   D. a football

2. A group of pandas is called
   A. a fuzz
   B. an embarrassment
   C. a newspaper
   D. a pud

3. A group of frogs is called
   A. a lily pad
   B. an army
   C. a wart
   D. an anthology

4. A group of owls is called
   A. a feather
   B. a night
   C. a parliament
   D. a hoot

5. A group of flamingos is called
   A. a stand
   B. a stack
   C. a stork
   D. a stuck

6. A group of jellyfish is called
   A. a glob
   B. a smack
   C. a sting
   D. an air

7. A group of sloths is called
   A. a slow
   B. an eery
   C. a bed
   D. a tail

8. A group of lemurs is called
   A. a conspiracy
   B. a ring
   C. a spiral
   D. a stinker

9. A group of bats is called
   A. a sight
   B. a fright
   C. a blight
   D. a cauldron

10. A group of snakes is called
   A. a slink
   B. a slither
   C. a nest
   D. a nurture

GAME 9
ELEMENT-ARY SCHOOL

I'll give you facts about an element on the periodic table along with an underlined anagram of that element within the clue. If you want to make the game even harder, have someone else read the clues aloud and emphasize the anagram. It's much more difficult to work with anagrams when you can't see them. Give yourself a point for every element you correctly identify.

1. If you're a <u>RICH LONE</u> swimmer, you'll probably add this chemical element to your private pool to kill waterborne diseases.
2. In pill form, this element is said to help with migraines, kidney stones, and <u>UMM EASING</u> constipation.
3. This mineral is a structural part of plant cell walls and may be helpful to humans, too. Some people take it as a supplement because they believe it leads to bone and brain health and helps estrogen and testosterone supplements work better. But is the science behind that definitive? <u>NO, BRO</u>!
4. In pill form, this can help people with bipolar disorder manage their moods. But don't take too much, there's an <u>UH, LIMIT</u>.
5. This shimmery metal was known as "kohl" in ancient times and used for cosmetics. Today in <u>MY NATION</u>, it's mostly used in flame retardants.
6. This gas is the most reactive on the periodic table and can be super dangerous. It's <u>FOULER IN</u> larger quantities, can lead to burns on the skin, and can even be fatal. But in teeny doses in our water supply, it makes our teeth stronger. Wild.
7. This light silver precious metal is even more expensive than gold. But gold isn't bad. I mean, it's better than a <u>LIMP TUNA</u>.

8. From the Roman Empire through the Renaissance, this chemical element was the poison of choice for one's enemies. I think it's <u>NICER AS</u> a natural part of rice. A tiny bit in your sushi won't hurt you.

9. This noble gas is the second most common element in the entire universe, but I prefer it in my birthday balloon. What color is my floaty balloon? <u>UH, LIME</u>!

10. This metal is the most common element on Earth and is used to make steel. Its gray color would be perfect for a film <u>NOIR</u>.

GAME 10
THE REAL NAME GAME

Match these celebrities to their real, given names. Give yourself a point for every one you get correct.

REAL NAMES

1. Stefani Joanne Angelina Germanotta
2. Ilyena Lydia Mironoff
3. Neta-Lee Hershlag
4. Ashley Frangipane
5. Elizabeth Woolridge Grant
6. Ella Marija Lani Yelich-O'Connor
7. Onika Tanya Maraj
8. Caryn Johnson
9. Katheryn Elizabeth Hudson
10. Melissa Jefferson

CELEBRITY NAMES

A. Lizzo
B. Lana Del Rey
C. Katy Perry
D. Lady Gaga
E. Nicki Minaj
F. Natalie Portman
G. Helen Mirren
H. Halsey
I. Whoopi Goldberg
J. Lorde

GAME 11
WHERE IN THE WORLD?

The United Nations recognizes **193** countries. How well do you know them? Time to find out! Each question will offer up five special facts about a particular country. Write down the country these facts belong to. When you're done, give yourself a point for every answer you get right.

1. Where actress Lupita Nyong'o was raised; Nairobi; the Great Rift Valley; the Great Wildebeest Migration; amazing long-distance runners. Is it:
   A. England
   B. Bulgaria
   C. Kenya
   D. Egypt

2. Gets named the safest country in the world almost every year; northern lights are visible; Elves Museum; zero mosquitoes; Kópavogur is its second largest city. Is it:
   A. Iceland
   B. Finland
   C. Greenland
   D. Blueland

3. World's largest island nation; 127 active volcanoes; Bali; the only place to see Komodo dragons in the wild; Sumatra. Is it:
   A. Japan
   B. Jamaica
   C. Indonesia
   D. Sri Lanka

4. Attracts more tourists than any other country; Mont Blanc; where the Mona Lisa lives; vintage wines; artist Henri Matisse. Is it:
   A. Switzerland
   B. Austria
   C. Luxembourg
   D. France

5. In the Top 10 smallest countries in the world; residents speak German; many castles; capital Vaduz; Rhätikon Mountains. Is it:
   A. Monaco
   B. Liechtenstein
   C. East Zimbanglia
   D. Cuba

6. Himalayas; non-rectangular flag; "Namaste" is a standard greeting here; has never been occupied by foreign invaders; Kathmandu. Is it:
   A. India
   B. China
   C. Laos
   D. Nepal

7. Highest proportion of redheads in the world; national animal is the unicorn; has 790 islands; golf was invented here; Ewan McGregor. Is it:
   A. Scotland
   B. Ireland
   C. Canada
   D. Norway

8. Picasso; the first modern novel—*Don Quixote*—takes place here; Penélope Cruz; architect Antoni Gaudí; four official languages: Castilian, Catalan, Basque, and Galician. Is it:

    A. Mexico
    B. Galicia
    C. Portugal
    D. Spain

9. Mount Kilimanjaro; Lake Victoria; Freddie Mercury was born here; almost 30 percent of this country is national parks; Zanzibar. Is it:

    A. England
    B. Tanzania
    C. Ethiopia
    D. Israel

10. Pato—a cross between basketball and polo on horseback—is the national sport; Patagonia; gnocchi is eaten on the twenty-ninth of every month; women here have more plastic surgeries per person than any other women in the world; country name comes from the Latin word for "silver." Is it:

    A. Brazil
    B. Italy
    C. Argentina
    D. Boonesia

GAME 12
SPORTY PHRASES

This game is about all the sports-related phrases we use off the field, in everyday life. I'll describe a popular phrase that originated in sports and tell you which sport it comes from. Your job is to figure out what everyday phrase I'm describing.

Example: From baseball: What's next

Answer: "On deck"

1. From baseball: To defend someone
2. From golf: Expected or typical
3. From boxing: To support someone
4. From baseball: To kiss
5. From sailing: To gain momentum or energy after being fatigued
6. From baseball: Really strange
7. From boxing: Broke and hopeless
8. From cricket: To have no clue or idea
9. From football: To intervene on behalf of someone else
10. From boxing: Showing you'd like to be considered for something

Bonus really hard one: From horse racing: A skilled imposter

Answer Section

Spoiler alert! This is an entire section of spoilers!

GAME 1: MODERN MYTHOLOGY ANSWERS

 1. F. Hera, goddess of marriage
 2. E. Aphrodite, goddess of beauty
 3. I. Poseidon, god of the sea
 4. D. Dionysus, god of revelry
 5. H. Zeus, god of all gods
 6. J. Hestia, goddess of the home
 7. C. Hermes, god of travel
 8. G. Athena, goddess of wisdom
 9. A. Demeter, goddess of agriculture and grains
10. B. Nike, goddess of speed and strength

GAME 2: MUSICAL SYNONYMS ANSWERS

1. The Seashore Male Youths = The Beach Boys
2. Fate's Kid = Destiny's Child
3. Sneaky and the Kinfolk Rock = Sly and the Family Stone
4. The Crimson Sweltering Nightshade Fruits = The Red Hot Chili Peppers
5. Male Duck = Drake
6. Soil, Breeze, and Blaze = Earth, Wind, and Fire
7. Singular Guidance = One Direction
8. The Fakers = The Pretenders
9. Most Powerful Chess Piece = Queen
10. Sodium Chloride 'n' the Flowering Vine Spice = Salt-N-Pepa

GAME 3: STATE THE FACTS ANSWERS

1. New Jersey
2. Washington
3. Massachusetts
4. Iowa
5. Nevada
6. Alaska
7. Alabama
8. Maryland
9. New Mexico
10. Wisconsin

GAME 4: MOVIE SYNONYMS ANSWERS

1. Intact Jewels = *Uncut Gems*
2. Dwelling Exclusively = *Home Alone*
3. Concealed Characters = *Hidden Figures*
4. Insomnia in the Emerald City = *Sleepless in Seattle*
5. Skirmish Mallet = *Fight Club*
6. Nearly Prominent = *Almost Famous*
7. Expire Solidly = *Die Hard*
8. Elegy for an Aspiration = *Requiem for a Dream*
9. Diminutive Gals = *Little Women*
10. Complete Absorption of Light on a Cat Genus = *Black Panther*

GAME 5: WHO SAID IT? ANSWERS

1. D. Malala Yousafzai
2. C. Virginia Woolf
3. F. Maya Angelou
4. J. Ruth Bader Ginsburg
5. H. Gloria Steinem
6. G. Betty Friedan
7. I. Michelle Obama
8. B. Shirley Chisholm
9. A. Dolly Parton
10. E. Laverne Cox

GAME 6: CELEBRITIES ARE ANIMALS ANSWERS

1. Lin-Manuel MiranDOVE (Lin-Manuel Miranda + DOVE)
2. Drew BarrymORCA (Drew Barrymore + ORCA)
3. Cardi BEE (Cardi B + BEE)
4. Jackie ChANTELOPE (Jackie Chan + ANTELOPE)
5. Demi LovaTOAD (Demi Lovato + TOAD)
6. Zooey DeschanELEPHANT (Zooey Deschanel + ELEPHANT)
7. Lil WANGEL FISH (Lil Wayne + ANGEL FISH)
8. Angelina JoLEMUR (Angelina Jolie + LEMUR)
9. Lana Del REINDEER (Lana Del Rey + REINDEER)
10. Jay-ZEBRA (Jay-Z + ZEBRA)

GAME 7: GREATEST MOMENTS IN NFL HISTORY ANSWERS

1. "THE CATCH" was the winning touchdown reception in the 1981 NFC championship game. For up to three points:
   ▷ Who threw it? Joe Montana
   ▷ Who caught it? Dwight Clark
   ▷ What team were they on/who won? The San Francisco 49ers
2. "THE MUSIC CITY MIRACLE" took place during a wild card playoff game in 2000 and featured a controversial lateral pass when there was sixteen seconds left in the game. For up to two points, which teams played in this game? The Tennessee Titans and the Buffalo Bills
3. "WIDE RIGHT" was a missed forty-seven-yard field goal attempt at the end of Super Bowl XXV on January 27, 1991. For up to three points:
   ▷ Which two teams played in this Super Bowl? The New York Giants and the Buffalo Bills
   ▷ Who missed the field goal? Scott Norwood

4. "THE IMMACULATE RECEPTION" is known as one of the greatest plays in NFL history. It took place on December 23, 1972. For up to three points:

   ▹ Which two teams played in this game? The Oakland Raiders and the Pittsburgh Steelers

   ▹ Who caught the Immaculate Reception? Franco Harris

5. "THE DRIVE" was an offensive series in the 4th quarter of the 1986 AFC Championship game. For up to three points:

   ▹ Which two teams played in this game? The Cleveland Browns and the Denver Broncos

   ▹ Who was the QB for the winning team? John Elway

6. "THE FUMBLE" was the sequel to "THE DRIVE," and featured the same two teams. This play occurred in the 1987 AFC Championship game.

   ▹ Which player fumbled the football? Earnest Byner

7. "THE MIRACLE AT THE MEADOWLANDS" was a fumble recovery after a botched handoff at the end of a game on November 19, 1978. For up to three points:

   ▹ Which teams played in this game? The New York Giants and the Philadelphia Eagles

   ▹ Who recovered the fumble that led to the winning score? Herman Edwards

8. "THE MONDAY NIGHT MIRACLE" happened at Giants Stadium on October 23, 2000, and was voted the Greatest Game Televised on ABC's *Monday Night Football*. For up to three points:

   ▹ Which teams played in this game? The Miami Dolphins and the New York Jets

   ▹ Who was the offensive lineman who caught a surprise touchdown pass? Jumbo Elliott

9. "THE TACKLE" was the final play of Super Bowl XXXIV and secured a Super Bowl win. For up to three points:

   ▹ Which teams played in this game? The St. Louis Rams and the Tennessee Titans

   ▹ Who made the tackle? Mike Jones

10. "THE COMEBACK" was an NFL playoff game on January 3, 1993, and featured the largest comeback in NFL history. For up to three points:
   - ▷ Which team made the comeback? The Buffalo Bills
   - ▷ Who did they beat? The Houston Oilers
   - ▷ What was the deficit at halftime? 25 points. The score was 28 to 3.

GAME 8: THE RAT PACK ANSWERS

1. A. An unkindness
2. B. An embarrassment
3. B. An army
4. C. A parliament
5. A. A stand
6. B. A smack
7. C. A bed
8. A. A conspiracy
9. D. A cauldron
10. C. A nest

GAME 9: ELEMENT-ARY SCHOOL ANSWERS

1. Chlorine
2. Magnesium
3. Boron
4. Lithium
5. Antimony
6. Fluorine
7. Platinum
8. Arsenic
9. Helium
10. Iron

GAME 10: THE REAL NAME GAME ANSWERS

1. Stefani Joanne Angelina Germanotta —D. Lady Gaga
2. Ilyena Lydia Mironoff—G. Helen Mirren
3. Neta-Lee Hershlag—F. Natalie Portman
4. Ashley Frangipane—H. Halsey
5. Elizabeth Woolridge Grant—B. Lana Del Rey
6. Ella Marija Lani Yelich-O'Connor—J. Lorde
7. Onika Tanya Maraj—E. Nicki Minaj
8. Caryn Johnson—I. Whoopi Goldberg
9. Katheryn Elizabeth Hudson—C. Katy Perry
10. Melissa Jefferson—A. Lizzo

GAME 11: WHERE IN THE WORLD? ANSWERS

1. C. Kenya
2. A. Iceland
3. C. Indonesia
4. D. France
5. B. Liechtenstein
6. D. Nepal
7. A. Scotland
8. D. Spain
9. B. Tanzania
10. C. Argentina

GAME 12: SPORTS PHRASES ANSWERS

1. To go to bat for
2. Par for the course
3. To be in someone's corner
4. First base (or second base—this varies by generation and location)
5. Get a second wind
6. Out of left field
7. Down and out
8. To be stumped
9. To run interference
10. Throw your hat in the ring

Bonus: A ringer

ACKNOWLEDGMENTS

Well! This is exciting.

First, I'd like to give credit to the sources and resources I found most inspiring and reliable during my research and writing process: *Smithsonian Magazine*, *The Atlantic*, *National Geographic*, and *Atlas Obscura*, as well as the podcasts *No Such Thing as a Fish*, *Curiosity Daily*, and *The Weirdest Thing I Learned This Week*. Information from these outlets sent me down fascinating rabbit holes, and I can't recommend them enough.

Thank you to my smart, kind, and practical agent, Lindsay Edgecombe at Levine Greenberg Rostan Literary Agency. And to my wise and talented editor at TarcherPerigee, Nina Shield. Thank you for thinking of me for this project. It gave me purpose and joy during extremely difficult times. I am so happy we got to work together.

Next up: Chris Calogero, a perfect human comedian who just so happens to be my husband. Chris, thank you for being unconditionally caring and encouraging, and for listening to me when I burst out of the office screaming, "Did you know porcupines impale themselves *all the time*?!" Thank you, too, for helping me research when I felt like I was at an information dead end and wanted to throw the entire internet at the wall and cry in a pizza pile.

Thank you to my supportive parents, Bob and Jan Winter, for

accepting that I don't have the constitution for a traditional career path and telling me to cash out my 401(k) and go for my dreams.

Thank you, Ophira Eisenberg and the team at NPR's *Ask Me Another,* for giving me the opportunity to write trivia and jokes for a show I've loved and admired since its inception.

And thank you to everyone else involved in this book: the cover artist Jess Morphew; the marketing and publicity teams; the designers; assistant editor Hannah Steigmeyer; copy editor Amy Brosey, who had a *lot* of work to do (sorry); the chapter introduction experts and former *Jeopardy!* contestants who were willing to share their favorite facts; and my sister, Lex, who made this book come alive with her incredible artwork.

Finally, thank *you* for reading this.

NOTES

On Failure & Rejection

2 **Schulz's drawings were rejected:** Chris Kaltenbach, "Creator of 'Peanuts' Comic Strip Dies; Charles M. Schulz's Passing Comes as Cartoon Ended," *The Baltimore Sun*, February 14, 2000, https://www.baltimoresun.com/news/bs-xpm-2000-02-14-0002140037-story.html.

2 **Oprah Winfrey was fired:** Rachel Sugar, Richard Feloni, and Ashley Lutz, "29 Famous People Who Failed Before They Succeeded," *The Independent*, August 14, 2017, https://www.independent.co.uk/news/people/success-29-famous-people-failed-jay-z-oprah-winfrey-steven-spielberg-isaac-newton-charles-darwin-a7892406.html.

2 **Gisele:** Isabelle Truman, "10 Supermodels on Bouncing Back After Being Rejected," *Elle Australia,* October 16, 2020, https://www.elle.com.au/fashion/supermodels-that-have-been-rejected-in-their-careers-24152.

2 **Tyra Banks:** "Tyra Banks Was Rejected by 'Six Agencies' At the Start of Her Modelling Career," *Irish Examiner*, November 6, 2015, https://www.irishexaminer.com/lifestyle/celebrity/arid-30704408.html.

2 **Sir James Dyson:** Madison Malone-Kircher, "James Dyson on 5,126 Vacuums That Didn't Work—and the One That Finally Did," *New York*, November 22, 2016, https://nymag.com/vindicated/2016/11/james-dyson-on-5-126-vacuums-that-didnt-work-and-1-that-did.html.

2 ***Mad Men*:** Alex Witchel, "'Mad Men' Has Its Moment," *The New York Times*, June 22, 2008, https://www.nytimes.com/2008/06/22/magazine/22madmen-t.html?pagewanted=all&_r=0.

2 **E. E. Cummings:** "E. E. Cummings Biography," *Encyclopedia of World Biography*, https://www.notablebiographies.com/Co-Da/Cummings-E-E.html.

2 **Spielberg was rejected:** Amethyst Tate, "Celebs Who Went from Failures to Success Stories," CBS News, July 19, 2012, https://www.cbsnews.com/pictures/celebs-who-went-from-failures-to-success-stories/9/.

2 **Elvis failed high school music class:** Elizabeth Nix, "7 Fascinating Facts About Elvis Presley," *History*, July 1, 2014, updated August 7, 2019, https://www.history.com/news/7-fascinating-facts-about-elvis.

2 **Uzo Aduba:** Antonia Blyth, "Uzo Aduba: Three Years Ago 'I Was Crying on the Subway–I Quit'—Emmys," *Deadline*, August 19, 2015, https://deadline.com/2015/08/uzo-aduba-orange-is-the-new-black-the-wiz-1201501689/.

2 **Shakira was cut:** Mabel Kabani, "Superstar Singer Shakira Once Teased by School Classmates for Singing 'Like a Goat,'" CBS News, January 5, 2020, https://www.cbsnews.com/news/superstar-singer-shakira-once-teased-by-school-classmates-for-singing-like-a-goat-60-minutes-2020-01-05/.

3 **Einstein didn't speak:** Yiyun Li, "Einstein Didn't Talk until He Was Four," *The Guardian*, March 2, 2005, https://www.theguardian.com/lifeandstyle/2005/mar/02/familyandrelationships.features11; Tate, "Celebs Who Went from Failures to Success Stories."

3 **Lady Gaga, Destiny's Child, Bruno Mars, and Katy Perry:** Rob Brunner, "Destiny's Child: Someday We'll Be Together," *Entertainment Weekly*, updated September 1, 2000, https://ew.com/article/2000/09/01/destinys-child-someday-well-be-together/; Sugar, Feloni, and Lutz, "29 Famous People Who Failed Before They Succeeded"; Elias Leight, "How Motown Records Got Its Groove Back," *Rolling Stone*, July 10, 2017, https://www.rollingstone.com/music/music-news/how-motown-records-got-its-groove-back-199011; Jenny Stevens, "Katy Perry to Launch Her Own Record Label," NME, June 21, 2012, https://www.nme.com/news/music/katy-perry-85-1275349.

3 **Emily Dickinson:** Alfred Habegger, "Emily Dickinson," *Britannica*, last updated January 7, 2021, https://www.britannica.com/biography/Emily-Dickinson.

3 **Claire Danes:** Yohana Desta, "8 Movie Stars with Unbelievable Contract Clauses," *Vanity Fair*, August 10, 2017, https://www.vanityfair.com/hollywood/photos/2017/08/stars-contract-clause-gallery.

3 **President Ulysses S. Grant:** "Ulysses S Grant," *The Independent*, January 18, 2009, https://www.independent.co.uk/news/presidents/ulysses-s-grant-1391125.html.

3 **Sidney Poitier:** Tate, "Celebs Who Went from Failures to Success Stories."

3 **Vera Wang:** Sugar, Feloni, and Lutz, "29 Famous People Who Failed Before They Succeeded."

3 **Early screen test of Fred Astaire:** Tate, "Celebs Who Went from Failures to Success Stories."

3 **Harvard freshmen:** Samantha Grossman, "It's Harder to Get a Job at Walmart Than It Is to Get into Harvard," *Time*, March 31, 2014, https://time.com/43750/walmart-acceptance-rate-lower-than-harvards/.

4 **Walmart takes 2.6 percent:** Grossman, "It's Harder to Get a Job at Walmart Than It Is to Get into Harvard."

4 **Jefferson anonymously submitted:** "Thomas Jefferson," Library of Congress, https://www.loc.gov/exhibits/jefferson/jefffed.html.

4 **Melville received a rejection letter:** Alice Vincent, "10 Classic Books that Got Famously Rejected," *Today*, June 6, 2014, updated June 06, 2014, https://www.todayonline.com/entertainment/arts/10-classic-books-got-famously-rejected.

4 **New Year's resolution:** Shireen Khalil, "You'll Fail at Your New Year's Resolution by This Date," News.com.au, December 22, 2019, https://www.news.com.au/lifestyle/real-life/youll-fail-your-new-years-resolutions-by-this-date/news-story/c05f7d2dd1a2c558e61d5f20322a0d5a.

4 **The Beatles were told:** "Listen to Audio of the Beatles' First-Ever Audition for Decca Records in 1962," *Far Out*, July 19, 2020, https://faroutmagazine.co.uk/the-beatles-first-ever-audition-audio/.

4 **Annie Murphy:** Noah Higgins-Dunn, "Actress Annie Murphy Had $3 in the Bank before Landing a Role in the Emmy-Nominated Show 'Schitt's Creek,'" CNBC, January 30, 2020, https://www.cnbc.com/2020/01/30/annie-murphy-had-3-in-the-bank-before-landing-schitts-creek.html.

4 **Stephen King's *Carrie*:** Tate, "Celebs Who Went from Failures to Success Stories"; Devon Geary, "'Carrie' by the Numbers," *The Seattle Times*, October 14, 2013, updated October 14, 2013, https://www.seattletimes.com/entertainment/lsquo carriersquo-by-the-numbers/.

5 **Successful people:** Karen Huang et al., "Mitigating Malicious Envy: Why Successful Individuals Should Reveal Their Failures," Working Paper 18-080, Harvard Business School, 2018, https://www.hbs.edu/faculty/Publication%20Files/18-080_56688b05-34cd-47ef-adeb-aa7050b93452.pdf.

Music

8 **Song of summer:** Phil Edwards, "The Surprising History of the 'Song of the Summer,'" Vox, updated June 15, 2016, https://www.vox.com/2015/6/17/8796289/summer-song-history.

8 ***Billboard* Hot 100:** Gary Trust, "Rewinding the Charts: In 1958, the Billboard Hot 100 Debuted with Ricky Nelson at No. 1," *Billboard*, August 3, 2018, https://www.billboard.com/articles/columns/chart-beat/8468557hot-100-ricky-nelson-poor-little-fool-rewinding-the-charts-1958.

8 **Chris Hadfield recorded:** Maya Rhodan, "Listen to the Single from Astronaut Chris Hadfield's Album Recorded in Space," *Time*, November 12, 2015, https://time.com/4111096/astronaut-chris-hadfield-song-space/.

8 **Shrimp Daddy:** "Nardwuar vs. Lil Wayne," NardwuarServiette, YouTube, https://www.youtube.com/watch?v=wgMUhI_SN68&list=UU8h8NJG9gacZ5lAJJvhD0fQ&index=21&feature=plcp.

8 **Beethoven's composing process:** Bill Smallwood, "Fun Fact Friday: Ludwig van Beethoven," Discovery Education, March 28, 2014, https://blog.discoveryeducation.com/blog/2014/03/28/fun-fact-friday-ludwig-van-beethoven/.

8 **Childish Gambino:** Edward Hyatt et al., "Childish Wonder: Who Is Childish Gambino aka Donald Glover?," *The Scottish Sun*, April 14, 2019, updated October 2, 2020, https://www.thescottishsun.co.uk/tvandshowbiz/celebrity/406886/childish-gambino-donald-glover/.

8 **"Wannabe" is the catchiest song:** Mark Kinver, "Spice Girls' Wannabe 'Is Catchiest Hit Single,'" BBC News, November 1, 2014, https://www.bbc.com/news/science-environment-29847739.

9 **Billie Eilish:** Patrick Hosken, "Billie Eilish Is the First Artist Born in the 2000s to Hit No. 1," MTV News, April 8, 2019, http://www.mtv.com/news/3119875/billie-eilish-no-1-album/.

9 **Billy Joel:** Miles in the Morning, 98.7 KLUV, "Billy Joel Refuses to Sell Front Row Tickets to His Shows, and Instead Gives Them Away to 'Real Fans' for Free," Radio.com, September 3, 2020, https://www.radio.com/kluv/blogs/miles-in-the-morning/billy-joel-refuses-to-sell-front-row-tickets-to-his-concerts.

9 **Panic! At the Disco:** Emily Zemler, "Spotlight: Panic! at the Disco," *SPIN*, October 3, 2005, https://www.spin.com/2005/10/panic-disco/.

9 **Boycotted the Grammys:** Hilary Lewis, "Oscars: Inside Will Smith's Boycott of the 1989 Grammys," *The Hollywood Reporter*, February 2, 2016, https://www.hollywoodreporter.com/news/oscars-will-smith-boycotted-grammys-861354.

9 **Pianos has 7,500 working parts:** "Five Interesting Facts About Musical Instruments," Associated Press, May 22, 2019, https://apnews.com/article/ca42ec54d14a44fc8d95abbc9275df12.

9 **"Jingle Bells":** Valerie Strauss, "'Jingle Bells'—Written for Thanksgiving?," *The Washington Post*, December 24, 2013, https://www.washingtonpost.com/news/answer-sheet/wp/2013/12/24/jingle-bells-written-for-thanksgiving/; Christopher Klein, "8 Things You May Not Know About 'Jingle Bells,'" History.com, December 16, 2016, updated August 31, 2018, https://www.history.com/news/8-things-you-may-not-know-about-jingle-bells.

9 **Leo Fender:** Alex A, "Leo Fender, Inventor of Fender Guitars, Never Learned How to Play the Guitar," *The Vintage News*, September 15, 2016, https://www.thevintagenews.com/2016/09/15/leo-fender-inventor-fender-guitars-never-learned-play-guitar/.

9 **Janis Joplin:** Melanie Dostis, "Looking Back on the Life of Janis Joplin 45 Years After Her Early Death," New York *Daily News*, October 4, 2015, https://www.nydailynews.com/entertainment/remembering-life-janis-joplin-35-years-death-article-1.2383613.

10 **"The Star-Spangled Banner":** "'Star-Spangled Banner' Born from a Drinking Song 200 Years Ago," *All Things Considered*, NPR, September 12, 2014, https://

www.npr.org/2014/09/12/348010268/star-spangled-banner-born-from
-a-drinking-song-200-years-ago.

10 **Lizzo's stage name:** Corinne Sullivan, "Just Cuz We Love Her, Here Are 10 Fascinating Facts About Lizzo," PopSugar, May 10, 2020, https://www.popsugar
.com/celebrity/photo-gallery/47422795/image/47423250/Her-Real-Name
-Is-Melissa-Jefferson.

10 **Lady Gaga's name:** "The Origin Stories Behind Gaga and Other Musicians'
Names," Dictionary.com, https://www.dictionary.com/e/origin-stories-behind
-musicians-names/.

10 **Mary did have a little lamb:** "Mary Had a Little Lamb—Yes, There Was a Mary
and She Did Have a Little Lamb," New England Historical Society, https://www
.newenglandhistoricalsociety.com/mary-little-lamb-yes-mary-little-lamb/.

10 **Sister Rosetta Tharpe:** "Sister Rosetta Tharpe, the First Gospel Recording Star,"
The New Yorker, August 26, 2016, https://www.newyorker.com/magazine
/2016/09/05/sister-rosetta-tharpe-the-first-gospel-recording-star; Erica Taylor,
"Little Known Black History Fact: Rosetta Tharpe," *The Tom Joyner Morning
Show*, Black America Web, https://blackamericaweb.com/2013/02/17/little
-known-black-history-fact-rosetta-tharpe/.

10 **Taylor Swift:** Lorena O'Neil, "Taylor Swift Tops Canadian iTunes Chart with
Eight Seconds of White Noise," *Billboard*, October 22, 2014, https://www.bill
board.com/articles/columns/pop-shop/6289411/taylor-swift-tops-canadian
-itunes-chart-eight-seconds-white-noise; Alice Vincent, "Why Taylor Swift and
Kanye West Hate Each Other," *The Telegraph*, August 28, 2017, https://www
.telegraph.co.uk/music/news/taylor-swift-kanye-west-hate/.

11 **Carly Simon:** Gavin Edwards, "10 Things We Learned from Carly Simon's Revealing New Memoir," *Rolling Stone*, November 24, 2015, https://www.rollingstone
.com/music/music-news/10-things-we-learned-from-carly-simons-revealing
-new-memoir-227520/.

11 **The Beastie Boys invented the word "mullet":** "Mullet," *Oxford English Dictionary*, https://www.oed.com/viewdictionaryentry/Entry/253382.

11 **"(You Gotta) Fight for Your Right (To Party!)":** Sean O'Neal, "A Brief Comedy History of the Beastie Boys," *Vulture*, November 6, 2018, https://www.vul
ture.com/2018/11/a-brief-comedy-history-of-the-beastie-boys.html.

11 **White gloves:** Alice Gordenker, "White Gloves," *The Japan Times*, March 19,
2013, https://www.japantimes.co.jp/news/2013/03/19/reference/white-gloves
/#.XvIkmPJJnUo.

11 **Audible only to dogs:** Paul Cashmere, "Paul McCartney Confirms the Beatles Recorded a Song for Dogs," *Noise 11*, November 4, 2013, http://www.noise11.com
/news/paul-mccartney-confirms-the-beatles-recorded-a-song-for-dogs-20131104.

11 **E flat:** Sharon & David Bowers, *Shop Class for Everyone* (New York: Workman
Publishing, 2021), 133.

11 **Aretha Franklin in 1987:** "Rock and Roll Hall of Fame Inducts First Woman," History.com, November 16, 2009, updated December 22, 2020, https://www .history.com/this-day-in-history/rock-and-roll-hall-of-fame-inducts-first -woman.

11 **Selena Gomez and Demi Lovato:** Megan Armstrong, "A Timeline of Demi Lovato & Selena Gomez's Friendship: From 'Barney' to the Pop Charts," *Billboard*, October 25, 2017, https://www.billboard.com/articles/columns/pop/8014026 /timeline-demi-lovato-selena-gomez-friendship.

12 **Tupac said his lyrics were inspired:** L-Fresh the Lion and Rosa Gollan, "Tupac Was One of the Greatest Rappers of All Time, and Here's Why," *The Music Show*, ABC Radio National, September 5, 2017, updated October 5, 2020, https://www .abc.net.au/news/2017-09-06/tupac-was-one-of-the-greatest-rappers-of-all -time-heres-why/8870400.

12 **Smoked his ashes:** "Tupac Shakur's Ashes Smoked," *The Independent*, October 23, 2011, https://www.independent.co.uk/news/people/news/tupac-shakurs -ashes-smoked-2346879.html.

12 **Anthony Kiedis was flagged down:** Evan Slead, "Carpool Karaoke: Red Hot Chili Peppers Singer Anthony Kiedis Saved Baby's Life While Filming," *Entertainment Weekly*, updated June 16, 2016, https://ew.com/article/2016/06/16 /anthony-kiedis-red-hot-chili-peppers-carpool-karaoke-save-baby/.

12 **Big Mama Thornton:** Olivia Riggio, "Women's History Month Profiles: Willie Mae 'Big Mama' Thornton, Blues Musician," DiversityInc, February 2, 2021, https://www.diversityinc.com/black-history-month-profiles-willie-mae-big -mama-thornton-blues-musician/.

12 **Tommy Cash:** "Tommy Cash—I Didn't Walk the Line," Armadillo Killer, YouTube, June 7, 2015, https://www.youtube.com/watch?v=kvhE7bgXaO0; "My Mother's Other Son by Tommy Cash and Tommy Jennings from 1983," On'ry Waymore, YouTube, September 28, 2016, https://www.youtube.com/watch?v=UPjZ9cT JHbg.

12 **"Old Town Road":** Mesfin Fekadu, "Lil Nas X's 'Old Town Road' Sets More Records on Billboard Charts," *USA Today*, August 12, 2019, https://www.usatoday .com/story/entertainment/music/2019/08/12/lil-nas-x-old-town-road-sets -more-billboard-hot-100-records/1990296001/.

13 **Freddie Mercury:** Corinne Sullivan, "OK, So We're Still Thinking About This Weird Detail from *Bohemian Rhapsody*," PopSugar, January 12, 2019, https:// www.popsugar.com/celebrity/Did-Freddie-Mercury-Really-Have-Too-Many -Teeth-45651844.

13 **Recall memories:** Taylor & Francis, "Music Brings Memories Back to the Injured Brain," ScienceDaily, December 10, 2013, https://www.sciencedaily.com/re leases/2013/12/131210072030.htm.

13 **Jay-Z:** Ryan Reed, "Jay Z Talks High School Rap Battle with Busta Rhymes on 'Kimmel,'" *Rolling Stone*, October 21, 2015, https://www.rollingstone.com/tv

/tv-news/jay-z-talks-high-school-rap-battle-with-busta-rhymes-on-kimmel-194181/.

13 **All That was performed by TLC:** Debbie Encalada, "The 'All That' Cast Reunited and Sang the Show's Theme Song," *Complex*, November 2, 2015, https://www.complex.com/pop-culture/2015/11/all-that-cast-reunites-sings-theme-song.

13 **"The Twelve Days of Christmas":** "The Maths Inside the Twelve Days of Christmas," Maths Careers, December 10, 2015, https://www.mathscareers.org.uk/article/the-maths-inside-the-twelve-days-of-christmas/.

13 **Ida Cox:** Greg Freeman, "Ida Cox (1894–1967)," New Georgia Encyclopedia, March 26, 2005, last edited May 4, 2020, https://www.georgiaencyclopedia.org/articles/arts-culture/ida-cox-1894-1967; "2019 Blues Hall of Fame Inductee—Ida Cox (Full)," The Blues Foundation, YouTube, December 3, 2019, https://www.youtube.com/watch?v=rroIkWZyTwM.

13 **Bruce Springsteen:** Dave Lifton, "How Bruce Springsteen's 'Born in the U.S.A.' Became First U.S.-Made CD," *Ultimate Classic Rock*, September 21, 2015, https://ultimateclassicrock.com/bruce-springsteen-born-in-the-usa-cd.

Art

15 **Basquiat:** "21 Facts About Jean-Michel Basquiat," Sotheby's, June 21, 2019, https://www.sothebys.com/en/articles/21-facts-about-jean-michel-basquiat.

16 **Banksy:** Scott Reyburn, "Banksy Painting Self-Destructs After Fetching $1.4 Million at Sotheby's," *The New York Times*, October 6, 2018, https://www.nytimes.com/2018/10/06/arts/design/uk-banksy-painting-sothebys.html.

16 **Mona Lisa:** Tobin Declan, "Fun Facts for Kids About Mona Lisa," *Easy Science for Kids*, January 2021, https://easyscienceforkids.com/mona-lisa-facts/.

16 **Most expensive painting:** "31 of the Most Expensive Paintings Ever Sold at Auction," *Invaluable*, last updated July 29, 2019, https://www.invaluable.com/blog/most-expensive-painting/.

16 **Children's art gallery:** Rebecca Speare-Cole, "London Bus Stop Transformed into Children's Art Gallery to Lift Spirits During Lockdown," *Evening Standard*, April 28, 2020, https://www.standard.co.uk/news/uk/london-bus-stop-art-gallery-children-coronavirus-a4426056.html.

16 **Painting was an Olympic event:** Matilda Jenkins, "5 Facts About Art That Will Impress Your Friends," Blue Thumb, May 14, 2020, https://bluethumb.com.au/blog/news-and-media/5-facts-about-art-that-will-impress-your-friends/.

16 **Dalí:** Rosie Lesso, "Salvador Dali: The Life and Work of an Icon," The Collector, October 1, 2019, https://www.thecollector.com/salvador-dali-the-life-and-work-of-an-icon/.

16 **Bedroom in Arles:** Chloe Riley, "Missed Out on the Van Gogh–Inspired Airbnb Room? Here's Your Second Chance," WTTW, March 8, 2016, https://news.wttw

.com/2016/03/08/missed-out-van-gogh-inspired-airbnb-room-heres-your -second-chance.

16 **The Starry Night:** "Vincent van Gogh: Paintings, Drawings, Quotes, and Biography," VincentVanGogh.org, https://www.vincentvangogh.org/starry-night .jsp.

16 **Graffiti and street art:** "The Difference Between Street Art and Graffiti," Schrift & Farbe Design Group, May 16, 2020, https://schriftfarbe.com/the-difference -between-street-art-and-graffiti.

17 **"Cornbread" McCray:** "Two Minutes with . . . Darryl 'Cornbread' McCray," *Worcester Magazine*, September 28, 2017, https://www.worcestermag.com /2017/09/28/two-minutes-darryl-cornbread-mccray.

17 **David's nose was too big:** "Michelangelo's David," *Italy Magazine*, September 9, 2009, https://www.italymagazine.com/featured-story/michelangelos-david.

17 **Kim Dong Yoo:** "Kim Dong Yoo," artsy.net, https://www.artsy.net/artist/kim -dong-yoo.

17 **Yves Klein:** Samuel Reilly, "Feeling Blue: Yves Klein at Blenheim Palace," *The Economist*, July 25, 2018, https://www.economist.com/1843/2018/07/25 /feeling-blue-yves-klein-at-blenheim-palace.

17 **Georgia O'Keeffe:** Mark Jacob, "10 Things You Might Not Know About Modern Art," May 10, 2009, *Chicago Tribune*, https://www.chicagotribune.com/news /ct-xpm-2009-05-10-10-things-modern-art-story.html.

17 **American art museums have a long way to go:** Brigit Katz, "Study Finds Art Museums Are Slowly Becoming More Diverse, but Progress Is 'Uneven,'" *Smithsonian Magazine*, January 29, 2019, https://www.smithsonianmag.com/smart -news/art-museums-are-becoming-more-diverse-progress-uneven-180971373/.

18 **Claude Monet:** Andrea Thompson, "The Blurry World of Claude Monet Recreated," Live Science, May 11, 2007, https://www.livescience.com/1512-blurry -world-claude-monet-recreated.html.

18 **A Greek painter named Zeuxis:** Ethel Dilouambaka, "This Greek Philosopher Died Laughing at His Own Joke," Culture Trip, March 18, 2018, https://thecul turetrip.com/europe/greece/articles/this-greek-philosopher-died-laughing -at-his-own-joke/.

18 **Patrick from *SpongeBob*:** Artemis Moshtaghian, "Vandals Give Soviet Star a SpongeBob SquarePants Makeover," CNN, November 14, 2016, updated November 15, 2016, https://www.cnn.com/2016/11/14/world/vandals-give-soviet -star-a-spongebob-makeover-trnd/index.html.

18 **Pineapple in the center of a table:** Roisin O'Connor, "Students Left a Pineapple in the Middle of an Exhibition and People Mistook It for Art," *The Independent*, May 8, 2017, https://www.independent.co.uk/arts-entertainment/art/news /pineapple-art-exhibition-scotland-robert-gordon-university-ruairi-gray-lloyd -jack-a7723516.html.

18 **Frida Kahlo:** Jessica Stewart, "8 Interesting Frida Kahlo Facts That May Surprise You," My Modern Met, August 14, 2018, https://mymodernmet.com/frida-kahlo-facts/.

18 **Most British thing ever:** Dirk Vanduffel, "A Question in Trivial Pursuit: Which Artist Created a Portrait of Queen Elisabeth II Using 1,000 Teabags? Answer: Andy Brown," *Artdependence Magazine*, March 1, 2018, https://www.artdependence.com/articles/a-question-in-trivial-pursuit-which-artist-created-a-portrait-of-queen-elisabeth-ii-using-1-000-teabags-answer-andy-brown/.

18 **"Non-visible" "sculpture":** Eyder Peralta, "Woman Pays $10,000 for 'Non-Visible' Work of Art," NPR, July 19, 2011, https://www.npr.org/sections/thetwo-way/2011/07/22/138513048/woman-pays-10-000-for-non-visible-work-of-art.

18 **Oldest known figurative painting:** Maya Wei-Haas, "40,000-Year-Old Cave Art May Be World's Oldest Animal Drawing," *National Geographic*, November 7, 2018, https://www.nationalgeographic.com/science/2018/11/news-oldest-animal-drawing-borneo-cave-art-human-origins/.

19 **"Lover's eye" jewelry:** Carly Silver, "19th-Century 'Lover's Eye' Jewelry Was the Perfect Accessory for Secret Affairs," *Atlas Obscura*, September 15, 2017, https://www.atlasobscura.com/articles/lovers-eye-jewelry.

19 **Lump was seventeen:** Alan Riding, "Picasso's Other Muse, of the Dachshund Kind," *The New York Times*, August 26, 2006, https://www.nytimes.com/2006/08/26/arts/design/26lump.html.

Sports

22 **Serena Williams:** David Lange, "Male Tennis Players with the Most Grand Slam Tournament Titles Won as of March 2021," Statista, March 1, 2021, https://www.statista.com/statistics/263034/male-tennis-players-with-the-most-victories-at-grand-slam-tournaments/; Claire Zillman, "Serena Williams: Another Pregnant Woman Just Doing Her Job," *Fortune*, April 20, 2017, https://fortune.com/2017/04/20/serena-williams-pregnant/.

22 **Tug-of-war:** Chandler Friedman, "Once an Olympic Sport, Tug-of-War Hopes for Reinclusion," CNN, August 10, 2012, https://www.cnn.com/2012/08/10/sport/olympics-tug-of-war/index.html.

22 **Babe Ruth:** "Korea Bans Baseball Cabbage Pitch," BBC News, June 22, 2005, http://news.bbc.co.uk/2/hi/asia-pacific/4117856.stm.

22 **Ice skates:** Karl Ove Knausgaard, "The Hidden Drama of Speedskating," *The New York Times Magazine*, March 6, 2018, https://www.nytimes.com/interactive/2018/01/30/magazine/winter-olympics-long-track-speed-skating-hidden-drama.html; Lesley Kennedy, "The Prehistoric Ages: How Humans Lived Before Written Records," History.com, September 27, 2019, updated October 21, 2019, https://www.history.com/news/prehistoric-ages-timeline.

22 **Wilma Rudolph:** "Wilma Rudolph Biography (1940–1994)," Biography, January 19, 2018, updated January 7, 2021, https://www.biography.com/athlete/wilma-rudolph.

22 **Elisha Manning:** "Manning Solution for Eli Confusion: 'Call Me Elisha,'" NFL .com, May 10, 2016, https://www.nfl.com/news/manning-solution-for-eli-confusion-call-me-elisha-0ap3000000661094.

22 **Eighteen minutes of action:** Steve Moyer, "In America's Pastime, Baseball Players Pass a Lot of Time," *The Wall Street Journal*, July 16, 2013, https://www.wsj .com/articles/SB10001424127887323740804578597932341903720.

22 **Abby Wambach:** Associated Press, "Soccer Star Abby Wambach Named Associated Press Female Athlete of the Year," Syracuse.com, December 20, 2011, updated March 22, 2019 https://www.syracuse.com/sports/2011/12/soccer_star_abby_wambach_named.html.

23 **Bob Hayes:** Ken Browne, "How 'Bullet' Bob Hayes Became the Only Man to Win Olympic Gold and NFL Super Bowl Glory," Olympic Channel, February 2, 2020, https://www.olympicchannel.com/en/stories/features/detail/bullet-bob-hayes-olympic-100m-gold-to-super-bowl-glory/.

23 **Seventeen million Americans take the day off:** Brett Molina, "If You Call In Sick Monday After the Super Bowl, You Aren't Alone. 'Super Bowl Fever' Is a Thing," *USA Today*, January 31, 2019, updated February 3, 2019, https://www .usatoday.com/story/money/2019/01/31/super-bowl-fever-why-many-people-skip-work-monday/2731405002/.

23 **Golf ball won't travel as far:** Brad Miller, "Does Weather Affect a Golf Ball's Distance?," Weather Works, September 3, 2020, https://weatherworksinc.com /news/weather-golf-ball-distance.

23 **Lisa Leslie:** "Lisa Leslie Throws Down WNBA's First Dunk," wnba.com, July 30, 2002, https://www.wnba.com/video/lisa-leslie-wnba-first-dunk/.

23 **William Penn:** Brooke Destra, "A Look at the Curse of Billy Penn on the Anniversary Where It All Began," NBC Sports Philadelphia, May 13, 2020, https://www.nbcs ports.com/philadelphia/eagles/philadelphia-sports-curse-billy-penn-anniversary.

24 **Shin kicking:** Neil Curry, "Cotswolds Olimpicks: Shin-Kicking at the 'Other' Games," CNN, June 9, 2012, https://www.cnn.com/2012/06/07/sport/cotswold-olimpicks-shin-kicking/index.html.

24 **Potential inclusion in the Olympics:** "Olympics May Soon Feature Pole Dancing, Foosball and Poker," Fox News, October 18, 2017, https://www.foxnews .com/sports/olympics-may-soon-feature-pole-dancing-foosball-and-poker.

24 **Sunita Williams:** Kelly Young, "Astronaut Completes Marathon in Space," *New Scientist*, April 16, 2007, https://www.newscientist.com/article/dn11617-astronaut-completes-marathon-in-space/.

24 **ESPN's twenty-fifth anniversary:** "Katie Nolan hosts four people named after ESPN," ESPN, YouTube, December 20, 2019, https://www.youtube.com/watch ?v=nxiQJmPMhec, https://www.fatherly.com/love-money/baby-names-2010s/.

24 **Rousey:** Alexandra Licata, "The 36 Most Iconic Female Athletes of the Past Century," *Business Insider*, July 12, 2019, https://www.businessinsider.com/iconic-female-athletes-women-sports-2019-7#ronda-rousey-9.

24 **Decide whether they're hitting a pitch:** David Kohn, "Scientists Examine What Happens in the Brain When a Bat Tries to Meet a Ball," *The Washington Post*, August 29, 2016, https://www.washingtonpost.com/national/health-science/scientists-examine-what-happens-in-the-brain-when-bat-tries-to-meet-ball/2016/08/29/d32e9d4e-4d14-11e6-a7d8-13d06b37f256_story.html.

24 **Printed with fans' tweets:** Shanna McCarriston, "Super Bowl 2020: Confetti Printed with Fans' Tweets Falls onto the Field in Miami After Chiefs Victory," CBS Sports, February 2, 2020, https://www.cbssports.com/nfl/news/super-bowl-2020-confetti-printed-with-fans-tweets-falls-onto-the-field-in-miami-after-chiefs-victory/.

24 **Golf ball and club onto Apollo 14:** Bryan Altman, "45 Years Ago Today, Astronaut Alan Shepard Hit a Golf Ball off the Moon," CBS Local Sports, February 6, 2016, https://sports.cbslocal.com/2016/02/06/45-years-ago-today-astronaut-alan-shepard-hit-a-golf-ball-off-the-moon/.

25 **Dock Ellis:** Jon Tayler, "Today Is the 47th Anniversary of Dock Ellis' Acid-Fueled No-Hitter," *Sports Illustrated*, June 12, 2017, https://www.si.com/mlb/2017/06/12/dock-ellis-acid-no-hitter-pittsburgh-pirates-anniversary.

25 **Original arena looked like an igloo:** "Last Hurrah for 'The Igloo?,'" nhl.com, May 28, 2008, https://www.nhl.com/penguins/news/last-hurrah-for-the-igloo/c-495976.

25 **Waffle maker:** "Bill Bowerman: Nike's Original Innovator," Nike News, September 2, 2015, https://news.nike.com/news/bill-bowerman-nike-s-original-innovator.

25 **Candace Parker:** "Sparks' Parker Wins MVP, Rookie of Year Honors," ESPN.com, October 3, 2018, https://www.espn.com/wnba/news/story?id=3623772.

25 **Highest Court in the Land:** "The Highest Court in the Land," *Atlas Obscura*, https://www.atlasobscura.com/places/highest-court-of-the-land.

25 **One single point in a professional women's tennis match:** Chris Chase, "101 Incredible Sports Facts That Will Blow Your Mind," For the Win, April 23, 2015, https://ftw.usatoday.com/2015/04/best-101-sports-facts-trivia-crazy-amazing-incredible-babe-ruth-michael-phelps-michael-jordan.

25 **Usain Bolt:** "Usain Bolt: The Fastest Man Who Has Ever Lived," BBC, https://www.bbc.co.uk/programmes/b00shlw7.

26 **Lexi Thompson:** Will Gray, "Major Champ Lexi Recalls First U.S. Open at 12," golfchannel.com, June 17, 2014, https://www.golfchannel.com/article/golf-central-blog/major-champ-lexi-recalls-first-us-open-12.

26 **White Sox:** David Adler, "The Longest Games in MLB History," MLB.com, June 16, 2020, https://www.mlb.com/news/longest-games-in-baseball-history-c275773542.

26 **Average NFL career:** Devin Gordon, "He Was 302 Pounds, but in This Battle, He's David and Not Goliath," *The New York Times*, November 16, 2018, https://www.nytimes.com/2018/11/16/business/nflpa-eric-winston-profile.html.

26 **A fan named Alice Roth:** David Seideman,"Lady Struck Twice by Foul Balls Hit by Phillies' Richie Ashburn in the Same At Bat," *Forbes*, September 21, 2017, https://www.forbes.com/sites/davidseideman/2017/09/21/richie-ashburn -once-struck-a-fan-twice-in-the-same-at-bat/#fae0f2a3b724.

26 **Air Jordans:** Matthew Ponsford, "Remember When the NBA Banned Michael Jordan's Sneakers?," CNN Style, November 1, 2019, https://www.cnn.com/style /article/remember-when-michael-jordan-sneakers/index.html.

27 **Simone Biles:** Laurel Wamsley, "Simone Biles Becomes the Most Decorated Gymnast in World Championship History," NPR, October 13, 2019, https://www.npr.org/2019/10/13/769896721/simone-biles-becomes-the-most -decorated-gymnast-in-world-championship-history.

27 **Steagles:** "Steelers/Eagles Combined Team During World War II: The Story of the Steagles," *Bleacher Report*, May 10, 2012, https://bleacherreport.com/ar ticles/1178949-steelerseagles-combined-team-during-world-war-ii-the -story-of-the-steagles.

27 **Ray Caldwell was struck:** Frank Hyde, "35 Years Ago Today Ray Caldwell Sur- vived Lightning to Beat A's," *The Post-Journal*, August 12, 1954, https://www .chautauquasportshalloffame.org/raycaldwell1954.php.

Animals

30 **Manatees the right of way:** Ashira Morris, "8 Things You Didn't Know About Manatees," *PBS NewsHour*, November 26, 2014, https://www.pbs.org/news hour/science/8-things-didnt-know-manatees.

30 **Baby elephants:** "Baby Elephants Are Just Like Humans," News24, May 28, 2014, https://www.news24.com/news24/green/news/Baby-elephants-are-just -like-humans-20140528.

30 **Cats have thirty-two muscles:** "Amazing Cat Facts," Cats International, https://catsinternational.org/amazing-cat-facts/.

31 **One big toe:** Giorgia Guglielmi, "Why Modern Horses Have Only One Toe," *Science*, August 22, 2017, https://www.sciencemag.org/news/2017/08/why -modern-horses-have-only-one-toe.

31 **The eyes of giant squids:** Nell Greenfieldboyce, "Just How Big Are the Eyes of a Giant Squid?," *All Things Considered*, NPR, March 15, 2012, https://www.npr .org/2012/03/15/148694025/just-how-big-are-the-eyes-of-a-giant-squid.

31 **California passed a law:** Christine Hauser, "California Forces Pet Stores to Sell Only Dogs and Cats from Shelters," *The New York Times*, January 2, 2019, https://www.nytimes.com/2019/01/02/us/california-pet-store-rescue-law.html.

31 **Can see colors we can't:** "How Do You Know if an Animal Can See Color?," Ask a Biologist, Arizona State University, https://askabiologist.asu.edu/colors -animals-see.

31 **Scallops have two hundred eyes:** Ed Yong, "Scallops Have Eyes, and Each One Builds a Beautiful Living Mirror," *The Atlantic*, November 30, 2017, https://www .theatlantic.com/science/archive/2017/11/scallops-have-eyes-and-each-one -builds-a-beautiful-living-mirror/547115/.

31 **Alaskan wood frogs:** "How (and Why) Wood Frogs Hold In Pee All Winter," Associated Press, CBC, May 2, 2018, https://www.cbc.ca/news/technology /wood-frogs-pee-1.4644522.

31 **Male white bellbird:** Daisy Hernandez, "This Bird Has a Serious Set of Pipes," *Popular Mechanics*, October 25, 2019, https://www.popularmechanics.com/sci ence/animals/a29565240/worlds-loudest-bird/.

31 **Swordfish are the fastest:** "What Makes Swordfish the Fastest Swimmers on Earth? It's All About the Lube!," Seriously, Science?, *Discover Magazine*, August 10, 2016, https://www.discovermagazine.com/planet-earth/what-makes-sword fish-the-fastest-swimmers-on-earth-its-all-about-the-lube.

31 **Porcupines regularly impale themselves:** Robin McKie, "Heal Thyself, Oh Fat and Prickly Porcupine," Scripps Howard News Service, *Chicago Tribune*, December 2, 1991, https://www.chicagotribune.com/news/ct-xpm-1991-12-02-9104180866 -story.html.

31 **Porcupines float:** Allison Keating, "Quirks and Quills!," *Wildlife Journal*, November/December 2018, https://www.wildlife.state.nh.us/pubs/documents /samples/quirks-quills.pdf.

31 **Catch yawns from humans:** Zoe Rossman et al., "Contagious Yawning in African Elephants (*Loxodonta africana*): Responses to Other Elephants and Familiar Humans," *Frontiers in Veterinary Science*, May 8, 2020, https://www.frontiersin .org/articles/10.3389/fvets.2020.00252/full.

32 **Rats are ticklish:** Emily Underwood, "Watch These Ticklish Rats Laugh and Jump for Joy," *Science*, November 10, 2016, https://www.sciencemag.org/news /2016/11/watch-these-ticklish-rats-laugh-and-jump-joy.

32 **Greta Thunberg:** "New Species of Beetle Named after Activist Greta Thunberg," press release, Natural History Museum, October 25, 2019, https://www.nhm .ac.uk/press-office/press-releases/new-species-of-beetle-named-after-activist -greta-thunberg-.html.

32 **Spider venom to create a pain reliever:** University of Queensland, "Spider Venom Key to Pain Relief Without Side-Effects," ScienceDaily, April 14, 2020, https://www.sciencedaily.com/releases/2020/04/200414105558.htm.

32 **Caesar the No Drama Llama:** Georgia Slater, "Caesar the 'No Drama Llama' Works to Keep the Peace and Comfort People at Portland Protests," *People*, August 7, 2020, https://people.com/pets/caesar-no-drama-llama-portland-protests/.

32 **Cow's weight can fluctuate:** Steve Lohr, "Robotic Milkers and an Automated Greenhouse: Inside a High-Tech Small Farm," *The New York Times*, January 13, 2019, https://www.nytimes.com/2019/01/13/technology/farm-technology-milkers-robots.html.

32 **Giraffe tongues:** "Giraffe Facts: Some of Your Most Frequently Asked Questions Answered," Giraffe Conservation Foundation, https://giraffeconservation.org/facts/how-long-is-a-giraffes-tongue-what-colour-is-it/.

32 **Butterflies drink the tears:** Charles Q. Choi, "Butterflies Caught Lapping Up Crocodile Tears," Live Science, May 1, 2014, https://www.livescience.com/45283-butterflies-drink-crocodile-tears.html.

32 **King bees:** Jordyn Cormier, "This Is *Exactly* Why We're So Obsessed with Queen Bees," Beekeeper's Naturals, March 20, 2019, https://beekeepersnaturals.com/blogs/blog/this-is-exactly-why-were-so-obsessed-with-queen-bees.

33 **Boxer crabs:** Ed Yong, "This Crab Clones Its Allies by Ripping Them in Half," *The Atlantic*, February 7, 2017, https://www.theatlantic.com/science/archive/2017/02/this-crab-clones-its-allies-by-ripping-them-in-half/515814/.

33 **Squirts blood from around its eyes:** "Short-Horned Lizard," *National Geographic*, https://www.nationalgeographic.com/animals/reptiles/s/short-horned-lizard/.

33 **Giraffes with darker spots:** Madelaine P. Castles et al., "Relationships Between Male Giraffes' Colour, Age and Sociability," ScienceDirect, November 2019, https://www.sciencedirect.com/science/article/pii/S0003347219302453?via%3Dihub.

33 **Have the ability to make honey:** glenfoerd, "Do Wasps Make Honey?," Philadelphia Honey Festival 2020, August 9, 2018, https://phillyhoneyfest.com/2018/08/09/do-wasps-make-honey/.

33 **Primary beneficiary:** "Dogs," World Animal Foundation, https://www.worldanimalfoundation.com/companions/dogs/.

33 **Can live more than two hundred years:** "Top 10 Longest Living Animals," OneKindPlanet, https://onekindplanet.org/top-10/top-10-worlds-longest-living-animals/.

33 **Goats love bonding:** Marc Silver, "What Does It Mean When a Goat Gazes into Your Eyes?," NPR, July 8, 2016, https://www.npr.org/sections/goatsandsoda/2016/07/08/485153844/what-does-it-mean-when-a-goat-gazes-into-your-eyes.

33 **Grizzly bears:** Michael Marshall, "Wild Bear Uses a Stone to Exfoliate," *New Scientist*, March 5, 2012, https://www.newscientist.com/article/dn21537-wild-bear-uses-a-stone-to-exfoliate/.

33 **Ribbon-tailed astrapia:** Ceri Perkins, "The Ten Sexiest Male Birds," BBC, May 1, 2015, http://www.bbc.com/earth/story/20150504-the-ten-sexiest-male-birds.

34 **Pregnant alpacas:** Stephen Greenhalgh and Graeme McPherson, "Camelid Husbandry and Common Veterinary Problems," *Larkmead Vets*, January 2010,

https://www.larkmead.co.uk/sites/larkmead.co.uk/files/Alpaca%20hus bandry%20handout%20amended.pdf.

34 **Bat poo:** Gwen Pearson, "Bats Have Sparkly Poop," *Wired*, May 30, 2014, https://www.wired.com/2014/05/scienceblogs0602bats/.

34 **Air Horse One:** Shelby Brown, "Kentucky Derby Horses Get First-Class Treatment on Air Horse One," CNET, May 2, 2019, https://www.cnet.com/news /kentucky-derby-horses-get-first-class-treatment-on-air-horse-one/.

34 **Albatross can stay airborne:** Adam Frost, "From One to a Billion: 10 Awesome but Totally Random Facts about Numbers," *The Guardian*, September 21, 2014, https://www.theguardian.com/childrens-books-site/2014/sep/21/top-10 -numbers-for-random-facts-adam-frost.

34 **Throwing rice:** Stephanie Pappas, "Does Wedding Rice Make Birds Explode?," Live Science, June 4, 2010, https://www.livescience.com/32624-does-wedding -rice-make-birds-explode.html.

34 **Blue whale can fit its weight:** Victoria Gill, "Blue Whale's Gigantic Mouthful measured," BBC Earth News, December 9, 2010, http://news.bbc.co.uk/earth /hi/earth_news/newsid_9265000/9265623.stm.

34 **Bird bones:** Ashley Hamer, "Why Do Birds Have Hollow Bones? It's Not to Make Them Lighter," Discovery.com, August 1, 2019, https://www.discovery.com /nature/Why-Do-Birds-Have-Hollow-Bones.

35 **Trained pigeons:** Justin Warner, "Pecking Birds Can Pick a Picasso," *New Scientist*, May 6, 1995, https://www.newscientist.com/article/mg14619761-000 -pecking-birds-can-pick-a-picasso/.

35 **Stink fights:** Mel Norris, "Oh Yeah? Smell This! Or, Conflict Resolution, Lemur-Style," Duke Lemur Center, March 16, 2012, https://lemur.duke.edu/oh-yeah -smell-this-or-conflict-resolution-lemur-style/.

35 **Butterflies can taste with their feet:** Liz Langley, "Some Insects Taste with Their Feet and Hear with Their Wings," *National Geographic*, September 14, 2018, https://www.nationalgeographic.com/animals/2018/09/insects-butter flies-anatomy-senses-animals/.

35 **Reduced noise pollution in cities:** Corryn Wetzel, "The Pandemic Shutdown in San Francisco Had Sparrows Singing Sexier Tunes," *Smithsonian Magazine*, September 25, 2020, https://www.smithsonianmag.com/science-nature/pan demic-shutdown-san-francisco-had-sparrows-singing-sexier-tunes-1809 75913/.

35 **Cats can't taste sweets:** "What Do Cats Drink? Common Milk Myths Dispelled," Purina, https://www.purina.co.uk/cats/health-and-nutrition/daily -feeding-guide/what-do-cats-drink; Richard Knox, "Cats Can't Taste Sweetness, Study Finds," *Morning Edition*, NPR, July 25, 2005, https://www.npr.org/tem plates/story/story.php?storyId=4766556.

35 **Bowerbird:** Perkins, "The Ten Sexiest Male Birds."

35 **Sloths poop:** Frost, "From One to a Billion."

35   **Elephants' footprints:** John R. Platt, "The Amazing Biodiversity Within an Elephant's Footprint," *Scientific American*, August 25, 2016, https://blogs.scientificamerican.com/extinction-countdown/elephant-footprint/; Erica Tennenhouse, "The Many Organisms that Inhabit an Elephant's Footprint," The Science Explorer, September 2, 2016, http://thescienceexplorer.com/nature/many-organisms-inhabit-elephant-s-footprint.

36   **Your pup would likely attempt:** Arizona State University, "Yes, Your Dog Wants to Rescue You," EurekAlert!, May 28, 2020, https://www.eurekalert.org/pub_releases/2020-05/asu-yyd052820.php.

36   **Wallaby that secretes purple dye:** Angela Heathcote, "The Wallaby with a Purple Neck," *Australian Geographic*, December 19, 2017, https://www.australiangeographic.com.au/topics/wildlife/2017/12/purple-necked-rock-wallaby/.

36   **Cow has eyes painted on its butt:** Lindsay Campbell, "Painting Eyes on Cows' Butts Can Scare Away Predators," *Modern Farmer*, August 23, 2020, https://modernfarmer.com/2020/08/painting-eyes-on-cows-butts-can-scare-away-predators/.

36   **Downtown rats:** Sarah Zhang, "New York City Has Genetically Distinct 'Uptown' and 'Downtown' Rats," *The Atlantic*, November 29, 2017, https://www.theatlantic.com/science/archive/2017/11/rats-of-new-york/546959/.

36   **Frogs close their eyes:** Seriously Science, "Frogs Use Their Eyes to Push Food Down While Swallowing," *Discover Magazine*, February 3, 2015, https://www.discovermagazine.com/planet-earth/frogs-use-their-eyes-to-push-food-down-while-swallowing.

36   **Jellyfish are being studied:** "The Immortal Jellyfish Might Find the Cure of Cancer," Scientific Scribbles, University of Melbourne, August 29, 2019, https://blogs.unimelb.edu.au/sciencecommunication/2019/08/29/the-immortal-jellyfish-might-find-the-cure-of-cancer/.

36   **Club-winged manakin birds:** Perkins, "The Ten Sexiest Male Birds."

36   **Goldfish are smart:** Anne Fawcett, "Fish Expert Says You Can Train Your Fish in Just Minutes Per Day," *Daily Telegraph*, November 26, 2016, https://www.dailytelegraph.com.au/newslocal/central-sydney/fish-expert-says-you-can-train-your-fish-in-just-minutes-per-day/news-story/85aa3916e94dcc363b09109d109a1e27.

36   **Osprey catches a fish:** "Osprey," Hawk Mountain, https://www.hawkmountain.org/raptors/osprey.

37   **Unpacking:** "Alpaca Facts," Lightfoot Alpacas, https://alpacabreeder.co.uk/alpaca-facts.

37   **Otters have a favorite rock:** "A Sea Otter's Toolkit," Oregon Coast Aquarium, https://aquarium.org/a-sea-otters-toolkit/.

37   **Blue manakin:** Perkins, "The Ten Sexiest Male Birds."

37   **Species of beetles:** "Beetlemania," *The Economist*, March 18, 2015, https://www.economist.com/science-and-technology/2015/03/18/beetlemania.

37 **Ostriches can run:** "Ostrich: *Struthio camelus*," Speed of Animals, https://www.speedofanimals.com/animals/ostrich?h=1.52; Dean Davis, "Average Sprinting Speed of a Human," Trackspikes, April 30, 2020, https://trackspikes.co.uk/average-sprinting-speed/.

37 **Octopuses:** "Can an Octopus Get to Know You?," Everyday Mysteries, Library of Congress, https://www.loc.gov/everyday-mysteries/item/can-an-octopus-get-to-know-you/.

37 **And honeybees:** Kate Wong, "Honeybees Can Recognize Individual Human Faces," *Scientific American*, December 1, 2013, https://www.scientificamerican.com/article/face-recognition-honeybees/.

37 **Leeches have thirty-two brains:** Rose George, "10 Stomachs, 32 Brains and 18 Testicles—a Day Inside the UK's Only Leech Farm," *The Guardian*, October 14, 2018, https://www.theguardian.com/lifeandstyle/2018/oct/14/10-stomachs-32-brains-and-18-testicles-a-day-inside-the-uks-only-leech-farm.

37 **Lightning bugs:** "Facts About Fireflies," Firefly Conservation and Research, https://www.firefly.org/facts-about-fireflies.html.

37 **Cats spend 30:** Jennifer Viegas, "7 Reasons Why Cats Are So Clean," *Reader's Digest Canada*, March 20, 2019, https://www.readersdigest.ca/home-garden/pets/7-reasons-why-cats-love-clean-themselves/.

37 **In Australia, the giant Gippsland:** Rob Blakemore, "Australian Earthworms," Australian Museum, February 25, 2019, https://australian.museum/learn/animals/worms/australian-earthworms/.

38 **Wallaroo:** "Wallaroo—*Macropus robustus*," Wildlife at Walkabout Park, http://www.walkaboutpark.com.au/mammals/wallaroo.

38 **Taste buds all over their bodies:** Reginald Chapman, "Taste Bud Anatomy," *Britannica*, https://www.britannica.com/science/taste-bud.

38 **Sloths are so slow:** Stacey Leasca, "A Sloth Can Hold Its Breath for 40 Minutes Underwater—and 6 Other Facts for International Sloth Day." *Travel + Leisure*, October 20, 2018, https://www.travelandleisure.com/animals/international-sloth-day.

38 **Almost 360 degrees:** Leasca, "A Sloth Can Hold Its Breath for 40 Minutes Underwater—and 6 Other Facts for International Sloth Day."

38 **Elephants can't jump:** Patrick Monahan, "Elephants Can't Jump—and Here's Why," *Science*, January 27, 2016, https://www.sciencemag.org/news/2016/01/elephants-can-t-jump-and-here-s-why.

38 **Intricate designs in their webs:** John Ezard, "From the Archive, 4 October 1971: Spiders on LSD Take a Tangled Trip," *The Guardian*, October 4, 2014, https://www.theguardian.com/science/2014/oct/04/spiders-lsd-drugs-experiment-1971.

38 **Dogs dream more often:** Liz Donovan, "Do Dogs Dream?," American Kennel Club, November 9, 2015, https://www.akc.org/expert-advice/lifestyle/do-dogs-dream/.

38 **Pigs are one of the cleanest:** Henry Nicholls, "The Truth About Pigs," BBC Earth, September 24, 2015, http://www.bbc.com/earth/story/20150924-the-truth-about-pigs.

38 **Eels reproduce:** "The Mysterious Life and Times of Eels," *The Economist*, December 21, 2019, https://www.economist.com/christmas-specials/2019/12/21/the-mysterious-life-and-times-of-eels.

39 **Weed-related dog names:** "The Most Popular Male and Female Dog Names," The Dog People, https://www.rover.com/blog/dog-names/#secondary-content.

39 **"Biologically immortal":** Ben Bryant, "Lobsters May Hold the Key to Eternal Life," *The Telegraph*, September 7, 2013, https://www.telegraph.co.uk/news/uknews/10294152/Lobsters-may-hold-the-key-to-eternal-life.html.

39 **A cat named Ketzel:** Associated Press, "Ketzel, NYC Cat That Wrote Piano Piece, Dies at 19," NBC New York, July 19, 2011, updated July 19, 2011, https://www.nbcnewyork.com/news/local/ketzel-nyc-cat-that-wrote-piano-piece-dies-at-19/2121030/.

39 **Bloodhounds can follow tracks:** "The Bloodhound's Amazing Sense of Smell," PBS, *Nature*, June 9, 2008, https://www.pbs.org/wnet/nature/underdogs-the-bloodhounds-amazing-sense-of-smell/350/.

39 **Humpback whales:** Jason Bittel, "Why Humpback Whales Protect Other Animals from Killer Whales," *National Geographic*, August 8, 2016, https://www.nationalgeographic.com/news/2016/08/humpback-whales-save-animals-killer-whales-explained/.

39 **Frogs can be frozen:** "Can Frogs Survive Being Frozen?," Live Science, September 6, 2012, https://www.livescience.com/32175-can-frogs-survive-being-frozen.html.

39 **Dolphins "sing":** Stephanie Pappas, "Mama Dolphins Sing Their Name to Babies in the Womb," Live Science, August 9, 2016, https://www.livescience.com/55699-mother-dolphins-teach-babies-signature-whistle.html.

39 **Three dogs survived:** "15 Amazing Dog Facts," Purina, https://www.purina.co.uk/dogs/behaviour-and-training/understanding-dog-behaviours/amazing-dog-facts.

39 **Ravens are known as:** Sindya N. Bhanoo, "Ravens Can Recognize Old Friends, and Foes, Too," *The New York Times*, April 23, 2012, https://www.nytimes.com/2012/04/24/science/ravens-can-recognize-old-friends-and-foes-too.html; Shaena Montanari, "We Knew Ravens Are Smart. But Not This Smart," *National Geographic*, July 13, 2017, https://www.nationalgeographic.com/news/2017/07/ravens-problem-solving-smart-birds/#close.

40 **Ants won't get hurt if they're microwaved:** Steve Myall, "Quite Interesting: 50 Amazing Facts to Celebrate 10 Years of QI," *Mirror*, January 19, 2013, updated January 19, 2013, https://www.mirror.co.uk/news/uk-news/qi-50-amazing-facts-from-10-1544434.

40 **Dogs sleep in their owners' beds:** "2019–2020 APPA National Pet Owners Survey," American Pet Products Association, https://www.americanpetproducts.org/pubs_survey.asp.

40 **Pigs are smarter:** Ellie Zolfagharifard, "Move Over Lassie: IQ Tests Reveal Pigs Can Outsmart Dogs and Chimpanzees," *Daily Mail*, June 12, 2015, updated June 13, 2015, https://www.dailymail.co.uk/sciencetech/article-3122303/Move-Lassie-IQ-tests-reveal-pigs-outsmart-dogs-chimpanzees.html.

40 **Elephants recognize themselves:** Ed Yong, "Elephants Recongise Themselves in Mirror," *National Geographic*, September 28, 2008, https://www.nationalgeographic.com/science/phenomena/2008/09/28/elephants-recognise-themselves-in-mirror/.

40 **Epaulette sharks:** Brian Hutchinson, "The Shark That Can Walk on Land," Oceanic Society, https://www.oceanicsociety.org/blog/1774/the-shark-that-can-walk-on-land.

40 **Flounder is a juvenile:** Liz Langley, "Flounders' Eyes Face Skyward. How Do They See the Ocean Floor?," *National Geographic*, August 13, 2016, https://www.nationalgeographic.com/news/2016/08/flatfish-animals-science-colors-flounders/.

40 **Green cat:** "Green Kitten Keeps the Vet Guessing," *New Scientist*, January 20, 1996, https://www.newscientist.com/article/mg14920131-800-green-kitten-keeps-the-vet-guessing/.

40 **Puppy born on the island:** "Rare Green Puppy 'Pistachio' Born in Italy," BBC News, October 22, 2020, https://www.bbc.com/news/world-europe-54650901.

40 **Dog is as intelligent:** Richard Gray, "Dogs as Intelligent as Two-Year-Old Children," *The Telegraph*, August 9, 2009, https://www.telegraph.co.uk/news/science/science-news/5994583/Dogs-as-intelligent-as-two-year-old-children.html.

40 **Wombat poop:** Tik Root, "Why Is Wombat Poop Cube-Shaped?," *National Geographic,* November 19, 2018, https://www.nationalgeographic.com/animals/2018/11/wombat-poop-cube-why-is-it-square-shaped/.

40 **Octopuses fought over the best "homes":** Nathaniel Scharping, "Octopuses Are Building Underwater 'Cities,'" *Discover Magazine*, September 19, 2017, https://www.discovermagazine.com/planet-earth/octopuses-are-building-underwater-cities.

40 **Dolphins jump out of the water:** "Why Do Dolphins Jump Out of the Water?," North American Nature, https://northamericannature.com/why-do-dolphins-jump-out-of-the-water/.

41 **Koala "bears" aren't bears:** "Interesting Facts," Australian Koala Foundation, https://www.savethekoala.com/about-koalas/interesting-facts.

41 **Puppies hit puberty:** Virginia Morell, "Dogs Get Difficult When They Reach Adolescence, Just Like Human Teenagers," *Science Magazine*, May 12, 2020, https://www.sciencemag.org/news/2020/05/dogs-get-difficult-when-they-reach-adolescence-just-human-teenagers.

41 **Ants have two stomachs:** Matt Reynolds, "Carpenter Ants 'Throw Up' on Each Other to Say Hello," *Wired*, November 29, 2016, https://www.wired.co.uk/ar ticle/ants-throwing-up-hormones-development.

41 **ManhattAnt:** Rachel Nuwer, "NYC Has Its Own Ant, the 'ManhattAnt,'" *Smithsonian Magazine*, September 5, 2012, https://www.smithsonianmag.com/smart -news/nyc-has-its-own-ant-the-manhattant-25741340/.

41 **Fish cough:** "Do Fish Cry?," Live Science, October 30, 2012, https://www.live science.com/32168-do-fish-cry.html.

41 **Red pandas use their tails as blankets:** "Red Panda," *National Geographic*, https://www.nationalgeographic.com/animals/mammals/r/red-panda/.

41 **Dog Ranger:** Zack Budryk, "George HW Bush Presidential Memo Asking Staff Not to Feed Overweight Dog Resurfaces for #InternationalDogDay," *The Hill*, August 26, 2019, https://thehill.com/blogs/blog-briefing-room/news/458851 -george-hw-bush-presidential-memo-asking-staff-not-to-feed.

41 **Dolphins can put one side of their brain to sleep:** "Dolphins Stay Awake for 15 Days by Sleeping with One Half of Brain," *The Telegraph*, October 18, 2012, https://www.telegraph.co.uk/news/earth/wildlife/9616671/Dolphins-stay-awake -for-15-days-by-sleeping-with-one-half-of-brain.html.

41 **Bird poop:** Carolyn Wilke, "Fish Eggs Can Hatch Even after Being Eaten and Excreted by Ducks," *The Washington Post*, July 4, 2020, https://www.washing tonpost.com/health/fish-eggs-can-hatch-even-after-being-eaten-and -pooped-out-by-ducks/2020/07/02/700761e4-baf0-11ea-bdaf-a129f921026f _story.html.

41 **Sea lion once saved:** "Kevin Hines Jumped Off the Golden Gate Bridge—and Lived," *Today*, June 12, 2018, https://www.youtube.com/watch?v=V3wvj DwpuDA.

42 **Koko:** Sarah Larson, "Remembering Koko, a Gorilla We Loved," *The New Yorker*, June 21, 2018, https://www.newyorker.com/culture/postscript/remembering -koko-a-gorilla-we-loved.

42 **Alpine bumblebee:** Laura Poppick, "Bumblebees Can Fly Higher Than Mount Everest," Live Science, February 5, 2014, https://www.livescience.com/43114 -bumble-bees-fly-higher-mount-everest.html.

42 **"Propose" by presenting:** Alex Potter, "Penguin Post Office: The Gift to Win a Penguin's Heart," BBC Earth, https://www.bbcearth.com/blog/?article=the-gift -to-win-a-penguins-heart.

42 **Armadillo shells:** Liz Langley, "These Animals Inspire Better Body Armor for Humans," *National Geographic*, February 21, 2019, https://www.nationalgeo graphic.com/animals/2019/02/animals-armor-bioinspiration/#close.

42 **Herrings communicate:** Mary Beckman, "Farting Fish Keep in Touch," *Science Magazine*, November 7, 2003, https://www.sciencemag.org/news/2003/11 /farting-fish-keep-touch.

42 **Lion's roar:** Sarah Crupi, "Ask the Expert: What Makes a Lion Roar?," Cleveland Zoological Society, November 30, 2017, https://www.clevelandzoosociety.org/z/2017/11/30/ask-the-expert-what-makes-a-lion-roar.

42 **Male cuttlefish:** "Persuading Others When Facts Don't Seem to Matter (w/ Lee Hartley Carter), Cross-Dressing Cuttlefish," *Curiosity Daily Podcast*, October 29, 2019, https://curiositydaily.com/persuading-others-when-facts-dont-seem-to-matter-w-lee-hartley-carter-cross-dressing-cuttlefish/.

42 **Rescue Ink:** Cedric Jackson, "American Biker Gang Hunts Dog Fight Rings and Saves Animals from Abusive Owners," Animal Channel, May 1, 2019, https://animalchannel.co/biker-gang-stops-dog-fighting-ring/.

42 **Cats spend up to 70:** Mary Kearl, "How Much Do Cats Sleep?," Pet Care Rx, January 10, 2021, https://www.petcarerx.com/article/how-much-do-cats-sleep/790.

43 **Sloth can hold its breath:** Stacey Leasca, "A Sloth Can Hold Its Breath for 40 Minutes Underwater—and 6 Other Facts for International Sloth Day," *Travel + Leisure*, October 20, 2018, https://www.travelandleisure.com/animals/international-sloth-day.

43 **Houseflies:** April Daley, "Do All Houseflies Hum in Key?," *Mental Floss*, October 14, 2015, https://www.mentalfloss.com/article/69639/do-all-houseflies-hum-key.

43 **It drank a full thirty-six cans:** Associated Press, "Bear Downs 36 Beers, Passes Out at Campground," NBC News, August 19, 2004, http://www.nbcnews.com/id/5756809/ns/us_news-weird_news/t/bear-downs-beers-passes-out-campground/#.XsLRw63MwdU.

43 **Goats have rectangular pupils:** Rachel Feltman, "Here's Why Goats Have Those Freaky Eyes," *The Washington Post*, August 10, 2015, https://www.washingtonpost.com/news/speaking-of-science/wp/2015/08/10/heres-why-goats-have-those-freaky-eyes/.

Celebs

46 **Selena Gomez:** Corinne Sullivan, "These 10 Fascinating Facts About Selena Gomez Prove She's So Rare," PopSugar, May 10, 2020, https://www.popsugar.com/celebrity/photo-gallery/47422164/embed/47422329/p.

46 **P-Willy:** Laura Roberts, "Royal Wedding: Former St. Andrews Student Discloses Details of Couple's Early Romance," *The Telegraph*, November 18, 2010, https://www.telegraph.co.uk/news/uknews/royal-wedding/8143014/Royal-wedding-former-St-Andrews-student-discloses-details-of-couples-early-romance.html.

46 **Dwayne "The Rock" Johnson:** Kyle Newport, "Dwayne 'The Rock' Johnson Eats 10 Lbs. of Food per Day, 821 Lbs. of Cod per Year," *Bleacher Report*, April 8, 2015, https://bleacherreport.com/articles/2424425-dwayne-the-rock-johnson-eats-10-lbs-of-food-per-day-821-lbs-of-cod-per-year.

46 **Michael B. Jordan:** Madison Malone Kircher, "Michael B. Jordan Offers to Replace the Retainer of a Teenager Who Broke Hers Clenching Her Jaw After Seeing His Pecs in *Black Panther*," *New York*, March 6, 2018, https://nymag.com/intel ligencer/2018/03/girl-breaks-retainer-from-michael-b-jordan-in-black-panther .html.

46 **Rebel Wilson:** Katy Brand, "Meet Rebel Wilson, the Actress Who Hallucinated She Won an Oscar," *The Telegraph*, December 21, 2012, https://www.telegraph .co.uk/women/womens-life/9761123/Meet-Rebel-Wilson-the-actress-who -hallucinated-she-won-an-Oscar.html.

46 **Samuel L. Jackson:** Desta, "8 Movie Stars with Unbelievable Contract Clauses."

46 **Jennifer Aniston:** Christine Rendon, "Jennifer Aniston Turned Down Being a *Saturday Night Live* Cast Member Because It Was a 'Boys Club': 'Women Need to Be Treated Better Here,'" *Daily Mail*, October 8, 2019, https://www.dailymail .co.uk/tvshowbiz/article-7551487/Jennifer-Aniston-reveals-turned-Saturday -Night-Live-cast-spot-boys-club.html.

47 **Beyoncé had only one:** Jaclyn Anglis, "Who Did Beyoncé Date Before Jay Z?," *Bustle*, October 27, 2015, https://www.bustle.com/articles/119689-who-did-bey once-date-before-jay-z-her-high-school-boyfriend-has-opened-up-about-dating.

47 **Julie Andrews:** Mary McNamara, "Julie Andrews Relives Her Glorious, Complicated, Very Real Hollywood Life in Her New Memoir," *The San Diego Union-Tribune*, October 15, 2019, https://www.sandiegouniontribune.com/enter tainment/books/story/2019-10-15/julie-andrews-relives-her-glorious -complicated-very-real-hollywood-life-in-her-new-memoir-home-work.

47 **Ryan Gosling:** "Swooooon: Ryan Gosling Knows How to Knit!," *Glamour*, January 16, 2013, https://www.glamour.com/story/swooooon-ryan-gosling-knows-ho.

47 **Florence Pugh:** Sophie Kemp, "Things You Didn't Know About Florence Pugh," *Vogue*, January 9, 2020, https://www.vogue.com/article/5-things-you-didnt -know-about-florence-pugh.

47 **Tyra Banks:** Grace Gavilanes, "All of Hollywood's Strangest Fears and Phobias, from Bellybuttons to . . . Dust in a Cup (?)," *People*, September 12, 2019, https:// people.com/celebrity/surprising-celeb-fears-phobias/?slide=5817013#5817013.

47 **Jennifer Lawrence:** Scarlett Conlon, "Jennifer Lawrence's Tattoo Fail," *Vogue*, July 15, 2015, https://www.vogue.co.uk/article/jennifer-lawrence-h20-tattoo -disaster.

47 **Bill Murray:** "Bill Murray Talks About His 1-800 Phone Number and What It Takes for Him to Respond," *Today*, April 12, 2018, https://www.today.com /video/bill-murray-talks-about-his-1-800-phone-number-and-what-it-takes -for-him-to-respond-1209389635553.

47 **Meghan Markle:** Sam Reed, "Here's a Video of 11-Year-Old Feminist Meghan Markle Taking On Procter & Gamble," *The Hollywood Reporter*, December 1, 2017, https://www.hollywoodreporter.com/news/heres-a-video-11-year-old -feminist-meghan-markle-taking-procter-gamble-1063357.

47 **Harry Styles:** Rosemary Donahue, "Harry Styles Has Four Nipples, and That's More Common Than You Think," *Allure*, July 19, 2017, https://www.allure.com /story/harry-styles-confirms-he-has-four-nipples.

47 **Matching tattoos:** "The Story Behind Ed Sheeran and Harry Styles' Matching Tattoos," *Inked*, May 15, 2015, updated October 10, 2018, https://www.inked mag.com/culture/harry-styles-ed-sheeran.

47 **Emma Roberts:** Devan Coggan and Cristina Everett, "Stars You Didn't Know Were Related," *Entertainment Weekly*, July 27, 2017, https://ew.com/gallery /stars-you-didnt-know-were-related/?slide=206986#206986.

47 **Julia Roberts's smile:** Julie Miller, "Mariah Carey Reportedly Insured Her Voice for an Outrageous Sum of Money," *Vanity Fair*, April 8, 2016, https://www.vani tyfair.com/hollywood/2016/04/mariah-carey-voice-insurance.

47 **Legs have been insured:** Sophie Shaw, "The Most Expensive Legs in History," *CR Fashion Book*, December 18, 2019, https://www.crfashionbook.com/celeb rity/g30247446/celebrity-legs-insured-betty-grable-rihanna/.

48 **Snoop Dogg and Brandy:** Devan Coggan and Cristina Everett, "Stars You Didn't Know Were Related," *Entertainment Weekly*, July 27, 2017, https://ew.com/gal lery/stars-you-didnt-know-were-related/?slide=206983#206983.

48 **Al Roker and Lenny:** Coggan et al., "Stars You Didn't Know Were Related."

48 **Lenny Kravitz and his actress:** "Lenny Kravitz & Daughter Zoe Get Tattoos Together—What Do They Say?," *TooFab*, September 26, 2014, https://toofab .com/2014/09/26/lenny-kravitz-zoe-kravitz-matching-tattoos/.

48 ***Fight Club* so much:** Allison Takeda, "Adam Driver Talks Starting His Own Fight Club, Making People Cry at Juilliard," *US Weekly*, June 3, 2014, https://www .usmagazine.com/celebrity-news/news/adam-driver-tells-m-magazine-about -starting-a-fight-club-juilliard-201436/.

48 **Santa:** Jacqueline Howard, "How Many Kids Still Believe in Santa?," CNN, December 19, 2017, https://www.cnn.com/2017/12/19/health/kids-santa-claus -belief-parent-curve-intl/index.html.

48 **Emily Blunt:** "Emily Blunt Talks About Stuttering," The Stuttering Foundation, https://www.stutteringhelp.org/emily-blunt-talks-about-stuttering.

48 **Danny DeVito:** Barbara Ellen, "Danny DeVito: 'It All Worked Out for Me. Life Is Good,'" *The Guardian*, April 14, 2012, https://www.theguardian.com/film /2012/apr/15/danny-devito-interview-sunshine-boys.

48 **Betty White:** Associated Press, CNN, "Celebrating 98 Years of Betty White, in Photos," Tucson.com, January 17, 2020, https://tucson.com/entertainment /celebrating-98-years-of-betty-white-in-photos/article_1ea3217a-7a2b-566b -b851-a184fd05a810.html.

48 **Eminem's Alcoholics Anonymous:** Janet Maslin, "Elton John Puts Down in Words How Wonderful (and Weird) Life Has Been," *The New York Times*, October 10, 2019, https://www.nytimes.com/2019/10/10/books/review-me-elton -john-memoir.html.

48   **Leonardo DiCaprio:** Yohana Desta, "The Role Leonardo DiCaprio Was Literally Born to Play," *Vanity Fair*, August 14, 2017, https://www.vanityfair.com/hollywood/2017/08/leonardo-dicaprio-da-vinci.

49   **Billy Crystal:** Hannah Warner, *Fascinating Celebrity Facts* (New York: Virgin Books, 2003).

49   **Lizzo dropped out of college:** Corinne Sullivan, "Just Cuz We Love Her, Here Are 10 Fascinating Facts About Lizzo," PopSugar, May 10, 2020, https://www.popsugar.com/celebrity/photo-gallery/47422795/image/47423251/She-Once-Took-3-Month-Vow-Silence.

49   **Michael J. Fox:** "Michael J. Fox Biography (1961–)," Biography, January 15, 2016, updated December 1, 2020, https://www.biography.com/actor/michael-j-fox.

49   **Asteroids:** Clara Moskowitz, "You've Got Asteroids: Tom Hanks & Meg Ryan Reborn as Space Rocks," Space.com, October 5, 2011, https://www.space.com/13184-asteroids-names-tom-hanks-meg-ryan.html.

49   **Madonna:** "Madonna Talks Her Rise to the Top, Dating Tupac, and Her Infamous VMAs Performance, During Her First Interview with Howard," Howard Stern, March 11, 2015, https://www.howardstern.com/news/2015/3/11/the-madonna-interview-ten-things-you-need-to-know/.

49   **Katy Perry's song:** Jesse Curti, "Scarlett Johansson Is Flattered She Inspired 'I Kissed a Girl,'" *People*, November 17, 2008, https://people.com/celebrity/scarlett-johansson-is-flattered-she-inspired-i-kissed-a-girl/.

49   **Will Smith:** "Will Smith Biography (1968–)," Biography, April 27, 2017, updated January 8, 2021, https://www.biography.com/actor/will-smith.

50   **Andrew Garfield:** Adrienne Tyler, "How Old Each Spider-Man Actor Was as Teenage Peter Parker," *Screen Rant*, July 10, 2010, https://screenrant.com/spiderman-peter-parker-teenager-holland-maguire-garfield-ages/.

50   **Audrey Hepburn:** *Breakfast at Tiffany's* (1961) Trivia," https://www.imdb.com/title/tt0054698/trivia.

50   **Moaning Myrtle:** "Shirley Henderson," https://www.imdb.com/name/nm0376602/?ref_=nmbio_bio_nm.

50   **John Cho:** "John Cho," https://www.imdb.com/name/nm0158626/.

50   ***Grease:*** Brian Boone, "How Old the Cast of *Grease* Actually Was During Filming," Looper, October 14, 2020, https://www.looper.com/261711/how-old-the-cast-of-grease-actually-was-during-filming/.

50   ***The Vampire Diaries:*** Anjelica Oswald, "How Old the Stars of 'The Vampire Diaries' Really Were When They Played Teen Characters," *Insider*, August 9, 2019, https://www.insider.com/vampire-diaries-stars-real-ages-teen-characters-2019-7.

51   ***Clueless:*** Jean Bentley, "Half of the *Clueless* Cast Were Actual Teens When the Movie Was Made," *Refinery29*, June 26, 2020, https://www.refinery29.com/en-us/2020/06/9877567/clueless-character-actor-ages-when-it-was-made.

51 ***Save the Last Dance:*** "Sean Patrick Thomas," https://www.imdb.com/name/nm0859503/.

51 ***Dirty Dancing:*** Nakeisha Campbell, "See How Old the Cast of 'Dirty Dancing' Was While Filming the Movie," Closer Weekly, April 6, 2017, https://www.closerweekly.com/posts/cast-of-dirty-dancing-ages-129297/.

51 ***Hannah Montana:*** "Jackson from *Hannah Montana* Is Turning 40 This Year!," News24, February 1, 2017, https://www.news24.com/channel/Gossip/News/jackson-from-hannah-montana-is-turning-40-this-year-20170131.

Food & Drink

54 **German chocolate cake:** "Celebrating Not-So-German Chocolate Cake," *All Things Considered,* NPR, June 23, 2007, https://www.npr.org/templates/story/story.php?storyId=11331541.

54 **Ice cream is solid, liquid, and gas:** "20 Favourite Facts from the QI Team," *The Guardian*, December 2, 2016, https://www.theguardian.com/books/2016/dec/02/20-favourite-facts-from-the-qi-team.

54 **Ripe bananas glow:** "Ripening Bananas Glow an Intense Blue Under Black Light," ScienceDaily, October 21, 2008, https://www.sciencedaily.com/releases/2008/10/081020093454.htm.

54 **"Cat pee aroma":** "Exploring the Philosophy of Food and Wine," https://foodandwineaesthetics.com/tag/sauvignon-blanc/.

55 **Mariya Russell:** Rachel Hinton, "Following Michelin Star Honor, 'Everything Has Changed Now' for Chef Mariya Russell," *Chicago Sun-Times*, December 10, 2019, https://chicago.suntimes.com/2019/12/10/20997893/first-african-american-woman-michelin-star-mariya-russell-chicago-kumiko-kikko.

55 **Cook broccoli:** Signe Dean, "Scientists Have Found a New, Healthier Way to Cook Broccoli," Science Alert, February 8, 2018, https://www.sciencealert.com/best-way-to-cook-broccoli-sulforaphane-stir-fry-healthy.

55 **Beer cans:** Shannon McMahon, "No One Can Crush Narragansett Like Quint. Literally . . . No One," Boston.com, February 13, 2017, https://www.boston.com/culture/movies/2015/06/17/no-one-can-crush-narragansett-like-quint-literally-no-one.

55 **Chef's hat:** Caroline Picard, "35 Coolest Random Pieces of Trivia That Will Impress Your Friends," *Good Housekeeping*, December 27, 2019, https://www.goodhousekeeping.com/life/g25692093/random-trivia/?slide=2.

55 **American cheese:** Lloyd L. Sponholtz, "Kraft, James Lewis (11 November 1874–16 February 1953)," American National Biography, February 2000, https://www.anb.org/view/10.1093/anb/9780198606697.001.0001/anb-9780198606697-e-1000942.

55 **Consuming hot sauce:** Edith Zimmerman, "Can Hot Peppers Make Me Happy?," The Cut, *New York*, December 19, 2018, https://www.thecut.com/2018/12/can-hot-chili-peppers-make-me-happy.html.

55 **Five percent of American adults are vegetarian:** Linda Searing, "The Big Number: 5 Percent of American Adults Consider Themselves Vegetarians," *The Washington Post*, May 6, 2019, https://www.washingtonpost.com/national /health-science/the-big-number5-percent-of-american-adults-consider-them selves-vegetarians/2019/05/03/5b7b0668-6cef-11e9-be3a-33217240a539_story .html.

55 **Doritos is the most popular brand:** Frank Olito and Yutong Yuan, "The Most Popular Brand of Chips in Every State," *Insider*, March 20, 2019, https://www .insider.com/most-popular-brand-of-chips-in-every-state-2019-3; Maggie Sheehan and Candace Braun Davison, "14 Things You Should Know Before Eating Doritos," Delish, February 2, 2017, https://www.delish.com/food/a42773 /things-you-didnt-know-about-doritos/.

55 **Sweet potato:** Carl Zimmer, "All by Itself, the Humble Sweet Potato Colonized the World," *The New York Times*, April 12, 2018, https://www.nytimes.com /2018/04/12/science/sweet-potato-pacific-dna.html.

55 **Flying saucers:** a a., "Streekproduct Series," Flanders Today, November 14, 2012, http://www.flanderstoday.eu/living/streekproduct-series-16.

56 **Professional chefs are women:** Kristen Hartke, "Women Chefs Still Walk 'a Fine Line' in the Kitchen," NPR, August 31, 2018, https://www.npr.org/sec tions/thesalt/2018/08/31/639398136/women-chefs-still-walk-a-fine -line-in-the-kitchen; Victoria Maranan, "US Census: Women Make Up Less Than a Quarter of Chefs," Spectrum News 1, February 3, 2020, https://spectrumlocal news.com/tx/san-antonio/news/2020/02/03/u-s--census--women-make -up-less-than-a-quarter-of-chefs.

56 **In 2010, Americans drank an average of:** Jan Conway, "Per Capita Consumption of Carbonated Soft Drinks (CSD) in the United States from 2010 to 2019," Statista, November 26, 2020, https://www.statista.com/statistics/306841 /us-per-capita-consumption-of-csd-by-state/.

56 **Mayonnaise isn't a common carrier:** "Debunking the Mayo Myth," Health and Wellness Alerts, UC Berkeley School of Public Health, August 8, 2019, https:// www.healthandwellnessalerts.berkeley.edu/topics/healthy-living/debunk ing-the-mayo-myth/.

56 **Watermelons are both fruits:** Jessie Szalay, "Watermelon: Health Benefits, Risks & Nutrition Facts," Live Science, May 11, 2017, https://www.livescience .com/46019-watermelon-nutrition.html.

56 **Malört:** *The Malört Times*, https://www.jeppsonsmalort.com/history/.

56 **Almond milk:** Jim Clarke, "In the Middle Ages, the Upper Class Went Nuts for Almond Milk," *Atlas Obscura*, December 8, 2017, https://www.atlasobscura .com/articles/almond-milk-obsession-origins-middle-ages.

56 **Brussels sprouts:** Andrea Beck, "It's Not Your Imagination, Brussels Sprouts Really Do Taste Better Now," *Better Homes & Gardens*, November 7, 2019, https://www.bhg.com/news/brussels-sprouts-less-bitter.

56 **It takes approximately seven hundred grapes:** Picard, "35 Coolest Random Pieces of Trivia That Will Impress Your Friends."

56 **Kagan had a fro-yo machine:** Jess Bravin, "Supreme Court's Junior Justice Has to Run the Cafeteria. Don't Eat There," *The Wall Street Journal*, July 20, 2017, https://www.wsj.com/articles/supreme-courts-junior-justice-has-to-run-the-cafeteria-dont-eat-there-1500567608.

57 **In America, the most popular ice cream:** Mary Ellen Shoup, "Vanilla Ranks as the Top-Selling Ice Cream Flavor in US Followed by Chocolate," Dairyreporter.com, July 7, 2017, updated October 20, 2017, https://www.dairyreporter.com/Article/2017/07/07/Vanilla-ranks-as-the-top-selling-ice-cream-flavor-in-US.

57 **Hybrid fruits:** Daniel Stone, "The Citrus Family Tree," *National Geographic*, https://www.nationalgeographic.com/magazine/2017/02/explore-food-citrus-genetics/.

57 **"Chicken feed":** Allie Koestler, "How Chicken Feed Became Candy Corn: An Underrated History," Spoon University, https://spoonuniversity.com/lifestyle/the-underrated-history-of-candy-corn.

57 **Grain alcohol:** Marko Ticak, "Whisky vs. Whiskey: What's the Difference?," Grammarly.com, https://www.grammarly.com/blog/whisky-vs-whiskey/.

57 **Girl Scout in San Diego:** Mark Saunders, "Girl Scout Sells More Than 300 Boxes of Cookies at San Diego Marijuana Dispensary," News 10 San Diego, February 2, 2018, updated February 3, 2018, https://www.10news.com/news/girl-scout-sells-more-than-300-boxes-of-cookies-at-san-diego-marijuana-dispensary.

57 **Women are twice as likely:** "Five Interesting Facts About Soup," Associated Press, January 30, 2019, https://apnews.com/09eb5363b0294aa2938fe6b0b25fe8cf.

57 **Apple pie isn't American:** Kat Eschner, "Apple Pie Is Not All That American," *Smithsonian Magazine*, May 12, 2017, https://www.smithsonianmag.com/smart-news/why-apple-pie-linked-america-180963515//.

57 **Lasagna Lady:** Cathy Free, "She Was Furloughed from Her Job. So She Became 'Lasagna Lady' and Made 1,200 Pans of Free Lasagna for Those in Need," *The Washington Post*, June 24, 2020, https://www.washingtonpost.com/lifestyle/2020/06/24/she-was-furloughed-her-job-so-she-became-lasagna-lady-gave-away-1200-pans-free-lasagna/.

57 **M&Ms:** Jamie Ballard, "M&Ms, Reese's Are the Most Popular Candies in the US," YouGov, October 30, 2018, https://today.yougov.com/topics/food/articles-reports/2018/10/30/most-popular-candies-halloween.

57 **The word *mocha*:** Kat Eschner, "Your Mocha Is Named After the Birthplace of the Coffee Trade," *Smithsonian Magazine*, September 29, 2017, https://www.smithsonianmag.com/smart-news/your-mocha-named-after-birthplace-coffee-trade-180965016/.

58 **Outback Steakhouse:** Dan Myers, "10 Things You Didn't Know About Outback Steakhouse," The Daily Meal, September 16, 2015, https://www.thedailymeal.com/eat/10-things-you-didn-t-know-about-outback-steakhouse.

58 **Soft drinks really *do* taste different:** "Why Soft Drinks Taste Different Out of Cans, Why Housecats Are Dangerous for Wildlife, and 100 Minor Planets Discovered Beyond Neptune," *Curiosity Daily Podcast*, April 29, 2020, https://curiosi tydaily.com/why-soft-drinks-taste-different-out-of-cans-why-housecats-are -dangerous-for-wildlife-and-100-minor-planets-discovered-beyond-neptune/.

58 **The raisin will bounce back and forth:** "Raisin in a Glass of Champagne," Yulia Taylor, YouTube, January 2, 2013, https://www.youtube.com/watch?v=DR4dCH WI5ZY.

59 **Licking ice cream than you do eating it with a spoon:** "Ice-Cream Better Licked Than Spooned Says Food Expert," Massey University, Phys.org, October 24, 2008, https://phys.org/news/2008-10-ice-cream-spooned-food-expert.html.

59 **New Zealand:** "Which Country Eats the Most Ice Cream?," WorldAtlas, https:// www.worldatlas.com/articles/the-top-ice-cream-consuming-countries-of-the -world.html; "New Zealand Consumes More Ice Cream per Capita Than Any Other Country, the US Is 2nd," *South Florida Reporter*, July 14, 2018, https://southflori dareporter.com/new-zealand-consumes-more-ice-cream-per-capita-than-any -other-country-the-us-is-2nd/.

59 **Beefeaters:** "Yeoman Warders at the Tower of London," Historic Royal Palaces, https://www.hrp.org.uk/tower-of-london/history-and-stories/yeoman-warders -at-the-tower-of-london/#gs.j7u15c.

59 **One hundred acres of pizza:** Lenny Bernstein, "We Eat 100 Acres of Pizza a Day in the U.S.," *The Washington Post*, January 20, 2015, https://www.washing tonpost.com/news/to-your-health/wp/2015/01/20/we-eat-100-acres-of -pizza-a-day-in-the-u-s/.

59 **Caviar was a *free bar snack*:** Peggy Trowbridge Filippone, "Caviar History," The Spruce Eats, updated January 20, 2020, https://www.thespruceeats.com /history-of-caviar-as-food-1807579.

59 **Primitive can openers:** Kat Eschner, "Why the Can Opener Wasn't Invented Until Almost 50 Years After the Can," *Smithsonian Magazine*, August 24, 2017, https://www.smithsonianmag.com/smart-news/why-can-opener-wasnt -invented-until-almost-50-years-after-can-180964590/.

59 **Granny Smith:** "Granny Smith," Big Oven, https://www.bigoven.com/article /recipe/granny-smith.

60 **Burger King was the first fast food chain to sell veggie burgers:** "A Brief and Meaty History of Vegetarian Fast Food," Portable Press, July 5, 2018, https:// www.portablepress.com/blog/2018/07/history-of-vegetarian-fast-food/.

60 **Red Lobster:** Paul Tharp, "Shellshock: 'Endless Crab' Is the End for Boss at Red Lobster," *New York Post*, September 26, 2003, https://nypost.com/2003/09/26 /shellshock-endless-crab-is-the-end-for-boss-at-red-lobster/.

60 **People will rate a wine:** Victoria Ward, "People Rate Wine Better if They Are Told It Is Expensive," *The Telegraph*, April 30, 2015, https://www.telegraph

.co.uk/news/shopping-and-consumer-news/11574362/People-rate-wine
-better-if-they-are-told-it-is-expensive.html.

60 **Bud Light:** Colman Andrews, "Most Popular Beer Brands in America Dominated
by Anheuser-Busch, Molson Coors," *USA Today*, March 18, 2020, https://www
.usatoday.com/story/money/2020/03/18/the-most-popular-beer-brands
-in-america/111416118/.

60 **First anniversary:** Erin Celletti, "Everything You Need to Know About Preserv-
ing the Top of Your Wedding Cake," *Brides*, updated May 17, 2020, https://www
.brides.com/story/why-we-preserve-the-top-layer-of-wedding-cakes.

60 **Guinness beer:** "Welsh Genius Behind Ireland's Favourite," BBC News, January
25, 2000, http://news.bbc.co.uk/2/hi/uk_news/wales/618355.stm.

60 **Putting sprinkles at the *bottom* of a cone:** "This Easy Trick Prevents Ice-
Cream Cones from Dripping," PureWow, reprinted by *Food & Wine*, updated July
14, 2016, https://www.foodandwine.com/news/how-keep-ice-cream-cone
-dripping.

60 **Hawaiian pizza:** "Greek-Canadian Sam Panopoulos, Inventor of Hawaiian Pizza
Dies," *The National Herald*, June 11, 2017, https://www.thenationalherald.com
/archive_whats_new/arthro/greek_canadian_sam_panopoulos_inventor_of
_hawaiian_pizza_dies-6122/.

60 **Food poisoning:** Patrick Allan, "Stop Blaming Food Poisoning on the Last Thing
You Ate," Lifehacker, November 20, 2019, https://lifehacker.com/stop-blaming
-food-poisoning-on-the-last-thing-you-ate-1796688099; "Peak Summer: More
Than One in Six People Likely to Get Food Poisoning," American Osteopathic
Association, July 2, 2019, https://osteopathic.org/2019/07/02/peak-summer
-more-than-one-in-six-people-likely-to-get-food-poisoning/.

60 **Wine bottle is called a "punt":** "Why Is There an Indentation in the Bottom of
a Wine Bottle?," Ask Dr. Vinny, *Wine Spectator*, February 10, 2012, https://www
.winespectator.com/articles/why-is-there-an-indentation-in-the-bottom
-of-a-wine-bottle-46387.

61 **Ben and Jerry:** Merrill Fabry, "Ben & Jerry's Is Turning 40. Here's How They
Captured a Trend That Changed American Ice Cream," *Time*, May 4, 2018,
https://time.com/5252406/ben-jerry-ice-cream-40/.

61 **Company does so well:** Priya Krishna, "There Is a Free Lunch, After All. It's at
the Office," *The New York Times*, January 7, 2019, https://www.nytimes.com
/2019/01/07/dining/free-food-employees.html.

61 **Teeny tiny air bubbles:** Anthony King, "Explaining Ice Cream," Chemistry
World, https://www.chemistryworld.com/news/whats-going-on-in-your-ice
-cream/3007790.article.

61 **Poppin' Fresh:** Alex Lasker, "The Pillsbury Doughboy Has an Actual Name and
You've Probably Never Heard It Before," AOL, July 10, 2017, https://www.aol
.com/article/lifestyle/2017/07/10/pillsbury-doughboy-real-name/23023865/.

61 **Chocolate bar has eight insect parts:** Lauren Torrisi, "Bugging Out: Chocolate Allergy Linked to Roaches," ABC News, March 26, 2012, https://abcnews.go .com/blogs/lifestyle/2012/03/bugging-out-chocolate-allergy-linked-to -roaches.

61 **Prince Albert's wedding cake:** Anne Ewbank, "You Can Still Buy the Actual Fruitcakes Served at British Royal Weddings," *Atlas Obscura*, December 9, 2019, https://www.atlasobscura.com/articles/royal-wedding-cake.

61 **Danishes:** Jan M. Olsen, "Danish Pastry: A Mistake That Conquered the World," *Los Angeles Times*, September 19, 1993, https://www.latimes.com/archives/la -xpm-1993-09-19-mn-36976-story.html.

61 **Chock Full o'Nuts:** James Barron, "What's in That Can of Chock Full o'Nuts? 'No Nuts,' Can Promises," *The New York Times*, November 27, 2017, https://www .nytimes.com/2017/11/27/nyregion/chock-full-o-nuts-coffee-can.html.

61 **Carrots do not improve your eyesight:** K. Annabelle Smith, "A WWII Propaganda Campaign Popularized the Myth that Carrots Help You See in the Dark," *Smithsonian Magazine*, August 13, 2013, https://www.smithsonianmag.com /arts-culture/a-wwii-propaganda-campaign-popularized-the-myth-that -carrots-help-you-see-in-the-dark-28812484/.

62 **Drinking coffee can lower your risk:** "Coffee Drinkers Have Lower Risk of Death," National Institutes of Health, June 4, 2012, https://www.nih.gov/news -events/nih-research-matters/coffee-drinkers-have-lower-risk-death.

62 **Square watermelons:** "Square Watermelons," *Atlas Obscura*, https://www.at lasobscura.com/foods/square-watermelons-japan.

62 **Bloody Mary:** John Mariani, "The Secret Origins of the Bloody Mary," *Esquire*, February 21, 2014, https://www.esquire.com/food-drink/drinks/recipes/a27481 /bloody-mary-origins-recipe/.

62 **Popcorn was discovered:** Adam Cole, "Aztec Gold: Watch the History and Science of Popcorn," NPR, January 19, 2016, https://www.npr.org/sections/thesalt /2016/01/19/463634834/aztec-gold-watch-the-history-and-science-of-popcorn.

62 **Coke contains a larger amount of sugar:** Cole, "Aztec Gold."

62 **Pound cake got its name:** Kat Eschner, "A Pound Cake Was Originally Made with Four Pounds of Ingredients," *Smithsonian Magazine*, March 3, 2017, https:// www.smithsonianmag.com/smart-news/pound-cake-was-originally-made-four -pounds-ingredients-180962308/.

62 **Bags O Mystery:** "Origin of 'Bag of Mystery' (Sausage)," https://wordhistories .net/2017/01/30/bag-of-mystery/.

62 **Ronald McDonald:** "Fast Food Nation," *PBS NewsHour* Extra, April 4, 2001, https://www.pbs.org/newshour/extra/2001/04/fast-food-nation/.

62 **Starbucks at the CIA:** Emily Wax-Thibodeaux, "At CIA Starbucks, Even the Baristas Are Covert," *The Washington Post*, September 27, 2014, https://www .washingtonpost.com/politics/at-cia-starbucks-even-the-baristas-are-covert/2014 /09/27/5a04cd28-43f5-11e4-9a15-137aa0153527_story.html.

63 **Prohibition, grape growers:** Erin Blakemore, "During Prohibition, Vintners Sold 'Wine Bricks' Rather Than Wine," *Smithsonian Magazine*, August 27, 2015, https://www.smithsonianmag.com/smart-news/ingenious-brick-helped-wine -industry-survive-prohibition-180956412/.

63 **The brand Pez:** "About Us," PEZ.com, https://us.pez.com/pages/history.

63 **Hippopotamus soup:** "Five Interesting Facts About Soup," Associated Press, January 30, 2019, https://apnews.com/09eb5363b0294aa2938fe6b0b25 fe8cf.

63 **Pineapple is named such because:** "A Pineapple Is an Apple (Kind Of)," Merriam-Webster, https://www.merriam-webster.com/words-at-play/word -history-pineapple.

63 **Refried beans:** ERICT_CULINARYLORE, "How Did Refried Beans Get Their Name?," Culinary Lore, January 2, 2018, https://culinarylore.com/food-history :how-did-refried-beans-get-their-name/.

63 **Chia seeds:** Jane E. Brody, "Drink Up! Most of Us Could Benefit from More Wa- ter," *The New York Times*, July 8, 2018, https://www.nytimes.com/2018/07/09 /well/hydration-thirst-water.html.

63 **Nerds breakfast cereal:** Dan Mitchell, "6 Weird Cereal Brands That Will Make You Nostalgic," *Fortune*, March 7, 2016, https://fortune.com/2016/03/07/ce real-brands-popular-disappear/; "17 Cereals That Were Too Sweet to Last Slide- show," The Daily Meal, July 25, 2012, https://www.thedailymeal.com/eat/17 -cereals-were-too-sweet-last-slideshow.

63 **Brown eggs are no better for you than white eggs:** Taylor Jones, "Brown vs. White Eggs—Is There a Difference?," Healthline, March 7, 2017, https://www .healthline.com/nutrition/white-vs-brown-eggs#section2.

63 **How many licks:** "Scientific Endeavors: Tootsie Gallery: How Many Licks Does It Take?," Tootsie Roll Inc., https://tootsie.com/howmanylick-experiments.

64 **Jell-O flavors:** Nancy Mock, "10 Vintage Jell-O Flavors You Won't Believe Ex- isted," *Taste of Home*, updated March 6, 2019, https://www.tasteofhome.com /article/vintage-jello-flavors/.

64 **Russia classified beer:** Fred Weir, "Why Russia Finally Decided That Beer Is Alcohol," *The Christian Science Monitor*, July 20, 2011, https://www.csmonitor .com/World/Europe/2011/0720/Why-Russia-finally-decided-that-beer-is -alcohol.

64 **Flamin' Hot Cheetos:** Kathleen Elkins, "How a Janitor Invented Flamin' Hot Cheetos and Became an Exec at PepsiCo," CNBC, March 27, 2018, updated June 29, 2018, https://www.cnbc.com/2018/03/27/a-janitor-invented-flamin-hot -cheetos-and-became-a-pepsico-exec.html.

64 **Milk Duds:** "Milk Duds Candy," Hershey's, https://www.hersheys.com/en_us /our-brands/milk-duds.html.

64 **Cornflakes:** Richard Cavendish, "The Battle of the Cornflakes," History Today, February 2006, https://www.historytoday.com/archive/battle-cornflakes.

64 **MSG:** Jessie Yeung, "MSG in Chinese Food Isn't Unhealthy—You're Just Racist, Activists Say," CNN, updated January 18, 2020, https://www.cnn.com/2020 /01/18/asia/chinese-restaurant-syndrome-msg-intl-hnk-scli/index.html.

64 **Mountain Dew:** Marissa Fessenden, "Mountain Dew Once Had Ties to Moonshine," *Smithsonian Magazine*, February 4, 2016, https://www.smithsonianmag .com/smart-news/mountain-dew-had-ties-moonshine-once-upon-time -180957978/.

64 **Avocados are berries:** "Avocado 101: Did You Know: The Avocado: Fruit or Vegetable?," California Avocados, February 12, 2015, https://www.californiaavo cado.com/blog/avocado-fruit-or-vegetable.

65 **Froot Loops:** Melissa Locker, "Breaking Breakfast News: Froot Loops Are All the Same Flavor," *Time*, January 21, 2014, https://time.com/1477/breaking-breakfast -news-froot-loops-are-all-the-same-flavor/.

65 **Popsicles were accidentally invented:** Shelby Pope, "How an 11-Year-Old Boy Invented the Popsicle," NPR, July 22, 2015, https://www.npr.org/sections/the salt/2015/07/22/425294957/how-an-11-year-old-boy-invented-the-popsicle.

65 **Cranberries bounce:** Bonnie S. Benwick, "It's Never Too Early to Start Bouncing Cranberries," *The Washington Post*, September 16, 2016, https://www.washing tonpost.com/lifestyle/food/its-never-too-early-to-start-bouncing-cranberries /2016/09/16/f35ca9c8-7b93-11e6-beac-57a4a412e93a_story.html.

Writers & Books

68 *Green Eggs and Ham***:** "Dr. Seuss Biography (1904–1991)," Biography, April 27, 2017, updated May 7, 2020, https://www.biography.com/news/dr-seuss-green -eggs-and-ham-bet https://www.seussville.com/dr-seuss/.

68 **Halley's Comet:** "Halley's Comet," twainquotes.com, http://www.twainquotes .com/Halley%27s_Comet.html.

68 **Twain didn't have an education:** Simran Khurana, "Mark Twain Education Quotes," ThoughtCo., updated June 21, 2019, https://www.thoughtco.com /mark-twain-education-2832664.

68 **Sophia Tolstoy:** "The Women Behind Great Russian Writers," *Russia Beyond*, January 22, 2014, https://www.rbth.com/arts/2014/01/22/the_women_be hind_great_russian_writers_32453.

68 **Lev Tolstoy:** "Leo Tolstoy," Britannica, https://www.britannica.com/biography /Leo-Tolstoy.

68 **Gwendolyn Brooks:** Selena Hill, "5 Black Pulitzer Prize Winners Who Made History," *Black Enterprise*, April 17, 2018, https://www.blackenterprise.com /5-black-pulitzer-prize-winners-history/.

69 *Beauty and the Beast***:** Sophie Gilbert, "The Dark Morality of Fairy-Tale Animal Brides," *The Atlantic*, March 31, 2017, https://www.theatlantic.com/entertain

ment/archive/2017/03/marrying-a-monster-the-romantic-anxieties-of-fairy
-tales/521319.

69 **Mary Shelley:** "Mary Shelley's 'Frankenstein' Is Published," A&E Television Networks, November 13, 2009, updated December 30, 2019, https://www.history.com
/this-day-in-history/frankenstein-published; "Mary Wollstonecraft Shelley," Britannica, https://www.britannica.com/biography/Mary-Wollstonecraft-Shelley; Ian
Irvine, "From Frankenstein's Monster to Franz Kafka: Vegetarians Through History," *Prospect*, June 13, 2019, https://www.prospectmagazine.co.uk/magazine
/from-frankensteins-monster-to-franz-kafka-vegetarians-through-history.

69 **Sleeping Beauty:** Steven Ford, "Original Story of Sleeping Beauty Would Have
Terrified Even Maleficent," *Orlando Sentinel*, May 29, 2014, https://www.orlan
dosentinel.com/travel/attractions/the-daily-disney/os-original-story-of
-sleeping-beauty-would-have-terrified-even-maleficent-20140529-story.html.

69 **Ancient Greek writing:** Keith Houston, "The Mysterious Origins of Punctuation," BBC, September 2, 2015, https://www.bbc.com/culture/article/20150902
-the-mysterious-origins-of-punctuation?.

69 **Toni Morrison:** "Toni Morrison, 'Beloved' Author and Nobel Laureate, Dies at
88," CNN Wire, August 6, 2019, https://www.wnep.com/article/news/local
/bradford-county/toni-morrison-beloved-author-and-nobel-laureate-dies
-at-88/.

69 **Cormac McCarthy:** "Castoff Typewriter Sells for a Quarter Million," Santa Fe
Institute, January 4, 2010, https://www.santafe.edu/news-center/news/castoff
-typewriter-sells-quarter-million.

69 **Shakespeare created the name Jessica:** "Jessica," Behind the Name, https://
www.behindthename.com/name/jessica.

70 **Zadie Smith:** Jeffrey Eugenides, "The Pieces of Zadie Smith," *The New York
Times Style Magazine*, October 17, 2016, https://www.nytimes.com/2016/10
/17/t-magazine/zadie-smith-swing-time-jeffrey-eugenides.html.

70 **Stuart Little:** Naomi Fry, "I Think About This a Lot: When Stuart Little Went on
a Date," The Cut, *New York*, February 19, 2018, https://www.thecut.com/2018
/02/i-think-about-this-a-lot-when-stuart-little-went-on-a-date.html.

70 *First Impressions:* Husna Haq, "'Pride and Prejudice': 5 Things You May Not
Know About the Classic Novel," *The Christian Science Monitor*, January 28, 2013,
https://www.csmonitor.com/Books/2013/0128/Pride-and-Prejudice-5-things
-you-may-not-know-about-the-classic-novel/Pride-and-Prejudice-was-almost
-published-as-First-Impressions.

70 **Stress-reducer:** "Reading for Stress Relief," Taking Charge of Your Health and
Wellbeing, University of Minnesota, https://www.takingcharge.csh.umn.edu
/reading-stress-relief.

70 **Pen names at some point:** Sara Semic, "Unmasking the Author Identities Behind the Aliases—Can the Real Elena Ferrante Please Stand Up?," *Elle*, May 10,
2016, https://www.elle.com/uk/life-and-culture/culture/articles/a32148/au

thor-aliases-unmasked/; Yohana Desta, "A Brief History of Female Authors with Male Pen Names," Mashable, March 1, 2015, https://mashable.com/2015/03 /01/female-authors-pen-names/.

70 **Fight Club:** Geoffrey Kleinman, "Chuck Palahniuk—Author of *Fight Club*," DVD Talk, https://www.dvdtalk.com/interviews/chuck_palahniuk.html.

70 **Most expensive book:** Tom Popomaronis, "Bill Gates Paid $30.8 Million for This Book 25 Years Ago—Here's Why It Still Inspires Him Today," CNBC, April 2, 2019, updated April 2, 2019, https://www.cnbc.com/2019/04/02/micrsoft-billionaire -bill-gates-paid-30-million-for-this-book-25-years-ago-and-it-still-inspires-him -today.html.

70 **Voltaire was said to drink:** Tori Avey, "The Caffeinated History of Coffee," PBS .org, April 8, 2013, https://www.pbs.org/food/the-history-kitchen/history -coffee/.

70 **Journalist Claude Sitton cut:** Jerry Mitchell, "Claude Sitton Would 'Go into Hell' to Get the Story," *Clarion Ledger*, March 10, 2015, https://www.clarionle dger.com/story/journeytojustice/2015/03/10/claude-sitton-remembered-as -stickler-for-accuracy/24713523/.

71 **Alice's Adventures in Wonderland:** Maria Popova, "Meet the Girl Who Inspired 'Alice in Wonderland,'" *The Atlantic*, July 5, 2012, https://www.theatlantic.com /entertainment/archive/2012/07/meet-the-girl-who-inspired-alice-in-wonderland /259474/.

71 **Sherlock Holmes:** "Results for Elementary—My-Dear-Watson," Dictionary .com, https://www.dictionary.com/browse/elementary—my-dear-watson.

71 **Proust:** "Longest Novel," Guinness World Records, https://www.guinnessworl drecords.com/world-records/longest-novel.

71 **Longest-ever title:** "Longest Title of a Book," Guinness World Records, https:// www.guinnessworldrecords.com/world-records/358711-longest-title-of -a-book.

71 **Phillis Wheatley:** Audrey Webster and Kelsey McConnell, "29 Facts About Black History That You Might Not Know," The Archive, January 31, 2019, updated January 26, 2021, https://explorethearchive.com/black-history-month-facts.

71 **Libraries per capita:** Kasia Kowalczyk, "The Best Cities in the World for Book Lovers, According to Numbers," Ebook Friendly, September 6, 2019, https://eb ookfriendly.com/best-cities-for-book-lovers-around-world/.

71 **R. L. Stine's fifty-eight-book horror series:** "Not My Job: We Quiz R. L. Stine on Ralph Lauren," *Wait Wait . . . Don't Tell Me!*, NPR, April 2, 2016, https:// www.npr.org/2016/04/02/472673808/not-my-job-we-quiz-r-l-stine-on-ralph -lauren.

71 **Of Mice and Men:** "101 Fun Facts You Never Knew, Guaranteed to Totally Blow Your Mind," *Parade*, October 20, 2020, https://parade.com/966564/parade /fun-facts/.

Word Origins & Language

74 **Nimrod:** Merrill Perlman, "When Good Words Go Bad," *Columbia Journalism Review*, August 8, 2016, https://www.cjr.org/language_corner/nimrod_nabob_mogul.php.

74 **OMG:** Rachel Nuwer, "The First Use of OMG Was in a 1917 Letter to Winston Churchill," November 27, 2012, https://www.smithsonianmag.com/smart-news/the-first-use-of-omg-was-in-a-1917-letter-to-winston-churchill-145636383/.

74 **Cryptophasia:** John Lackman, "Dugon, Haus You Dinikin, Du-Ah," *Slate*, August 23, 2011, https://slate.com/human-interest/2011/08/cryptophasia-the-secrets-of-twin-speak.html.

74 **Crossword puzzles:** Adrienne Raphel, "Crosswords Have Always Been a Solace in Times of Trouble. Here's How the 20th Century's Toughest Moments Shaped the Puzzle's History," *Time*, March 27, 2020, https://time.com/5811396/crossword-history/.

74 **"Sinful waste":** Stephen Hiltner, "'Relaxation' in a Time of War: How the *New York Times* Crossword Puzzle Got Its Start," *The New York Times*, December 18, 2017, https://www.nytimes.com/2017/12/18/insider/how-the-new-york-times-crossword-puzzle-got-its-start-in-a-time-of-war.html.

74 **Thai Internet slang:** Megan Garber, "55555, or, How to Laugh Online in Other Languages," *The Atlantic*, December 12, 2012, https://www.theatlantic.com/technology/archive/2012/12/55555-or-how-to-laugh-online-in-other-languages/266175/.

74 **Forte, meaning something you're good at:** Victor Mather, "We Use Sports Terms All the Time. But Where Do They Come From?," *The New York Times*, August 6, 2018, https://www.nytimes.com/2018/08/06/sports/sports-cliches-metaphors.html.

75 **Factoid to mean information:** "Are 'Factoids' the Same as 'Facts'?," Merriam-Webster, https://www.merriam-webster.com/words-at-play/some-facts-about-factoids.

75 **Honeymoon may have come from:** "What Is the Origin of the Word 'Honeymoon'?," *The Times of India*, November 6, 2005, https://timesofindia.indiatimes.com/What-is-the-origin-of-the-word-honeymoon/articleshow/1285765.cms?.

75 **In 2019, stan:** Jon Blistein, "Eminem-Inspired Use of 'Stan' Added to Merriam-Webster's Dictionary," *Rolling Stone*, April 24, 2019, https://www.rollingstone.com/music/music-news/eminem-stan-merriam-websters-dictionary-entry-826557/.

75 **"Passion pits":** Nancy Wride, "O.C. Theater's Double Feature: Love Seats," *Los Angeles Times*, July 11, 1996, https://www.latimes.com/archives/la-xpm-1996-07-11-mn-23222-story.html.

75 **Paint the town red:** Evan Andrews, "10 Common Sayings with Historical Origins," History.com, April 23, 2013, updated August 22, 2018, https://www.history.com/news/10-common-sayings-with-historical-origins.

75 *Chuckaboo:* Fraser McAlpine, "20 Victorian Terms That Seem Oddly Modern," BBC America, https://www.bbcamerica.com/anglophenia/2014/08/20-victorian-terms-seem-oddly-modern.

75 *Hipster:* "What's the Origin of the Term Hipster?," Dictionary.com, https://www.dictionary.com/e/hipster/.

76 *Long in the tooth:* "The Meaning and Origin of the Expression: Long in the Tooth," The Phrase Finder, https://www.phrases.org.uk/meanings/long-in-the-tooth.html.

76 *Nomophobia:* Tim Elmore, "Nomophobia: A Rising Trend in Students," *Psychology Today*, September 18, 2014, https://www.psychologytoday.com/us/blog/artificial-maturity/201409/nomophobia-rising-trend-in-students.

76 *Sneakers* **was in England in 1862:** "Sneaker (n.)," Online Etymology Dictionary, https://www.etymonline.com/word/sneaker.

76 **Smell of rain:** Elizabeth Palermo, "Why Does Rain Smell Good?," Live Science, June 21, 2013, https://www.livescience.com/37648-good-smells-rain-petrichor.html.

76 *Octothorpe:* Picard, "35 Coolest Random Pieces of Trivia That Will Impress Your Friends."

76 *Backlog:* "Backlog (n.)," Online Etymology Dictionary, https://www.etymonline.com/word/backlog.

77 *Karoshi:* Zaria Gorvett, "Can You Work Yourself to Death?," BBC, September 13, 2016, https://www.bbc.com/worklife/article/20160912-is-there-such-thing-as-death-from-overwork.

77 **Life expectancy:** "Life Expectancy of the World Population," Worldometer, https://www.worldometers.info/demographics/life-expectancy/.

77 *Literally:* "Did We Change the Definition of 'Literally'?," Merriam-Webster, https://www.merriam-webster.com/words-at-play/misuse-of-literally.

77 *Fizzle:* "Fizzle," Lexico, https://www.lexico.com/definition/fizzle.

77 *By and large:* Evan Andrews, "10 Common Sayings with Historical Origins," History.com, April 23, 2013, updated August 22, 2018, https://www.history.com/news/10-common-sayings-with-historical-origins.

77 **"Twitter" was an abscess:** Ana Samways, "Sideswipe: October 18: Not a Squeak?," *The New Zealand Herald*, October 17, 2017, https://www.nzherald.co.nz/entertainment/news/article.cfm?c_id=1501119&objectid=11934057.

77 **"Zugzwang":** "Zugzwang," Lexico, https://www.lexico.com/en/definition/zugzwang.

77 **"Top of the mornin'":** "Top of the Morning to Yourself," Macmillan Dictionary Blog, https://www.macmillandictionaryblog.com/top-of-the-morning-to-yourself.

78 ***Goodbye* originated from *God bye*:** "Goodbye," Lexico, https://www.lexico.com/en/definition/goodbye.

78 ***Bootylicious*:** Elizabeth J. Pyatt, "How Bootylicious Got into the Oxford English Dictionary," A Linguist in the Wild, April 9, 2008, http://www.personal.psu.edu/ejp10/blogs/thinking/2008/04/how-bootylicious-got-into-the.html.

78 ***Pushing the envelope*:** Caroline Bologna, "Here's Why We Say 'Pushing the Envelope,'" *HuffPost*, July 24, 2018, https://www.huffpost.com/entry/heres-why-we-say-pushing-the-envelope_n_5af9bf9ae4b044dfffb4bdf1?.

78 **Hippopotomonstrosesquippedaliophobia:** Annamarya Scaccia, "What Is Hippopotomonstrosesquippedaliophobia?," Healthline, updated September 12, 2017, https://www.healthline.com/health/hippopotomonstrosesquippedaliophobia.

78 ***Griffonage*:** "Griffonage," Merriam-Webster, https://www.merriam-webster.com/dictionary/griffonage.

78 **There are two verbs for eating in Germany:** John Gould, "Lobsters Debut and Disappear in Germany," *The Christian Science Monitor*, November 22, 1996, https://www.csmonitor.com/1996/1122/112296.home.home.2.html.

78 **They said "Ahoy":** Robert Krulwich, "A (Shockingly) Short History of 'Hello,'" NPR, February 17, 2011, www.npr.org/sections/krulwich/2011/02/17/133785829/a-shockingly-short-history-of-hello.

78 **The word *karaoke*:** "Your Say—Weird words: Empty Orchestra," BBC, http://www.bbc.co.uk/languages/yoursay/weird_words/japanese/empty_orchestra.shtml.

78 **"Butt violin":** Steph Koyfman, "Cursing Abroad: German Insults to Round Out Your Studies," *Babbel Magazine*, November 9, 2019, https://www.babbel.com/en/magazine/cursing-abroad-german-insults-to-round-out-your-studies.

79 **"Get someone's goat":** "Get Someone's Goat," Dictionary.com, https://www.dictionary.com/browse/get-someone-s-goat.

79 ***Muppet*:** Eleanor Blau, "Jim Henson, Puppeteer, Dies; The Muppets' Creator Was 53," *The New York Times*, May 17, 1990, https://www.nytimes.com/1990/05/17/obituaries/jim-henson-puppeteer-dies-the-muppets-creator-was-53.html.

79 **Tittle:** "What's the Name for the Dot Over 'i' And 'j'?," Dictionary.com, https://www.dictionary.com/e/tittle/.

79 ***Espresso*:** Amanda Hawkins and Caroline Picard, "21 Surprising Coffee Facts That Will Perk Up Your Afternoon," *Good Housekeeping*, December 3, 2018, https://www.goodhousekeeping.com/health/diet-nutrition/a30303/facts-about-coffee/.

79 ***AC/DC*:** "AC/DC," Dictionary.com, https://www.dictionary.com/browse/ac-dc.

79 ***FOMO*:** Michael Dirda, "Oxford Dictionaries Adds 'Twerk,' 'FOMO,' 'Selfie,' and Other Words That Make Me Vom," *The Washington Post*, August 28, 2013, https://www.washingtonpost.com/lifestyle/style/oxford-dictionaries-adds-twerk-fomo-selfie-and-other-words-that-make-me-vom/2013/08/28/678ddd48-102c-11e3-8cdd-bcdc09410972_story.html.

79 ***Happy as a clam***: Meghan Jones, "Here's Where Your Favorite Animal-Related Sayings Come From," *Reader's Digest*, updated August 29, 2019, https://www.rd.com/list/where-animal-sayings-come-from/.

79 ***Computer bug***: "This Day in History: What Happened on September 9th," Computer History Museum, https://www.computerhistory.org/tdih/september/9/.

79 ***Sauce-box***: "The 25 Best Victorian Slang Terms," History Hustle, November 12, 2018, https://historyhustle.com/victorian-slang-terms/.

79 **Punctuation mark to denote irony**: Erin McKean, "Yeah, Right: Do We Need a New Punctuation Mark?," Boston.com, February 7, 2010, http://archive.boston.com/bostonglobe/ideas/articles/2010/02/07/yeah_right/.

80 **"Boxing rings"**: "Why Is a Boxing Ring Square?," Wonderopolis, https://www.wonderopolis.org/wonder/why-is-a-boxing-ring-square.

80 **KFC:** Chad Brooks, "Lost in Translation: 9 International Marketing Fails," Fox Business, October 8, 2013, https://www.foxbusiness.com/features/lost-in-translation-9-international-marketing-fails.

80 ***Testify***: Dario Maestripieri, "Testify" Comes from the Latin Word for Testicle," *Psychology Today*, December 11, 2011, https://www.psychologytoday.com/us/blog/games-primates-play/201112/testify-comes-the-latin-word-testicle.

80 **"Canapés":** "Canapé," Wordreference.com, https://www.wordreference.com/definition/canapé.

80 **Before Present:** "The Radioactive Clock: Radiocarbon Dating," Time Team America, PBS, https://www.pbs.org/time-team/experience-archaeology/radioactive-dating/.

80 **Elvish and Klingon:** Maryn Liles, "100 Wild and Wacky WTF Facts That Are So Shocking They'll Have You Saying, 'Whoa,'" *Parade*, April 3, 2020, https://parade.com/1019661/marynliles/wtf-facts/.

80 **We call it a "toast":** "Why Do We Clink Glasses And Say 'Cheers'?," *Farmers' Almanac*, updated January 1, 2021, https://www.farmersalmanac.com/why-do-we-say-cheers-30416.

80 **"Frog sticks":** Albie Yuravich, "Diner Lingo: How to Talk Like a Short Order Cook," *Connecticut Magazine*, June 1, 2017, https://www.connecticutmag.com/food-drink/diner-lingo-how-to-talk-like-a-short-order-cook/article_6dce37f0-3a7d-11e7-b0df-4f4d5326a3d1.html.

81 **Classic diner lingo:** Yuravich, "Diner Lingo: How to Talk Like a Short Order Cook."

81 ***Chicks on a raft***: Patrick Allan, "A Quick Lesson in Essential Diner Lingo," Lifehacker, September 29, 2017, https://lifehacker.com/a-quick-lesson-in-essential-diner-lingo-1818975167.

81 ***Karate***: Tulane Karate Club, https://www.tulane.edu/~karate/karate.htm.

81 **"Nurdle":** Jonathan Stempel, "Colgate, Glaxo Sue Over Toothpaste 'Nurdle,'" Reuters, https://www.reuters.com/article/us-colgate-glaxo-nurdle/colgate-glaxo-sue-over-toothpaste-nurdle-idUSTRE66S5RD20100729.

81 **It took Webster twenty-eight years:** "The History of Webster's Dictionary," *American Dictionary of the English Language*, http://webstersdictionary1828 .com/NoahWebster.

81 **Hangover is often referred to:** Joan Acocella, "A Few Too Many," *The New Yorker*, May 19, 2008, https://www.newyorker.com/magazine/2008/05/26 /a-few-too-many.

81 *Bow wow mutton:* "6 Handy Victorian Words & Phrases You'll Need This Summer," The Long Victorian, https://thelongvictorian.com/2016/06/04/6-handy -victorian-words-phrases-youll-need-this-summer/.

81 *Muscle* **comes from the Latin:** Hannah Jeon, "The Surprising Origins of 15 Commonly-Used Words in the English Language," *Good Housekeeping*, December 11, 2019, https://www.goodhousekeeping.com/life/g30186775/surprising -word-origins/?slide=8.

81 *In the ketchup:* "Full text of 'Thesaurus Of Slang,'" Internet Archive, https:// archive.org/stream/ThesaurusOfSlang/Thesaurus%20of%20Slang_djvu.txt.

81 **No official language:** Harmeet Kaur, "FYI: English Isn't the Official Language of the United States," CNN, updated June 15, 2018, https://www.cnn.com/2018 /05/20/us/english-us-official-language-trnd/index.html.

Morbid Facts for Know-It-All Goths

84 **Pringles can:** Jeremy Caplan, "The Man Buried in a Pringles Can," *Time*, June 4, 2008, http://content.time.com/time/business/article/0,8599,1811730,00.html.

84 **Ford began advertising in Belgium:** Skye Schooley, "Lost in Translation: 10 International Marketing Fails," *Business News Daily*, August 12, 2019, https:// www.businessnewsdaily.com/5241-international-marketing-fails.html.

84 **A cat named Oscar:** Angela Lutz, "Meet Oscar, a Nursing Home Cat Who Predicts Death," Catster, September 10, 2015, https://www.catster.com/lifestyle /oscar-nursing-home-therapy-cat-predicts-death.

84 **Fear of the number 13:** Marika Gerken, "Friday the 13th: How It Came to Be and Why It's Considered Unlucky," CNN, December 13, 2019, https://www.cnn .com/2019/12/13/us/friday-the-13th-history-why-trnd/index.html.

84 **La Isla de las Muñecas:** "The Island of the Dolls," Isla de las Muñecas, https:// isladelasmunecas.com.

85 **"Have you been decapitated?":** "Episode 714: Can a Game Show Lose?," *Planet Money*, NPR, July 27, 2016, https://www.npr.org/transcripts/487654380.

85 **Belcher's sea snake:** "What Is the Most Poisonous Snake?," *The Petri Dish*, October 27, 2017, https://thepetridish.my/2017/10/27/what-is-the-most-poisonous -snake/.

85 **107 billion people:** Wesley Stephenson, "Do the Dead Outnumber the Living?," BBC News, February 4, 2012, https://www.bbc.com/news/magazine-1687 0579.

85 **Frozen Dead Guy Days:** "What Goes on at FDGD?," Frozen Dead Guy Days, https://frozendeadguydays.org/about-the-festival.

85 **During the Salem Witch Trials:** Evan Andrews, "Were Witches Burned at the Stake During the Salem Witch Trials?," History.com, August 13, 2014, updated September 1, 2018, https://www.history.com/news/were-witches-burned-at -the-stake-during-the-salem-witch-trials.

85 **A chicken named Mike:** "The Chicken That Lived for 18 Months Without a Head," BBC News, September 9, 2015, https://www.bbc.com/news/magazine -34198390.

85 *Mortgage* **comes from French words:** Libby Kane, "The Origins of the Word 'Mortgage' Will Make You Think Twice About Buying a House," *Business Insider*, https://www.businessinsider.com/mortgage-means-death-pledge-2016-3.

85 *The Exorcist:* "Creepy Tales from Cursed Movies," CBS News, https://www.cb snews.com/pictures/creepy-strange-tales-cursed-movies/13/.

86 **Great Fire of London:** Rose Eveleth, "Officially, More People Died Falling Off the Great Fire of London Monument Than in the Fire—but Only Officially," *Smithsonian Magazine*, March 4, 2014, https://www.smithsonianmag.com/smart-news /no-more-people-have-not-died-falling-monument-great-fire-london-fire-itself -180949960/.

86 **Jack-o'-lanterns:** Kayla Hertz, "Original Irish Jack-o-Lanterns Made of Turnips Were Truly Terrifying," Irish Central, October 25, 2020, https://www.irishcentral .com/roots/history/jack-o-lantern-turnips-ireland.

86 **Female black widow:** Ed Yong, "How Male Black Widow Spiders Avoid Being Cannibalized During Sex," *National Geographic*, September 20, 2016, https:// www.nationalgeographic.com/news/2016/09/animals-spiders-black-widows -cannibals/.

86 **Fingernails don't continue to grow:** Claudia Hammond, "Do Your Hair and Fingernails Grow After Death?," BBC, May 27, 2013, https://www.bbc.com/fu ture/article/20130526-do-your-nails-grow-after-death.

86 *Miniature teeth:* Dani Matias, "Surgeons Remove More Than 500 Teeth from Boy in India," NPR, August 2, 2019, https://www.npr.org/2019/08/02/7476 14435/surgeons-remove-more-than-500-teeth-from-boy-in-india.

86 **Forty-five percent of American adults believe demons:** H. Alan Scott, "More Than 45 Percent of Americans Believe Demons and Ghosts Are Real: Survey," *Newsweek*, October 21, 2019, https://www.newsweek.com/more-45-per cent-americans-believe-demons-ghosts-are-real-survey-1466743.

86 **Peter the Great:** Natasha Frost, "What Happened to the Severed Head of Peter the Great's Wife's Lover," *Atlas Obscura*, October 20, 2017, https://www.atlas obscura.com/articles/kunstkamera-museum-head-jar-peter-great-lover-wife.

86 **Kiss Kaskets:** Zach Shaw, "New Kiss Kaskets Revealed, Fans Rejoice?," Metal Insider, February 15, 2011, https://www.metalinsider.net/douchetastic/new-kiss -kaskets-revealed-fans-rejoice.

86 **Owls eat other owls:** Arthur Cleveland Bent, *Life Histories of North American Birds of Prey: Orders Falconiformes and Strigiformes* (Washington, D.C.: U.S. Government Printing Office, 1961), 191.

86 **Thanatology is the scientific study:** "Thanatology," Britannica, https://www.britannica.com/science/thanatology.

87 **4 is unlucky:** Jaclyn Skurie, "Superstitious Numbers Around the World," *National Geographic*, September 14, 2013, https://www.nationalgeographic.com/news/2013/9/130913-friday-luck-lucky-superstition-13/#close.

87 **9 is unlucky:** Heather Whipps, "Why 09/09/09 Is So Special," Live Science, September 8, 2009, https://www.livescience.com/5679-09-09-09-special.html.

87 **Bedbugs have been around:** Becky Ferreira, "Bedbugs Menaced the Dinosaur Age Before Moving into Our Mattresses," *The New York Times*, May 16, 2019, https://www.nytimes.com/2019/05/16/science/bedbugs-dinosaurs-evolution.html.

87 **Washington was terrified of:** Becky Little, "Why Many Famous Figures Feared They'd Be Buried Alive," History.com, November 13, 2017, updated August 23, 2018, https://www.history.com/news/why-many-famous-figures-feared-theyd-be-buried-alive.

87 **A cockroach can live:** Charles Choi, "Fact or Fiction?: A Cockroach Can Live without Its Head," *Scientific American*, March 15, 2007, https://www.scientificamerican.com/article/fact-or-fiction-cockroach-can-live-without-head/.

87 **John and Yoko:** William Plummer, "What's in a Name? Actor Mark Lindsay Finds Out," *People*, updated July 15, 1985, https://people.com/archive/whats-in-a-name-actor-mark-lindsay-finds-out-vol-24-no-3/.

87 **JFK's brain went missing:** Emind Saner, "The President's Brain Is Missing and Other Mysteriously Mislaid Body Parts," *The Guardian*, October 21, 2013, https://www.theguardian.com/world/shortcuts/2013/oct/21/presidents-brain-missing-mislaid-body-parts.

87 **Her husband's body was discovered:** Leah Simpson, "Utah Man, 75, Found in Wife's Freezer Ten Years After He'd Died Left Notarized Letter Claiming She Had Nothing to Do with His Death, as It's Revealed She Went on to Claim $117K in Veteran Benefits," Dailymail.com, December 17, 2019, https://www.dailymail.co.uk/news/article-7802477/Utah-mans-body-freezer-11-years-left-notarized-letter-stating-wife-didnt-kill-him.html.

87 **Russian prisoners used to tattoo:** Fiona Macdonald, "Secret Meanings of Russian Prisoner Tattoos," BBC, October 21, 2014, https://www.bbc.com/culture/article/20140424-decoding-russian-criminal-tattoos.

87 **Human sheds about seventy-seven:** "How Are Tattoos Permanent, When Humans Shed So Much Skin?," Science Alert, December 9, 2016, https://www.sciencealert.com/watch-how-are-tattoos-permanent-when-humans-shed-so-much-skin.

88 **A "dancing plague":** Evan Andrews, "What Was the Dancing Plague of 1518?," History.com, August 31, 2015, updated March 25, 2020, https://www.history.com/news/what-was-the-dancing-plague-of-1518.

88   **"Twelve plus one":** Mark Hanks, *Usefully Useless: Everything You'd Never Learn at School (But May Like to Know)* (London: Square Peg, 2011).

88   **Lady Dai:** "Lady Dai: The 2,000+ Year Old, Beautifully Preserved Mummy," History 101, March 18, 2020, https://www.history101.com/lady-dai-xin-zhui/.

88   **Being scared releases dopamine:** Allegra Ringo, "Why Do Some Brains Enjoy Fear?," *The Atlantic*, October 31, 2018, https://www.theatlantic.com/health/archive/2013/10/why-do-some-brains-enjoy-fear/280938/.

88   ***Confederacy of Dunces:*** Bradford Evans, "10 Actors Who Came Close to Starring in 'A Confederacy of Dunces,'" *Vulture*, March 28, 2013, https://www.vulture.com/2013/03/8-actors-who-came-close-to-starring-in-a-confederacy-of-dunces.html.

88   **Human brain remains conscious after decapitation:** Josh Clark, "Do You Really Stay Conscious After Being Decapitated?," How Stuff Works, https://science.howstuffworks.com/science-vs-myth/extrasensory-perceptions/lucid-decapitation.htm.

88   **Capsized tugboat:** Marc Lallanilla, "Undersea Miracle: How Man in Sunken Ship Survived 3 Days," Live Science, December 4, 2013, https://www.livescience.com/41688-how-to-survive-underwater-for-3-days.html.

88   **Morbid sense of humor:** Brandon Specktor, "If You Laugh at These Dark Jokes, You're Probably a Genius," *Reader's Digest*, October 15, 2020, https://www.rd.com/article/dark-sense-of-humor-and-intelligence/.

89   **Oscar than you are to be struck:** Sarah Long, "17 Random Statistics That Will Actually Surprise You," SheKnows, May 3, 2018, https://www.sheknows.com/living/articles/1023453/what-are-the-odds-21-statistics-that-will-surprise-you/.

89   **Bowl a perfect game:** Joseph, "The 300 Club: Tips to Help You Bowl a Perfect Game," Beginner Bowling Tips, https://beginnerbowlingtips.com/the-300-club-tips-to-help-you-bowl-a-perfect-game; Long, "17 Random Statistics That Will Actually Surprise You."

89   **Champagne cork than you are by a shark:** Megan Denny, "18 Things More Dangerous Than Sharks," Padi.com, https://blog.padi.com/2017/05/04/18-things-dangerous-sharks/.

89   **Ants than you are by a shark:** Denny, "18 Things More Dangerous Than Sharks."

89   **Coconut than you are by a shark:** Amanda Onion, "Coconuts Called Deadlier Than Sharks," ABC News, January 7, 2006, https://abcnews.go.com/Technology/story?id=97993&page=1.

89   **Freshwater snail:** Elizabeth Shockman, "Why Snails Are One of the World's Deadliest Creatures," Science Friday, The World, August 13, 2016, https://www.pri.org/stories/2016-08-13/why-snails-are-one-worlds-deadliest-creatures.

89   **Dance party than you are to be killed by a black bear:** "Your Chances of Dying," https://www.besthealthdegrees.com/health-risks/; Christine Dell'Amore and Todd Wilkinson, "How to Not Get Attacked by a Bear," *Na-*

tional Geographic, September 16, 2019, https://www.nationalgeographic.com
/news/2015/09/150916-bears-attacks-animals-science-north-america-grizzlies/.

89 **Famous than you are to be killed by an alligator:** Jim Hanas, "You Are Not
Going to Be Famous," *New York Post*, July 25, 2009, https://nypost.com/2009
/07/25/you-are-not-going-to-be-famous/; Michael Greshko, "Ailligator Attacks
Can Be Deadly but Are Quite Rare," *National Geographic*, June 15, 2016, https://
www.nationalgeographic.com/news/2016/06/alligator-attack-toddler-disney
-world-grand-floridian/.

89 **Firearm than you are by a shark:** "Facts + Statistics: Mortality Risk," Insurance
Information Institute, https://www.iii.org/fact-statistic/facts-statistics-mor
tality-risk; Kelly McLaughlin, "Here Are the Chances of Getting Bitten by a Shark
While You're Swimming at the Beach," *Insider*, July 21, 2018, https://www.in
sider.com/shark-attacks-what-are-odds-of-getting-bitten-2018-7.

89 **Human-to-human bites:** Bryan Walsh, "In the War Between Sharks and People,
Humans Are Killing It," *Time*, December 03, 2013, https://science.time.com
/2013/12/03/in-the-war-between-sharks-and-people-humans-are-killing-it/.

TV & Movies

92 **Zendaya:** April Siese, "Zendaya Is the Youngest Lead Drama Actress Winner in
Emmys History at 24," CBS News, updated September 21, 2020, https://www
.cbsnews.com/news/emmys-2020-zendaya-is-the-youngest-to-win-the-award
-for-lead-actress-in-a-drama-for-her-role-in-euphoria-2020-09-20/.

92 *Parasite* **was built on a water tank:** Gabriella Paiella, "*Parasite* Director Bong
Joon-ho on the Art of Class Warfare," *GQ*, October 8, 2019, https://www
.gq.com/story/parasite-director-bong-joon-ho-interview.

92 **Phyllis Vance:** Natalie Stone, "*The Office*'s Phyllis Smith Was a Burlesque Dancer!
'She Has a Great Shimmy,' Angela Kinsey Says," *People*, November 18, 2019,
https://people.com/tv/the-office-jenna-fischer-angela-kinsey-talk-phyllis-smith
-burlesque-dancer.

92 **Krasinski shot the footage:** Oriana Schwindt, "Scranton Says Goodbye to *The
Office*," *TV Guide*, May 4, 2013, https://www.tvguide.com/news/the-office
-wrap-party-scranton-says-goodbye-1064969/.

93 *Jaws:* "QI Fan? Here Are 40 of the Best Facts Chosen by the Team Behind the BBC
Show," i, December 13, updated August 21, 2020, https://inews.co.uk/culture
/television/qi-bbc-elves-40-best-facts-235022; Cory Turner, "'Jaws' Shark Gets
His Bite Back: A Love Story," NPR, August 9, 2019, https://www.npr.org/2019
/08/09/745651910/jaws-shark-gets-his-bite-back-a-love-story.

93 *Dazed and Confused:* I noticed this while watching the movie on (legal)
edibles!

93 **Lice breaks out like crazy:** Gabriela Quirós, "Video: Head Lice Up Close, and All Too Personal," MPR News, March 27, 2019, https://www.mprnews.org/story /2019/03/27/npr-video-head-lice-up-close-and-all-too-personal.

93 **Sinatra was offered the role of John McClane:** Steve Palace, "Frank Sinatra Almost Became an 80s Action Hero," *The Vintage News*, December 23, 2018, https://www.thevintagenews.com/2018/12/23/frank-sinatra-die-hard/.

93 **Joaquin Phoenix:** Annie Thompson, "Joaquin Phoenix Talks About Finding His 'Joker': Dropping Weight, Facing Fear, and 'Testing Boundaries,'" IndieWire, October 1, 2019, https://www.indiewire.com/2019/10/joaquin-phoenix-the-joker -todd-phillips-mirror-1202177432/.

93 *Terminator* **to producer Gale Anne Hurd:** Taryn Smee, "Hasta La Vista, Dollar— James Cameron Sold the Original Terminator Script for $1," The Vintage News, November 1, 2018, https://www.thevintagenews.com/2018/11/01/terminator/.

93 **Youngest executive producer:** Shereen Marisol Meraji, "Meet Marsai Martin, The Youngest Executive Producer in Hollywood," *Morning Edition*, NPR, April 11, 2019, https://www.npr.org/2019/04/11/711942538/meet-marsai-martin -the-youngest-executive-producer-in-hollywood.

93 **Queen Latifah:** Desta, "8 Movie Stars with Unbelievable Contract Clauses."

93 **Murray was bitten by the groundhog:** "Happy 'Groundhog Day': Here's 5 Things You Didn't Know About the Movie," *The Hollywood Reporter*, February 2, 2015, https://www.hollywoodreporter.com/news/happy-groundhog-day -heres-5-769137.

94 **Whoopass Girls:** "Whoopass Stew! (1992)," IMDB.com, https://www.imdb .com/title/tt0253941/.

94 *The Owl House:* Lynn Elber, "Bisexual Character Luz on Animated 'The Owl House' Is a Disney TV Series Rarity," Associated Press, *USA Today*, https://www .usatoday.com/story/entertainment/tv/2020/08/17/bisexual-character -animated-owl-house-disney-tv-series-rarity/3387896001/.

94 **John Singleton:** Theodora Aidoo, "John Singleton: Youngest Ever Filmmaker to Be Nominated for the Best Director Oscar," Face 2 Face Africa, February 19, 2020, https://face2faceafrica.com/article/john-singleton-youngest-ever-filmmaker -to-be-nominated-for-the-best-director-oscar.

94 *The Matrix:* Mayukh Sen, "That Trippy Green Code in 'The Matrix' Is Just a Bunch of Sushi Recipes," *Vice*, October 26, 2017, https://www.vice.com/en_us/article /mb3vxp/that-trippy-green-code-in-the-matrix-is-just-a-bunch-of-sushi-recipes.

94 **Cookie Monster has a name:** Colin Schultz, "Cookie Monster's First Name Is Sid, and Other Icon's 'Real' Names," *Smithsonian Magazine*, March 14, 2014, https://www.smithsonianmag.com/smart-news/cookie-monsters-first-name -sid-and-other-icons-real-names-180950099/.

95 **Bradley Cooper cast his own dog:** Elyse Wanshel, "The Breakout Star of 'A Star Is Born' Is Bradley Cooper's Real-Life Dog," *HuffPost*, October 10, 2018, https://

www.huffpost.com/entry/bradley-cooper-dog-star-is-born_n_5bbe1643e4b0
876edaa483b4.

95 **25 percent of American cowboys:** Katie Nodjimbadem, "The Lesser-Known
History of African-American Cowboys," *Smithsonian Magazine*, February 13,
2017, https://www.smithsonianmag.com/history/lesser-known-history-african
-american-cowboys-180962144/.

95 **Apple will not allow villains:** Victoria Song, "Apple Bans Bad Guys from Using
iPhones in Movies, Says *Knives Out* Director," Gizmodo, February 26, 2020,
https://gizmodo.com/apple-bans-bad-guys-from-using-iphones-in-movies
-says-1841929887.

95 ***The Empire Strikes Back:*** John Wenz, "Some Asteroids in 'The Empire Strikes
Back' Were Actual Potatoes," *Popular Mechanics*, April 13, 2015, https://www
.popularmechanics.com/culture/movies/a15063/empire-strikes-back-asteroids
-were-potatoes/.

95 **Joe Pesci turned down his role:** James Hibberd, "Martin Scorsese: *The Irishman*
Interview," *Entertainment Weekly*, October 24, 2019, https://ew.com/movies
/2019/10/24/martin-scorsese-irishman-interview/.

95 **"Lisa the Vegetarian":** Alan Siegel, "Celebrating 'Lisa the Vegetarian,' the *Simpsons* Episode That Changed the Image of Vegetarians on TV," *Slate*, October 12,
2015, https://slate.com/culture/2015/10/the-simpsons-lisa-the-vegetarian
-episode-changed-the-image-of-vegetarians-on-tv.html.

95 ***The Simpsons* is the oldest:** "'The Simpsons' and Other Longest-Running Prime-
Time Scripted Series," *USA Today*, https://www.usatoday.com/picture-gallery
/life/tv/2018/04/26/the-simpsons-and-other-longest-running-prime-time
-scripted-series/34167149/.

95 **Leno ate a bite of:** Associated Press, "Leno Eats 125-Year-Old Fruitcake," *Today*,
December 24, 2003, https://www.today.com/popculture/leno-eats-125-year
-old-fruitcake-wbna3802979.

95 ***The Golden Girls:*** Andrea Park, "'The Golden Girls' Turns 30: 10 Things You
Didn't Know," CBS News, September 14, 2015, https://www.cbsnews.com/me
dia/golden-girls-turns-30-10-things-you-didnt-know/.

96 ***Raiders of the Lost Ark:*** Steve Kovach, "Harrison Ford Explained the Story Behind the Best Scene in 'Indiana Jones,'" *Business Insider Australia*, April 14, 2014,
https://www.businessinsider.com.au/harrison-ford-reddit-ama-2014-4.

96 ***16 and Pregnant:*** Melissa S. Kearney and Phillip B. Levine, "Media Influences on
Social Outcomes: The Impact of MTV's *16 and Pregnant* on Teen Childbearing,"
January 2014, revised August 2015, https://www.nber.org/papers/w19795.

96 ***Space Jam:*** https://www.spacejam.com.

96 **Contact lenses to change his eye color:** JD Kraemer, "The Eyes Have It,"
the Alcone archives, October 1, 2019, https://alconemakeup.com/the-alcone
-archives/the-eyes-have-it.

96 **Little Women:** "Saoirse Ronan, Timothée Chalamet, Laura Dern & Greta Gerwig Break Down a Scene from 'Little Women,'" December 17, 2019, *Vanity Fair*, YouTube, https://www.youtube.com/watch?v=Li9ff4rQlck&feature=youtu.be &t=571.

96 **Laverne Cox:** "20 LGBTQ+ People Who Changed the World," Out.com, https://www.out.com/lifestyle/2019/5/29/20-lgbtq-people-who-changed-world #media-gallery-media-1.

96 **Eddie from *Frasier*:** "Frasier's Dog Eddie Dies Aged 16," BBC, updated June 28, 2006, http://news.bbc.co.uk/2/hi/entertainment/5124104.stm.

96 **Robin Williams:** "Robin Williams Dead: Actor 'Always Required Film Companies to Hire Homeless People,'" *Huffington Post UK*, August 13, 2014, https://www.huffingtonpost.co.uk/2014/08/13/robin-williams-dead-rider-film_n_5674896.html.

96 **Wouldn't let his kids watch TV:** Cristobal Gomez, "Fun with Languages: Fun Facts About Television," K Blog, Kaplan International Languages, October 6, 2020, https://www.kaplaninternational.com/blog/fun-facts-about-television.

97 **2001: A Space Odyssey:** Bill Higgins, "Hollywood Flashback: In 1968, '2001: A Space Odyssey' Confounded Critics," *The Hollywood Reporter*, May 7, 2018, https://www.hollywoodreporter.com/news/hollywood-flashback-1968-2001-a-space-odyssey-confounded-critics-1109385.

97 **Friends:** Claire Hodgson, "34 Things You Never Knew About Friends," *Cosmopolitan*, April 7, 2016, https://www.cosmopolitan.com/uk/entertainment/news/a29836/friends-facts-33-things-you-never-knew/.

97 **Aladdin was Chinese:** Manal Khan, "Top Ten Things You Didn't Know about Aladdin," *National Geographic*, May 23, 2019, https://www.nationalgeographic.com/culture/2019/05/aladdin-origins-arabian-nights/.

97 **Doctor Dolittle:** Brian Viner, "If You Can Talk to the Animals, Tell Your Squirrel to Lay Off the Gin! Brian Viner on the Chaos of Creating a £135m Remake of Dr Dolittle," *Daily Mail*, January 29, 2020, https://www.dailymail.co.uk/tvshowbiz/article-7945115/BRIAN-VINER-chaos-creating-135m-remake-Dr-Dolittle.html.

97 **most-viewed show on Netflix:** Samuel Spencer, "Netflix Reveals Its Five Most-Watched Shows Ever," *Newsweek*, January 5, 2021, https://www.newsweek.com/netflix-shows-viewing-figures-most-watched-bridgerton-witcher-tiger-king-stranger-things-money-heist-1558968.

97 **Michael Myers's mask in *Halloween*:** "Was Michael Myers' Halloween Mask William Shatner's Face?," StarTrek.com, October 31, 2020, https://www.startrek.com/article/was-michael-myers-halloween-mask-william-shatners-face.

97 **Pet lizard was run over:** Jo-Anne Rowney, "41 Facts About Titanic the Movie—from Leonardo DiCaprio's Lizard to Kate Winslet's Bid for the Role," *Mirror*, December 19, 2017, updated May 28, 2018, https://www.mirror.co.uk/tv/tv-news/titanic-movie-facts-anniversary-cameron-11720855.

97 **Voiced by the same person, Frank Oz:** "101 Fun Facts You Never Knew, Guaranteed to Totally Blow Your Mind."

97 **Directed by women:** Cara Buckley, "Study of TV Directors Finds Record Level of Diversity," *The New York Times*, November 19, 2019, https://www.nytimes.com/2019/11/19/arts/television/tv-directors-diversity-report.html.

98 *I Love Lucy:* Erik Adams et al., "More Than 60 Years Ago, a Pregnant Lucille Ball Couldn't Call Herself 'Pregnant,'" AV Club, July 24, 2013, https://tv.avclub.com/more-than-60-years-ago-a-pregnant-lucille-ball-couldn-1798239435.

98 **Won more Emmys:** "Which Shows Have Won the Most Emmys of All Time?," AS English, September 20, 2020, https://en.as.com/en/2020/09/19/latest_news/1600526784_007808.html.

98 **Doc Brown's first name:** Brad Frenette, "'Heavy, Doc': 25 Facts About Back to the Future," *National Post*, October 26, 2010, https://nationalpost.com/arts/this-is-heavy-doc-25-facts-about-the-back-to-the-future-trilogy/.

98 **Ewoks in *Star Wars*:** "Short Takes: Family's Dog Helped Inspire 'Jedi' Ewoks, Lucas Testifies," *Los Angeles Times*, January 18, 1990, https://www.latimes.com/archives/la-xpm-1990-01-18-ca-587-story.html.

98 *Jurassic Park:* Kyle Buchanan, "You'll Never Guess How the Dinosaur Sounds in *Jurassic Park* Were Made," *Vulture*, June 9, 2019, https://www.vulture.com/2013/04/how-the-dino-sounds-in-jurassic-park-were-made.html.

98 **Alan Smithee:** Thomas Harlander, "What Ever Happened to Alan Smithee, Hollywood's Worst Director?," *Los Angeles Magazine*, June 4, 2018, https://www.lamag.com/culturefiles/alan-smithee/.

98 **Fred Astaire loved to skateboard:** Martin Chilton, "Hollywood's Seventysomething Skateboarder: Why Fred Astaire's Late-Life Obsession Ended in Disaster," *The Telegraph*, May 8, 2019, https://www.telegraph.co.uk/films/0/hollywoods-seventysomething-skateboarder-fred-astaires-late/.

98 **Redd Pepper:** "Meet Gravesend Man Redd Pepper, the Voice Behind World Famous Film Trailers for *Armageddon*, the *Blair Witch Project* and *Saw*," *Kent Online*, June 2, 2016, https://www.kentonline.co.uk/gravesend/news/meet-the-voice-behind-world-96733/.

99 **"Play it again, Sam":** Matt Goddard, "'Play It Again, Sam' and More Completely Misquoted Famous Lines from Film History to Mark *Casablanca*'s 70th Anniversary," *Mirror*, November 26, 2012, https://www.mirror.co.uk/lifestyle/going-out/film/casablanca-70th-anniversary-the-most-misquoted-1458034.

99 **Scoobert Doo:** Anthony Smith, "Scooby Doo's Real Name Isn't Really Scoobert Doobert," *Business Insider*, July 21, 2017, https://www.businessinsider.com/scooby-doo-real-name-scoobert-doobert-2017-7.

99 **"Let's get out of here":** Janice, "Let's Get out of Here!"—the Most-Used Piece of Dialog in Film History," *Seattle P-I*, May 21, 2010, https://blog.seattlepi.com/movielady/2010/05/21/lets-get-out-of-here-the-most-used-piece-of-dialog-in-film-history/.

The Human Body

102 **Four to six dreams:** "How Often Do We Dream?," Sleep.org, https://www
.sleep.org/how-often-dreams/.

102 **Work out only on weekends:** Ian Sample, "Weekend Workouts Can Benefit
Health as Much as a Week of Exercise, Say Researchers," *The Guardian*, January
9, 2017, https://www.theguardian.com/science/2017/jan/09/weekend-work
outs-nearly-as-good-as-whole-week-of-excercise-researchers-say.

102 **Déjà vu:** Patrick Chauvel, "Deja Vu: What It Is, When It May Be Cause for Concern," The Cleveland Clinic Health Essentials, January 27, 2017, https://health
.clevelandclinic.org/deja-vu-what-it-is-and-when-it-may-be-cause-for-concern/.

102 **Bacteria living on their skin:** Bill Bryson, *A Short History of Nearly Everything:
Special Illustrated Edition* (New York: Crown, 2010).

102 **Body contains 0.2 milligrams of gold:** Molly Oldfield and John Mitchinson,
"QI: Quite Interesting Facts About Gold," *The Telegraph*, July 28, 2011, https://
www.telegraph.co.uk/men/the-filter/qi/8667421/QI-Quite-interesting-facts
-about-gold.html.

102 **Pregnancy uses the same amount of energy:** "Being Pregnant Is Like Running a 40-Week Marathon, Study Says," Fox 8, June 12, 2019, updated June 12,
2019, https://fox8.com/news/being-pregnant-is-like-running-a-40-week-mara
thon-study-says/.

102 **Eating carbs releases the hormone insulin:** Tanya Lewis, "Thanksgiving Myth
Busted: Eating Turkey Won't Make You Sleepy," Live Science, November 26,
2013, https://www.livescience.com/41543-thanksgiving-myth-busted-eating
-turkey-won-t-make-you-sleepy.html.

102 **Femurs are stronger than concrete:** Astrid Lange, "Thigh Bone, Connected
to the Hip Bone, Is Hard as Concrete," *Toronto Star*, February 18, 2013, https://
www.thestar.com/life/health_wellness/2013/02/18/thigh_bone_connected
_to_the_hip_bone_is_hard_as_concrete.html.

102 **Body weight consists of bacteria:** Natalie Wolchover, "Your Body Harbors
Pounds of Microbes, Study Reveals," Live Science, June 15, 2012, https://www
.livescience.com/34004-microbes-human-body.html.

102 **Parent loses approximately 350 hours:** "Sleep Deprivation and New Parents,"
HealthDay News, December 31, 2019, https://consumer.healthday.com/encyclo
pedia/parenting-31/parenting-health-news-525/sleep-deprivation-and-new
-parents-643886.html.

103 **Tickle yourself:** David Robson, "Why Can't You Tickle Yourself?," BBC, January
9, 2015, https://www.bbc.com/future/article/20150109-why-you-cant-tickle
-yourself.

103 **Goose bumps:** George A. Bubenik, "Why Do Humans Get 'Goosebumps' When
They Are Cold, or Under Other Circumstances?," *Scientific American*, September

1, 2003, https://www.scientificamerican.com/article/why-do-humans-get-goosebu/.

103 **Turns food into alcohol:** Megan Henry, "How a Rare Condition Causes a Columbus Man to Produce Alcohol in His Gut, Act Drunk," *The Columbus Dispatch,* June 20, 2020, https://www.dispatch.com/story/lifestyle/health-fitness/2020/06/20/how-rare-condition-causes-columbus-man-to-produce-alcohol-in-his-gut-act-drunk/112773580/.

103 **Blue eyes has a common ancestor:** Hans Eiberg et al., "Blue Eye Color in Humans May Be Caused by a Perfectly Associated Founder Mutation in a Regulatory Element Located Within the HERC2 Gene Inhibiting OCA2 Expression," *Human Genetics,* ScienceDaily, https://www.sciencedaily.com/releases/2008/01/080130170343.htm.

103 **Shed about 1.5 pounds of skin:** Nina Bell, "You Do Shed Your Skin and It's Good for You!," *The Meadville Tribune,* October 15, 2013, updated September 4, 2014, https://www.meadvilletribune.com/archives/you-do-shed-your-skin-and-its-good-for-you/article_125ee27f-31bf-58c2-892b-d155258174ac.html.

103 **When you blush:** Tony Yeung, "When You Blush, the Lining of Your Stomach Also Turns Red," *Toronto Star,* November 20, 2012, https://www.thestar.com/life/2012/11/20/when_you_blush_the_lining_of_your_stomach_also_turns_red.html.

103 **Cancer patients treated in the United States:** Jane E. Brody, "Cancer Treatment at the End of Life," *The New York Times,* August 5, 2019, https://www.nytimes.com/2019/08/05/well/live/cancer-treatment-at-the-end-of-life.html.

103 **Cured of HIV:** Maria Cohut, "2nd Person Cured of HIV Thanks to Stem Cell Transplant," Medical News Today, March 11, 2020, https://www.medicalnewstoday.com/articles/2nd-person-cured-of-hiv-thanks-to-stem-cell-transplant.

103 "**Muscle confusion**": Brad Stulberg, "'Muscle Confusion' Is Mostly a Myth," The Cut, *New York,* https://www.thecut.com/2016/08/workout-plans-based-on-muscle-confusion-dont-work.html.

103 **Blind has ever been diagnosed with schizophrenia:** Shayla Love, "People Born Blind Are Mysteriously Protected from Schizophrenia," *Vice,* February 11, 2020, https://www.vice.com/en_us/article/939qbz/people-born-blind-are-mysteriously-protected-from-schizophrenia.

104 **Taller in the morning:** Michael Hinck, "Are We Taller in the Morning?," Jamaica Hospital Medical Center, May 8, 2015, https://jamaicahospital.org/newsletter/are-we-taller-in-the-morning/.

104 **Save up to three people's lives:** "Blood Needs & Blood Supply," Blood Services, American Red Cross, https://www.redcrossblood.org/donate-blood/how-to-donate/how-blood-donations-help/blood-needs-blood-supply.html.

104 **Gum, it'll be there for a day or two:** "Swallowing Gum: Is It Harmful?," Mayo Clinic, https://www.mayoclinic.org/digestive-system/expert-answers/faq-20058446.

104 **We blink so often:** Joseph Stromberg, "Why Do We Blink So Frequently?," *Smithsonian Magazine*, December 24, 2012, https://www.smithsonianmag.com /science-nature/why-do-we-blink-so-frequently-172334883/.

104 **Men sweat more:** Todd R. Nelson, "Myth or Fact: Men Sweat More Than Women," Aurora Health Care, October 12, 2016, https://www.aurorahealthcare .org/patients-visitors/blog/myth-or-fact-men-sweat-more-than-women.

104 **Sleeping on their side:** E. S. Skarpsno, "Sleep Positions and Nocturnal Body Movements Based on Free-Living Accelerometer Recordings: Association with Demographics, Lifestyle, and Insomnia Symptoms," Dove Press, November 1, 2017, https://www.dovepress.com/sleep-positions-and-nocturnal-body-move ments-based-on-free-living-acce-peer-reviewed-fulltext-article-NSS.

104 **Fist bumps spread only:** Shirley Li, "Science Proves Fist Bumps Are Better Than High Fives," *The Atlantic*, July 28, 2014, https://www.theatlantic.com/cul ture/archive/2014/07/science-proves-fist-bumps-are-better-than-high-fives /375179/.

104 **Tooth is the only body part that can't repair:** Nathaniel Scharping, "Teaching Our Teeth to Heal Themselves," *Discover Magazine*, January 9, 2017, https:// www.discovermagazine.com/health/teaching-our-teeth-to-heal-themselves.

104 **Flu shot:** Samantha Lauriello, "How Long Does It Take for the Flu Shot to Be Effective?," Health, updated January 29, 2021, https://www.health.com/condi tion/cold-flu-sinus/how-long-for-flu-shot-effective.

104 **Lose a pound every night while sleeping:** Lauriello, "How Long Does It Take?"

104 **Hair to grow back thicker:** "Does Shaving Unwanted Body Hair Make It Grow Back Thicker and Darker?," Mayo Clinic, https://www.mayoclinic.org/healthy -lifestyle/adult-health/expert-answers/hair-removal/faq-20058427.

105 **Seven percent of your body weight:** Rachel Nall, "How Much Blood Is in Your Body and How Much You Can Lose," Healthline, updated July 18, 2017, https:// www.healthline.com/health/how-much-blood-in-human-body.

105 **Dimples are caused by:** Alicia Ault, "Ask Smithsonian: What Is a Dimple?," *Smithsonian Magazine*, August 30, 2016, https://www.smithsonianmag.com /smithsonian-institution/ask-smithsonian-what-is-dimple-180960272/.

105 **Sneeze travels about 100:** "How Fast Is a Sneeze Versus a Cough? Cover Your Mouth Either Way!," Each Breath, American Lung Association, May 12, 2016, https://www.lung.org/blog/sneeze-versus-cough.

105 **Men to lactate:** Joseph Castro, "Can Men Lactate?," Live Science, May 31, 2014, https://www.livescience.com/45732-can-men-lactate.html.

105 **Humans are the only animals with chins:** Ed Yong, "We're the Only Animals with Chins, and No One Knows Why," *The Atlantic*, January 28, 2016, https:// www.theatlantic.com/science/archive/2016/01/were-the-only-animals-with -chins-and-no-one-knows-why/431625/.

105 **White blood cells, to be specific:** Emma Davies, "What Are the Wiggly Things I See in My Eyes When I Look at the Sky?," Science Focus, https://www.science

focus.com/the-human-body/what-are-the-wiggly-things-i-see-in-my-eyes -when-i-look-at-the-sky/.

105 **Causing more bloat:** Ashley Mateo, "Why Am I Bloated After a Workout and How Do I Get Rid of It?," *Runner's World*, June 18, 2020, https://www.runner sworld.com/nutrition-weight-loss/a25949096/why-am-i-bloated/; Zoe Weiner, "Trainers Say the 'Superman Exercise' Is the Best Way to Work Your Obliques and Back," Well + Good, June 2, 2020, https://www.wellandgood.com/superman -exercises/; Samantha Lauriello, "Is Workout Bloat a Thing? An Expert Explains," Health, updated January 29, 2021, https://www.health.com/fitness/bloated -after-workout.

105 **A lot of eyelashes:** Sarah Aumond and Etty Bitton, "The Eyelash Follicle Features and Anomalies: A Review," *Journal of Optometry*, US National Library of Medicine, National Institutes of Health, July 17, 2018, https://www.ncbi.nlm .nih.gov/pmc/articles/PMC6147748/.

105 **You cannot snore and dream:** Clayton Dillon, "Is It Possible to Snore and Dream at the Same Time?," Snoring Source, updated January 12, 2021, https:// www.snoringsource.com/can-you-snore-and-dream/.

105 **Thumbs have their own pulse:** "Taking a Pulse (Heart Rate)," MyHealth.Alberta, https://myhealth.alberta.ca/Health/Pages/conditions.aspx?hwid=hw201 445&lang=en-ca.

History

107 **President James Garfield:** Sarah Pruitt, "The First Left-handed President Was Ambidextrous and Multilingual," History.com, August 13, 2018, updated September 1, 2018, https://www.history.com/news/first-left-handed-president -ambidextrous-multilingual.

108 **Women gladiators:** Natalie Haynes, "Did Female Gladiators Exist?," BBC, November 24, 2015, https://www.bbc.com/culture/article/20151120-did-female -gladiators-exist.

108 **Harriet Tubman:** Allison Keyes, "Harriet Tubman, an Unsung Naturalist, Used Owl Calls as a Signal on the Underground Railroad," Audubon, February 25, 2020, https://www.audubon.org/news/harriet-tubman-unsung-naturalist-used -owl-calls-signal-underground-railroad.

108 **Nobel Prize was created as part:** Lawrence K. Altman, "Alfred Nobel and the Prize That Almost Didn't Happen," *The New York Times*, September 26, 2006, https://www.nytimes.com/2006/09/26/health/26docs.html.

108 *I have a dream:* "USF Professor Recalls Role In King's 'I Have a Dream' Speech," KPIX 5, August 20, 2013, https://sanfrancisco.cbslocal.com/2013/08/20/usf -professor-recalls-role-in-kings-i-have-a-dream-speech/.

108 **Winston Churchill came to the:** Natasha Geiling, "The Day Winston Churchill Lost His Cigar," *Smithsonian Magazine*, November 19, 2013, https://www.smith

sonianmag.com/smithsonian-institution/the-day-winston-churchill-lost-his
-cigar-180947770/; Justine Sterling, "Winston Churchill Got a Prescription for
Alcohol During Prohibition," *Food & Wine*, updated May 24, 2017, https://www
.foodandwine.com/news/winston-churchill-got-prescription-alcohol-during
-prohibition.

108 **Several small children were mailed:** Danny Lewis, "A Brief History of Children
Sent Through the Mail," *Smithsonian Magazine*, June 14, 2016, updated December
21, 2016, https://www.smithsonianmag.com/smart-news/brief-history
-children-sent-through-mail-180959372/.

108 **Bush and Senator John Kerry:** Matt Sedensky, "Bush vs. Kerry? They're Distant
Cousins," NBC News, February 17, 2004, http://www.nbcnews.com/id/4286105
/ns/technology_and_science-science/t/bush-vs-kerry-theyre-distant-cousins/#
.XzmQ3C2z0_U.

108 **All citizens of New Jersey:** Jennifer Schuessler, "On the Trail of America's First
Women to Vote," *The New York Times*, February 24, 2020, updated August 7,
2020, https://www.nytimes.com/2020/02/24/arts/first-women-voters-new
-jersey.html.

108 **Egyptians shaved off their eyebrows:** "Cats Rule in Egypt," *National
Geographic,* https://kids.nationalgeographic.com/explore/cats-rule-in-ancient
-egypt/.

109 **Napoleon was a little over 5'5":** Barbara Stepko, "Napoleon and the Battle of
the Rabbits: Faced with the Implacable Animal Horde, the Emperor Beat a Hasty
Retreat," *The Vintage News*, May 18, 2018, https://www.thevintagenews.com
/2018/05/18/napoleon-and-the-battle-of-the-rabbits/.

109 **President Boris Yeltsin:** Becky Little, "When a Russian President Ended Up
Drunk and Disrobed Outside the White House," History.com, April 3, 2018, updated August 30, 2018, https://www.history.com/news/bill-clinton-boris
-yeltsin-drunk-1994-russian-state-visit.

109 **Theodore Roosevelt was shot:** Christopher Klein, "When Teddy Roosevelt
Was Shot in 1912, a Speech May Have Saved His Life," History.com, October 12,
2012, updated July 21, 2019, https://www.history.com/news/shot-in-the-chest
-100-years-ago-teddy-roosevelt-kept-on-talking.

109 **Caligula:** Elizabeth Nix, "Did Caligula Really Make His Horse a Consul?," History
.com, June 21, 2016, updated August 30, 2018, https://www.history.com/news
/did-caligula-really-make-his-horse-a-consul.

109 **Freddie and Truus Oversteegen:** Becky Little, "This Teenager Killed Nazis with
Her Sister During WWII," History.com, September 19, 2018, updated March 1,
2019, https://www.history.com/news/dutch-resistance-teenager-killed-nazis
-freddie-oversteegen.

109 **Horoscope is from 410 BCE:** J. V. Stewart, *Astrology: What's Really in the Stars*
(Amherst, NY: Prometheus Books, 1996).

110 **"She sells seashells":** Fiona Pepper and Julie Street, "Mary Anning Inspired 'She Sells Sea Shells'—but She Was Actually a Legendary Fossil Hunter," Late Night Live, ABC Radio National, May 5, 2019, https://www.abc.net.au/news/2019-05 -06/mary-anning-legendary-female-fossilist-inspired-seashell-rhyme/11055404.

110 **Ronald Reagan saved:** Ted Gregory, "Ronald Reagan Lifeguard-Statue Plan Standing Still in Dixon," *Chicago Tribune*, January 5, 2017, https://www.chicago tribune.com/news/ct-ronald-reagan-lifeguard-statue-met-20170104-story.html.

110 **Domestic partners:** Judith Scherr, "Berkeley, Activists Set Milestone for Domestic Partnerships in 1984," *East Bay Times*, June 28, 2013, https://www.eastbay times.com/2013/06/28/berkeley-activists-set-milestone-for-domestic-partner ships-in-1984/.

110 **America has used fireworks:** "Fourth of July—Independence Day," History.com, December 16, 2019, updated January 8, 2021, https://www.history .com/topics/holidays/july-4th.

110 **Ancient Mayans most likely used:** Joshua Rapp, "The Maya Civilization Used Chocolate as Money," *Science Magazine*, June 27, 2018, https://www.science mag.org/news/2018/06/maya-civilization-used-chocolate-money?.

110 **Vote from space:** Hillary Brady and Amy Stamm, "How Do Astronauts Vote from Space?," Smithsonian National Air and Space Museum, November 2, 2020, https://airandspace.si.edu/stories/editorial/how-do-astronauts-vote-space.

110 **Lincoln had grown his signature beard:** "Handwritten Letters Which Made History," Pen Heaven, https://www.penheaven.co.uk/blog/handwritten-letters -which-made-history/.

110 **Employment-based healthcare:** Aaron E. Carroll, "The Real Reason the U.S. Has Employer-Sponsored Health Insurance," *The New York Times*, September 5, 2017, https://www.nytimes.com/2017/09/05/upshot/the-real-reason-the -us-has-employer-sponsored-health-insurance.html.

111 **$10,000 bill:** Cindy Perman, "10 Things You Probably Don't Know About Money," CNBC, February 1, 2011, updated September 13, 2013, https://www.cnbc.com /2011/02/01/10-Things-You-Probably-Dont-Know-About-Money.html.

111 **Al Capone:** Christopher Klein, "Mobster Al Capone Ran a Soup Kitchen During the Great Depression," History.com, April 5, 2019, https://www.history.com /news/al-capone-great-depression-soup-kitchen.

111 **Kings of a playing card deck:** "How Did Playing Cards Get Their Symbols?," Vanishing Inc., https://www.vanishingincmagic.com/playing-cards/articles/how -did-playing-cards-get-their-symbols/.

111 **Coffee for their caffeine fix:** Tori Avey, "The Caffeinated History of Coffee," PBS.org, April 8, 2013, https://www.pbs.org/food/the-history-kitchen/history -coffee/.

111 **He once accidentally left nuclear:** John Donovan, "President Bill Clinton Lost Nuclear Codes While in Office, New Book Claims," ABC News, October 20, 2010,

https://abcnews.go.com/WN/president-bill-clinton-lost-nuclear-codes-office
-book/story?id=11930878&page=2.

111 **Milky Way stopped forming stars:** Matt Williams, "We're in the Milky Way's
Second Life. Star Formation Was Shut Down for Billions of Years," Universe Today,
August 26, 2018, https://www.universetoday.com/139823/were-in-the-milky
-ways-second-life-star-formation-was-shut-down-for-billions-of-years/.

112 **John Harvard in Harvard Yard:** "The 3 Lies of Harvard," Harvard Division of
Continuing Education, July 31, 2015, https://blog.dce.harvard.edu/summer
/3-lies-harvard.

112 **Launch a rocket in the rain:** Chelsea Gohd, "50 Years Ago: NASA's Apollo 12 Was
Struck by Lightning Right After Launch . . . Twice!," Space.com, November 14, 2019,
https://www.space.com/apollo-12-lightning-strike-twice-launch-video.html.

112 **Name all hurricanes after women:** Sam Roberts, "Roxcy Bolton, Feminist Cru-
sader for Equality, Including in Naming Hurricanes, Dies at 90," *The New York
Times*, May 21, 2017, https://www.nytimes.com/2017/05/21/us/roxcy-bolton
-dead-feminist-hurricane-names.html.

112 **Plato's name wasn't Plato:** Damon Young, "Plato Said Knock You Out," *Psychology Today*, February 9, 2015, https://www.psychologytoday.com/us/blog
/how-think-about-exercise/201502/plato-said-knock-you-out.

112 **Cleopatra:** Stacy Schiff, *Cleopatra* (New York: Little, Brown and Company, 2011).

112 **Jackson had a parrot:** "Polly Want a WHAT?! Andrew Jackson's Pet Parrot,"
Presidential Pet Museum, March 3, 2016, http://www.presidentialpetmuseum
.com/pets/andrew-jacksons-pet-parrot/.

112 **"Uncle Sam":** "The United States Gets the Nickname Uncle Sam," History.co.uk,
https://www.history.co.uk/this-day-in-history/07-september/the-united-states
-gets-the-nickname-uncle-sam.

112 **"Knocker upper":** Sitala Peek, "Knocker Uppers: Waking Up the Workers in In-
dustrial Britain," BBC News, March 27, 2016, https://www.bbc.com/news/uk-en
gland-35840393.

112 **Queen Isabella of Castile:** Meghan Ferrara, "Spain's Catholic Chess Queen," *Regina
Magazine*, April 8, 2015, https://reginamag.com/spains-catholic-chess-queen/.

113 **First woman in space:** Nick Clark, "First Woman in Space Reveals What Crucial
Piece of Kit Was Missing on Her 1963 Mission," *The Independent*, September 17,
2015, https://www.independent.co.uk/news/people/first-woman-in-space
-reveals-what-crucial-piece-kit-was-missing-her-1963-mission-10506688.html.

113 **Sally Ride:** Erin Blakemore, "When Sally Ride Took Her First Space Flight, Sexism
Was the Norm," History.com, June 18, 2018, updated March 6, 2019, https://
www.history.com/news/sally-ride-first-astronaut-sexism.

113 **Hitler's food to "feminize" him:** "The 'Bizarre' Plan to Turn Hitler into a
Woman," *The Week*, August 17, 2011, https://theweek.com/articles/482449
/bizarre-plan-turn-hitler-into-woman.

113 **Pirates wore earrings:** Remy Melina, "Why Did Pirates Wear Earrings?," Live Science, March 8, 2011, https://www.livescience.com/33099-why-did-pirates -wear-earrings-.html.

113 **"Posture photos":** Ron Rosenbaum, "The Great Ivy League Nude Posture Photo Scandal," *The New York Times Magazine*, January 15, 1995, https://www.ny times.com/1995/01/15/magazine/the-great-ivy-league-nude-posture-photo -scandal.html.

113 **Vikings didn't have horns:** Elizabeth Nix, "Did Vikings Really Wear Horned Helmets?," History.com, March 20, 2013, updated September 4, 2018, https:// www.history.com/news/did-vikings-really-wear-horned-helmets.

114 **The handshake was created:** Evan Andrews, "The History of the Handshake," History.com, August 9, 2016, updated March 16, 2020, https://www.history .com/news/what-is-the-origin-of-the-handshake.

114 **Pauline Wayne:** Brian Resnick and National Journal, "For Years, the Washington Post Tried to Interview a Cow," *The Atlantic*, February 5, 2015, https://www .theatlantic.com/politics/archive/2015/02/for-years-the-washington-post -tried-to-interview-a-cow/453507/.

114 **The Leaning Tower of Pisa:** Brigit Katz, "The Leaning Tower of Pisa Has Gotten a Little Straighter," *Smithsonian Magazine*, November 23, 2018, https://www .smithsonianmag.com/smart-news/leaning-tower-pisa-has-gotten-little -straighter-180970882/.

114 **Founding fathers John Adams and:** Natasha Frost, "Two Presidents Died on the Same July 4: Coincidence or Something More?," History.com, July 3, 2018, updated September 4, 2018, https://www.history.com/news/july-4-two -presidents-died-same-day-coincidence.

114 **July 2, 1776:** "1776: July 04: Continental Congress Adopts the Declaration of Independence," History.com, https://www.history.com/this-day-in-history/ameri can-colonies-declare-independence.

114 **Hundred Years' War:** Laura Schumm, "How Long Was the Hundred Years' War?," History.com, April 11, 2016, updated August 30, 2018, https://www .history.com/news/how-long-was-the-hundred-years-war.

114 **Vikings gave kittens:** Amanda Scherker, "5 Obscure Wedding Traditions We Should Definitely Bring Back," *HuffPost*, November 12, 2014, updated December 6, 2017, https://www.huffpost.com/entry/wedding-traditions-to-bring-back _n_6139992.

115 **Debated laws twice:** Chunka Mui, "Big Decision? Consider It Both Drunk and Sober," *Forbes*, March 22, 2016, https://www.forbes.com/sites/chunkamui /2016/03/22/wine-and-sleep-make-for-better-decisions/#66d9e8a124b1.

115 **Caesar was once captured:** "The Time Julius Caesar Was Captured by Pirates," Britannica, https://www.britannica.com/story/the-time-julius-caesar-was -captured-by-pirates.

115 **Napoleon Bonaparte penned a romance:** Chris Irvine, "Napoleon Bonaparte—
the Romantic Novelist," *The Telegraph*, May 8, 2009, https://www.telegraph
.co.uk/news/worldnews/europe/france/5293757/Napoleon-Bonaparte-the
-romantic-novelist.html.

115 **Alice Roosevelt Longworth:** Leah Silverman, "Alice Roosevelt Longworth: The
Original White House Wild Child," All That's Interesting, March 26, 2019,
updated June 12, 2020, https://allthatsinteresting.com/alice-roosevelt-long
worth.

115 **The Roman goddess of sorcery:** David Arthur Walters, "The Goddess Trivia,"
AuthorsDen, September 17, 2006, updated September 17, 2006, http://www
.authorsden.com/visit/viewarticle.asp?id=24212.

Love the Lewk (On Beauty, Style & Fashion)

118 **"Beauty sleep":** University of Manchester, "Beauty Sleep Could Be Real, Say
Body Clock Biologists," ScienceDaily, January 15, 2020, https://www.sciencedaily
.com/releases/2020/01/200115120626.htm.

118 **Colored their hair:** Sarah Marshall, "When, and Why, Did Women Start Dyeing
Their Gray Hair?," *Elle*, September 18, 2015, https://www.elle.com/beauty/hair
/news/a30556/when-and-why-did-women-start-dyeing-their-gray-hair/.

119 **The left side of our face:** Kashmira Gander, "The 'Good Side' of a Person's Face
Revealed in New Study," *The Independent*, April 17, 2017, https://www.indepen
dent.co.uk/life-style/best-side-how-find-selfie-attractive-left-psychology
-photo-instagram-brain-a7686891.html.

119 **"Black Friday":** Sarah Pruitt, "What's the Real History of Black Friday?," History
.com, November 23, 2015, updated November 13, 2020, https://www.history
.com/news/whats-the-real-history-of-black-friday.

119 **Early years of the Roman Empire:** Rebecca Guenard, "Hair Dye: A History,"
The Atlantic, January 2, 2015, https://www.theatlantic.com/health/archive
/2015/01/hair-dye-a-history/383934/.

119 **Phoenicians used to "dye":** Marshall, "When, and Why, Did Women Start
Dyeing Their Gray Hair?"

119 **Mark Twain invented the bra clasp:** Rebecca Greenfield, "Celebrity Invention:
Mark Twain's Elastic-Clasp Brassiere Strap," *The Atlantic*, July 1, 2011, https://
www.theatlantic.com/technology/archive/2011/07/celebrity-invention-mark
-twains-elastic-clasp-brassiere-strap/241267/.

119 **Pink and blue:** Jeanne Maglaty, "When Did Girls Start Wearing Pink?," *Smithsonian Magazine*, April 7, 2011, https://www.smithsonianmag.com/arts-culture
/when-did-girls-start-wearing-pink-1370097/.

119 **When the bikini was first:** "Bikini Atoll Revolutionized the Swimsuit 70 Years
Ago," NBC News, updated July 5, 2016, https://www.nbcnews.com/slideshow
/bikini-atoll-revolutionized-swimsuit-70-years-ago-n604156.

119 **Vein that ran directly from your heart:** Jessie Mooney DiGiovanna, "Everything You Need to Know About Ring Fingers," *Brides*, updated September 11, 2020, https://www.brides.com/story/why-are-wedding-rings-worn-on-left-hand.

120 **The color purple:** Remy Melina, "Why Is the Color Purple Associated with Royalty?," Live Science, June 3, 2011, https://www.livescience.com/33324-purple-royal-color.html.

120 **Male-pattern baldness:** Hilary Brueck, "A Bald Head Is Not All Your Mom's Fault—These Are the Other Factors That Can Cause You to Lose Your Hair," *Business Insider*, March 27, 2018, https://www.businessinsider.com/baldness-genes-going-bald-isnt-all-your-mothers-fault-2018-3.

120 **Yoko Ono married:** Rebecca Carhart, "Keds Has Been Around for 102 Years, and the Brand's History Is Fascinating," PopSugar UK, October 11, 2008, https://www.popsugar.co.uk/fashion/photo-gallery/45368994/image/45368990/Rise-Popularity.

120 **Jeans were called "jean":** "History of Jeans and Denim," History of Jeans, http://www.historyofjeans.com.

120 **The oldest evidence of human tattoos:** Cate Lineberry, "Tattoos: The Ancient and Mysterious History," *Smithsonian Magazine*, January 1, 2007, https://www.smithsonianmag.com/history/tattoos-144038580/.

120 **Wear high heels were men:** Ariana Marsh, "High Heeled Shoes Were Originally Created for Men," *Teen Vogue*, July 12, 2017, https://www.teenvogue.com/story/heels-history-men.

120 **Illegal to wear stripes:** Emily Eakin, "When Fashion Decreed Stripes a Capital Crime," *The New York Times*, June 9, 2001, https://www.nytimes.com/2001/06/09/books/when-fashion-decreed-stripes-a-capital-crime.html.

120 **"Pop Goes the Weasel":** "The Meaning and Origin of the Expression: Pop Goes the Weasel," The Phrase Finder, https://www.phrases.org.uk/meanings/pop-goes-the-weasel.html.

120 **"Liquid stockings":** Emily Spivack, "Paint-on Hosiery During the War Years," *Smithsonian Magazine*, September 10, 2012, https://www.smithsonianmag.com/arts-culture/paint-on-hosiery-during-the-war-years-29864389/.

121 **Imposed a beard tax during their reigns:** Kat Eschner, "Why Peter the Great Established a Beard Tax," *Smithsonian Magazine*, September 5, 2017, https://www.smithsonianmag.com/smart-news/why-tsar-peter-great-established-beard-tax-180964693/.

121 **Marc Jacobs has a SpongeBob:** Amy Larocco, "Marc Jacobs on Tattoos in the Fashion Industry," The Cut, *New York*, August 11, 2013, https://www.thecut.com/2013/08/marc-jacobs-on-tattoos-in-the-fashion-industry.html.

121 **Ancient Greek dramatic actors:** Renee Jacques, "11 Facts About Shoes That Will Knock Your Socks Off," *HuffPost*, January 15, 2015, updated December 6, 2017, https://www.huffpost.com/entry/facts-about-shoes-knocked-socks-off_n_6456712.

121 **Fastest-growing hair:** Joseph Castro, "How Fast Does Hair Grow?," Live Science, January 27, 2014, https://www.livescience.com/42868-how-fast-does-hair-grow.html.

121 **American owns seven pairs of jeans:** Leah Melby Clinton, "You Probably Own WAY Too Many Pairs of Jeans," *Glamour*, December 9, 2014, https://www.glamour.com/story/how-many-jeans-owned-average.

121 **Men really do prefer ladies in red:** "Red on Women Drives Men Wild," Live Science, October 28, 2008, https://www.livescience.com/5136-red-women-drives-men-wild.html.

121 **Elizabeth Taylor's last wishes:** Jonathan Brown, "As a Final Act, Elizabeth Taylor Is Late for Her Own Funeral," *The Independent*, March 26, 2011, https://www.independent.co.uk/news/world/americas/as-a-final-act-elizabeth-taylor-is-late-for-her-own-funeral-2253475.html.

121 **Dyed socks used to contain arsenic:** Joe Schwarcz, "The Right Chemistry: The Case of the Toxic Socks," *Montreal Gazette*, February 10, 2017, https://montrealgazette.com/technology/science/the-right-chemistry-the-case-of-the-toxic-socks.

121 **"Aloha Friday":** Megan Garber, "Casual Friday and the 'End of the Office Dress Code,'" *The Atlantic*, May 25, 2016, https://www.theatlantic.com/entertainment/archive/2016/05/casual-friday-and-the-end-of-the-office-dress-code/484334/.

121 **Tiny pocket within your jeans':** Anna De Souza, "Why Do Jeans Have That Tiny Pocket? There Is a Reason," *Today*, June 28, 2017, https://www.today.com/style/why-do-jeans-have-tiny-pocket-t113216.

Technology

124 **World's smallest commercial camera:** Chris George, "World's Smallest Camera Is the Size of a Grain of Sand," Digital Camera World, February 6, 2020, https://www.digitalcameraworld.com/news/worlds-smallest-camera-is-the-size-of-a-grain-of-sand.

124 **Larry Bird:** Rosa Golijan, "The Twitter Bird Has a Name: Larry," *Today*, February 28, 2012, https://www.today.com/money/twitter-bird-has-name-larry-235179.

124 **Zuckerberg is red-green colorblind:** Hayley Tsukayama, "10 Surprising Facts About Mark Zuckerberg," *The Washington Post*, May 30, 2012, https://www.washingtonpost.com/business/technology/10-surprising-facts-about-mark-zuckerberg/2012/05/30/gJQAJ9yJ2U_story.html.

124 **Sony came out with a camera:** "Sony's Naked Cam Scam?," CNN Money, August 14, 1998, https://money.cnn.com/1998/08/14/technology/camera_pkg/.

124 **Video games three or more hours per week:** Andrew Stern, "Surgeons Who Play Video Games More Skilled: Study," Reuters, September 15, 2016, https://www.reuters.com/article/us-surgery-games/surgeons-who-play-video-games-more-skilled-study-idUSN2J30397820070219.

124 **Steve Jobs (intentionally) dropped the first iPod:** David W. Brown, "In Praise of Bad Steve," *The Atlantic*, October 6, 2011, https://www.theatlantic .com/technology/archive/2011/10/in-praise-of-bad-steve/246242/.

124 **MikeRoweSoft.com:** Munir Kotadia, "MikeRoweSoft Settles for an Xbox," CNET, January 26, 2004, https://www.cnet.com/news/mikerowesoft-settles-for -an-xbox/.

125 **Flashing a peace sign:** Lars Rehm, "Flashing a Peace Sign in a Photo Could Lead to Identity Theft," *DP Review*, January 17, 2017, https://www.dpreview.com/news /1806278172/flashing-a-peace-sign-in-a-photo-could-lead-to-identity-theft.

125 **Amazon rating:** Sapna Maheshwari, "When Is a Star Not Always a Star? When It's an Online Review," *The New York Times*, November 28, 2019, https://www .nytimes.com/2019/11/28/business/online-reviews-fake.html.

125 **Air curtains:** "Selection Guide," Air Curtains for Less, https://aircurtainsforless.com.

125 **VCR:** Yazhou Sun and Sophia Yan, "R.I.P.: The World's Last VCR Will Be Manufactured This Month," CNN Business, July 22, 2016, https://money.cnn.com /2016/07/22/technology/vcr-funai-last/index.html.

125 **Pokémon:** Katy Steinmetz, "The Surprising History Behind the Word *Pokémon*," *Time*, July 19, 2016, https://time.com/4411912/pokemon-go-word-origin/.

125 **Instagram filters became popular:** "8 Strange Baby Name Trends That Defined the 2010s," Fatherly, December 11, 2019, https://www.fatherly.com/love -money/baby-names-2010s/.

125 **Google's original name:** "101 Fun Facts You Never Knew, Guaranteed to Totally Blow Your Mind."

125 *Donkey Kong* **as Jumpman:** Tom Huddleston Jr., "'Super Mario Bros.' Debuted 33 Years Ago—Here's How Mario Accidentally Became a Gaming Superstar," CNBC, September 13, 2018, updated September 13, 2018, https://www.cnbc .com/2018/09/13/super-mario-bros-how-shigeru-miyamoto-created-mario-for -nintendo.html.

125 **Six thousand tweets:** David Sayce, "The Number of Tweets Per Day in 2020," https://www.dsayce.com/social-media/tweets-day/.

126 **Ninety percent of texts:** Cheryl Conner, "Fifty Essential Mobile Marketing Facts," *Forbes*, November 12, 2013, https://www.forbes.com/sites/cherylsnap pconner/2013/11/12/fifty-essential-mobile-marketing-facts/#64e97a527475.

126 **Nokia made everything:** Kline Finley, "Hey, Nokia Isn't Just a Company That Used to Make Phones," *Wired*, April 27, 2016, https://www.wired.com/2016/04 /hey-nokia-isnt-just-company-used-make-phones/.

126 **Allied forces had at their disposal:** Michio Kaku, "Your Cell Phone Has More Computing Power Than NASA Circa 1969," excerpt from *Physics of the Future* (New York: Doubleday, 2011).

126 **Fax machine was invented in 1843:** "The Invention of the Fax Machine," Ency clopedia.com, updated February 2, 2021, https://www.encyclopedia.com/sci ence/encyclopedias-almanacs-transcripts-and-maps/invention-fax-machine.

126 **Robots seem more trustworthy:** Dan Robitzski, "Scientists Built a Robot with a Sense of Irony. It's Insufferable," Futurism, June 12, 2019, https://futurism.com /the-byte/scientists-insufferable-robot-irony.

126 **Bill Gates invested $150 million:** Catherine Clifford, "When Microsoft Saved Apple: Steve Jobs and Bill Gates Show Eliminating Competition Isn't the Only Way to Win," CNBC, August 29, 2017, updated June 12, 2020, https://www .cnbc.com/2017/08/29/steve-jobs-and-bill-gates-what-happened-when-micro soft-saved-apple.html.

126 **Crash test dummies:** DE Guest, "Crash Test Dummies Get Older, and Better," Digital Engineering 247, July 1, 2018, https://www.digitalengineering247.com /article/crash-test-dummies-get-older-and-better/.

126 **We touch our phones:** Natasha Singer, "How Companies Scour Our Digital Lives for Clues to Our Health," *The New York Times*, February 25, 2018, https://www.nytimes.com/2018/02/25/technology/smartphones-mental -health.html.

126 **Measured in a unit called Mickeys:** Picard, "35 Coolest Random Pieces of Trivia That Will Impress Your Friends."

126 **Rubik's Cube in under:** Kacey Deamer, "New Record! Robot Solves Rubik's Cube in Less Than a Second," Live Science, November 11, 2016, https://www.live science.com/56828-robot-sets-rubiks-cube-world-record.html.

126 **Playing *Tetris* after a traumatic:** Ruhr-University Bochum, "Post-Traumatic Stress Disorder: Alleviating Flashbacks by Playing Tetris," ScienceDaily, January 8, 2019, https://www.sciencedaily.com/releases/2019/01/190108095114.htm.

127 **Impossible to block Mark Zuckerberg:** Ashley Carman, "Facebook Quietly Fixed an Error that Prevented You from Blocking Mark Zuckerberg," *The Verge*, December 15, 2017, https://www.theverge.com/2017/12/15/16782352/block -mark-zuckerberg-facebook.

127 **Instagram's original name:** Megan Garber, "Instagram Was First Called 'Burbn,'" *The Atlantic*, July 2, 2014, https://www.theatlantic.com/technology /archive/2014/07/instagram-used-to-be-called-brbn/373815/.

127 **Typing speed is getting faster all the time:** Aalto University, "Smartphone Typing Speeds Catching Up with Keyboards," ScienceDaily, October 2, 2019, https://www.sciencedaily.com/releases/2019/10/191002075925.htm.

127 **More than half of the elements:** Madison Margolin, "The Periodic Table of iPhone Elements," *Vice*, November 29, 2016, https://www.vice.com/en_us /article/nz7kwm/the-periodic-table-of-iphone-elements.

127 **CIA reads 5 million of our tweets:** Tim Mak, "AP: CIA Eyes up to 5M Tweets a Day," *Politico*, November 4, 2011, https://www.politico.com/story/2011/11 /ap-cia-eyes-up-to-5m-tweets-a-day-067619.

127 ***Castlevania*:** Nick Wanserski et al., "30 Years of Night: A Musical History of Castlevania," AV Club, September 26, 2016, https://games.avclub.com/30 -years-of-night-a-musical-history-of-castlevania-1798252346.

127 **Internet access a basic human right:** Catherine Howell and Darrell M. West, "The Internet as a Human Right," Brookings, November 7, 2016, https://www .brookings.edu/blog/techtank/2016/11/07/the-internet-as-a-human-right/.

Human Nature

130 **Compassion is instinctive:** Emma Seppälä, "Compassion: Our First Instinct," *Psychology Today*, June 3, 2013, https://www.psychologytoday.com/us/blog /feeling-it/201306/compassion-our-first-instinct.

130 **Spending money on experiences:** Ilya Pozin, "The Secret to Happiness? Spend Money on Experiences, Not Things," *Forbes*, March 3, 2016, https://www.forbes .com/sites/ilyapozin/2016/03/03/the-secret-to-happiness-spend-money-on -experiences-not-things/#37e584f439a6.

130 **Making more eco-friendly choices:** "Americans Say They're Becoming More Environmentally Conscious Each Year—and Their Green Changes Are Conta- gious," Good News Network, July 2, 2020, https://www.goodnewsnetwork.org /americans-becoming-more-eco-conscious-as-they-age/.

130 **Adults laugh somewhere:** Pamela Gerloff, "You're Not Laughing Enough, and That's No Joke," *Psychology Today*, June 21, 2011, https://www.psychologyto day.com/us/blog/the-possibility-paradigm/201106/youre-not-laughing -enough-and-thats-no-joke.

130 **People change their sheets:** Alina Bradford, "Do You Wash Your Sheets Enough? Probably Not," CNET, January 17, 2018, https://www.cnet.com /how-to/do-you-wash-your-sheets-enough-probably-not/.

130 **People who volunteer report:** Melissa Dahl, "People Who Volunteer Are Hap- pier with Their Work-Life Balance," The Cut, *New York*, February 17, 2015, https://www.thecut.com/2015/02/time-expanding-magic-of-volunteering .html.

130 **Narcissistic after their teen years:** Bob Curley, "The Older You Are, the Less Narcissistic You Tend to Be," Healthline, December 17, 2019, https://www .healthline.com/health-news/older-less-narcissistic.

130 **Smiling is not learned:** Jeanna Bryner, "Smiles Are Innate, Not Learned," Live Science, December 29, 2008, https://www.livescience.com/5254-smiles-innate -learned.html.

130 **Candles are bought by women:** Meda Kessler, "A Few Burning Candle Ques- tions," New York Times News Service, *Chicago Tribune*, December 21, 2003, https://www.chicagotribune.com/news/ct-xpm-2003-12-21-0312210478-story .html.

131 **"Short sleepers":** Megan Schmidt, "Short Sleeper 'Syndrome': When You Can Get By on Just a Few Hours of Sleep," *Discover Magazine*, September 20, 2019, https://www.discovermagazine.com/health/short-sleeper-syndrome-when-you -can-get-by-on-just-a-few-hours-of-sleep.

131 **Eight minutes in the shower:** "Save Water and Energy by Showering Better," EPA Water Sense, https://www.epa.gov/sites/production/files/2017-02/docu ments/ws-ourwater-shower-better-learning-resource_0.pdf.

131 **Prayed for a good parking spot:** Kevin Drum, "5 Percent of Religious Americans Routinely Try to Fool God," *Mother Jones*, October 6, 2014, https://www.motherjones.com/kevin-drum/2014/10/5-percent-religious-americans-routinely-try-fool-god/.

131 **Best friend is twenty-one:** Clare Ansberry, "At What Age Do You Meet Your Best Friend?," *The Wall Street Journal*, July 14, 2019, https://www.wsj.com/ar ticles/at-what-age-do-you-meet-your-best-friend-11563109200.

131 **Altruism stimulate the same parts:** Jenny Santi, "The Secret to Happiness Is Helping Others," *Time*, August 4, 2017, https://time.com/collection/guide-to -happiness/4070299/secret-to-happiness/.

131 **Babies are born in the summer:** Remy Melina, "In Which Month Are the Most Babies Born?," Live Science, July 27, 2010, https://www.livescience.com/32728 -baby-month-is-almost-here-.html.

131 **Most common birthday:** Abigail Abrams, "This Is the Most Common Birthday," *Time*, September 8, 2017, https://time.com/4933041/most-popular-common -birthday-september/.

131 **Romantic kissing:** Lindsey Bever, "A Kiss Is Not a Kiss. In Some Cultures It's Just Gross, Researchers Find," *The Wall Street Journal*, July 27, 2015, https://www.washingtonpost.com/news/morning-mix/wp/2015/07/27/romantic-kissing -is-not-a-shared-practice-across-cultures-research-shows/.

131 **Snooze button:** Gisela Wolf, "People Who Hit the Snooze Button Are More Intelligent, More Creative and Happier," *The Independent*, January 24, 2017, https://www.independent.co.uk/life-style/snooze-button-alarm-sleep-longer -happier-more-creative-intelligent-a7543986.html.

131 **Millennials donate to charity:** Jason Notte, "Why Millennials Are More Charitable Than the Rest of You," The Street, January 25, 2018, https://www.thes treet.com/lifestyle/why-millennials-are-more-charitable-14445741.

132 **Men tend to view their exes:** Mark Travers, "Why Men Think More Fondly of Their Exes Than Women Do," *Psychology Today*, October 30, 2019, https://www.psychologytoday.com/us/blog/social-instincts/201910/why-men -think-more-fondly-their-exes-women-do.

132 **Fewer workers are taking their full vacation days:** Allen Kim, "A Record 768 Million US Vacation Days Went to Waste Last Year, a Study Says," CNN, August 19, 2019, https://www.cnn.com/travel/article/unused-vacation-days-trnd/index .html.

132 **Teenage laziness is innate:** Louise Carpenter, "Revealed: The Science Behind Teenage Laziness," *The Telegraph*, February 14, 2015, https://www.telegraph .co.uk/news/science/science-news/11410483/Revealed-the-science-behind -teenage-laziness.html.

132 **Superstitious relieves anxiety:** Neil Dagnall, "The Scientific Reason You Still Believe in Superstitions," Quartz, July 2, 2018, https://qz.com/1319382/why -do-people-believe-in-superstitions-its-all-a-trick-of-the-mind/.

132 **Humans are hardwired for empathy:** Azadeh Aalai, "Facts About Human Behavior That Defy Our Assumptions," *Psychology Today*, July 28, 2018, https:// www.psychologytoday.com/us/blog/the-first-impression/201807/facts-about -human-behavior-defy-our-assumptions.

132 **Curse words are more honest:** Alex Orlando, "Worried About Swearing Too Much? Science Says You Shouldn't Be," *Discover Magazine*, January 14, 2020, https://www.discovermagazine.com/health/worried-about-your-foul-mouth -swearing-could-actually-be-good-for-you.

132 **Teens type ten words per minute faster:** Jack Guy, "People Are Now Texting Nearly as Fast as They Type," CTV News, October 2, 2019, https://www.ct vnews.ca/sci-tech/people-are-now-texting-nearly-as-fast-as-they-type-1.46 20252.

132 **Junk food when you're exhausted:** Northwestern University, "Why We Crave Junk Food After a Sleepless Night: Blame Your Nose, Which Sniffs Out High Fat, Calorie-Dense Food," ScienceDaily, October 8, 2019, https://www.sciencedaily .com/releases/2019/10/191008165821.htm.

132 **Babies laugh on their exhales:** Meilan Solly, "Babies Share Same Laugh Patterns as Chimpanzees," *Smithsonian Magazine*, November 8, 2018, https:// www.smithsonianmag.com/smart-news/babies-share-same-laugh-patterns -chimpanzees-180970757/.

133 **Left-handed people win fights more:** Sebastian Ocklenburg, "Left-Handers Are Better Fighters Than Right-Handers," *Psychology Today*, December 22, 2019, https://www.psychologytoday.com/us/blog/the-asymmetric-brain/201912 /left-handers-are-better-fighters-right-handers.

133 **Meditate has been steadily rising:** Peter Dockrill, "There's a Strange Explosion of Certain Meditative Practices in America Right Now," Science Alert, November 12, 2018, https://www.sciencealert.com/yoga-and-meditation-in-the-us-are -totally-exploding-right-now.

133 **Blind people may "see":** Helder Bértolo et al., "Rapid Eye Movements (REMs) and Visual Dream Recall in Both Congenitally Blind and Sighted Subjects," SPIE Digital Library, August 22, 2017, https://www.spiedigitallibrary.org/conference -proceedings-of-spie/10453/2276048/Rapid-Eye-Movements-REMs-and-visual -dream-recall-in-both/10.1117/12.2276048.short?SSO=1.

133 **"Collective narcissism":** Christian Jarrett, "How 'Collective Narcissism' Is Directing World Politics," BBC, March 3, 2017, https://www.bbc.com/future/article /20170303-how-collective-narcissism-is-directing-world-politics.

133 **Fail at multitasking:** Kristin Piombino, "Infographic: Only 2 Percent of People Can Multitask Effectively," Ragan's PR Daily, August 21, 2012, https://www .prdaily.com/infographic-only-2-percent-of-people-can-multitask-effectively/.

133 **Receiving paper greeting cards:** Alia Wong, "Millennials Are Keeping Family Holiday Cards Alive," *The Atlantic*, December 19, 2018, https://www.theatlantic.com/family/archive/2018/12/family-christmas-cards/578506/.

133 **Laugh track behind them:** Nell Greenfieldboyce, "A Study Confirms That Laugh Tracks Make Jokes Seem Funnier," *Morning Edition*, NPR, July 23, 2019, https://www.npr.org/2019/07/23/744335651/a-study-confirms-that-laugh-tracks-make-jokes-seem-funnier.

133 **Sleep twice per night:** Melinda Jackson and Siobhan Banks, "Humans Used to Sleep in Two Shifts, and Maybe We Should Do It Again," Science Alert, April 4, 2018, https://www.sciencealert.com/humans-used-to-sleep-in-two-shifts-maybe-we-should-again.

133 **Birth order does not determine:** Susan Newman, "Does Your Birth Order Actually Matter?," *Psychology Today*, November 17, 2015, https://www.psychologytoday.com/us/blog/singletons/201511/does-your-birth-order-actually-matter.

134 **Drunk driving is still a big problem:** "Drunk Driving Fatality Statistics," Foundation for Advancing Alcohol Responsibility, https://www.responsibility.org/alcohol-statistics/drunk-driving-statistics/drunk-driving-fatality-statistics/.

134 **Ambivert:** Rena Goldman, "5 Signs That You May Be an Ambivert," Healthline, November 6, 2018, https://www.healthline.com/health/health-ambivert.

134 **Elevator wait times:** Ana Swanson, "What Really Drives You Crazy About Waiting in Line (It Actually Isn't the Wait at All)," *The Wall Street Journal*, November 27, 2015, https://www.washingtonpost.com/news/wonk/wp/2015/11/27/what-you-hate-about-waiting-in-line-isnt-the-wait-at-all/.

134 **The act of smiling:** Ronald E. Riggio, "There's Magic in Your Smile," *Psychology Today*, June 25, 2012, https://www.psychologytoday.com/us/blog/cutting-edge-leadership/201206/there-s-magic-in-your-smile.

134 **Women remember their dreams more often:** Patrick McNamara, "The Dreams of Men and Women," *Psychology Today*, September 9, 2011, https://www.psychologytoday.com/us/blog/dream-catcher/201109/the-dreams-men-and-women.

134 **Manage their household's finances:** Alicia Adamczyk, "Younger Women Are Twice as Likely to Make Their Families' Financial Decisions Than Previous Generations," NBC News, August 31, 2020, https://www.nbcnews.com/know-your-value/feature/younger-women-are-twice-likely-make-their-families-financial-decisions-ncna1238859.

134 **Rainy days make us sleepier:** James Hale, "There's Actually a Scientific Reason for Why You're Always Sleepy When It's Rainy Out," *Bustle*, March 29, 2018, https://www.bustle.com/p/why-am-i-so-tired-when-its-raining-we-asked-expert-this-is-what-they-said-8646746.

134 **Conspiracy theories:** Matthew Hutson, "Conspiracy Theorists May Really Just Be Lonely," *Scientific American*, May 1, 2017, https://www.scientificamerican.com/article/conspiracy-theorists-may-really-just-be-lonely/.

134 **"Optimism bias":** Steve Paulson, "The Science of Looking on the Bright Side," Wisconsin Public Radio, April 19, 2019, https://www.wpr.org/science-looking -bright-side.

135 **Fear of public speaking:** Theo Tsaousides, "Why Are We Scared of Public Speaking?," *Psychology Today*, November 27, 2017, https://www.psychologyto day.com/us/blog/smashing-the-brainblocks/201711/why-are-we-scared-public -speaking.

135 **Earned their money are happier:** Peter Cohan, "This Harvard Study of 4,000 Millionaires Revealed Something Surprising About Money and Happiness," *Inc.*, https://www.inc.com/peter-cohan/will-10-million-make-you-happier-harvard -says-yes-if-you-make-it-yourself-give-it-away.html.

135 **Happiest age:** Raven Saunt, "Life Begins at 80! Major Study Reveals People Reach Their Happiest at 82 and Parts of the Brain Improve as We Get Older," *Daily Mail*, March 1, 2020, updated March 3, 2020, https://www.dailymail.co.uk /news/article-8061877/Study-reveals-people-reach-happiest-82-parts-brain -improve-older.html.

Love

138 **Marry their best friend:** Rebecca Adams, "New Study Says You Should Marry Your Best Friend," *HuffPost*, January 9, 2015, https://www.huffpost.com/entry /married-people-happier_n_6436420.

138 **Romantic partners hold hands:** University of Colorado at Boulder, "When Lovers Touch, Their Breathing, Heartbeat Syncs, Pain Wanes, Study Shows," Science-Daily, June 21, 2017, https://www.sciencedaily.com/releases/2017/06/1706211 25313.htm.

138 **Jack Benny:** Felicity Hannah, "10 of the Strangest Wills of All Time," *The Guardian*, August 25, 2015, https://www.theguardian.com/money/2015/aug/25 /10-strangest-wills-finances-death.

138 **Couples who post photos with their partner:** Gwendolyn Seidman, "Is Social Media PDA a Sign of Happiness or Overcompensation?," *Psychology Today*, November 25, 2018, https://www.psychologytoday.com/us/blog/close-encounters /201811/is-social-media-pda-sign-happiness-or-overcompensation.

138 **Opposites don't attract:** Matthew D. Johnson, "No, Opposites Do Not Attract," The Conversation, February 12, 2018, https://theconversation.com /no-opposites-do-not-attract-88839.

138 **On the bow of the *Titanic*:** "Titanic Couple Take the Plunge," BBC News, July 28, 2001, http://news.bbc.co.uk/2/hi/americas/1461368.stm.

138 **Crying for an hour burns:** Kathryn Watson, "How Many Calories Does Crying Burn?," Healthline, June 18, 2020, https://www.healthline.com/health/does-cry ing-burn-calories#how-many-calories-do-you-burn-crying.

138 **Divorce rates have been declining:** Joe Pinsker, "The Not-So-Great Reason Divorce Rates Are Declining," *The Atlantic*, September 25, 2018, https://www.theatlantic.com/family/archive/2018/09/millennials-divorce-baby-boomers/571282/.

138 **Apple at a woman:** Brad Smithfield, "In Ancient Greece, Throwing an Apple at Someone Was Considered a Marriage Proposal," *The Vintage News*, September 10, 2016, https://www.thevintagenews.com/2016/09/10/ancient-greece-throwing-apple-someone-considered-marriage-proposal/.

139 **Same-sex relationships:** Bonnie J. Morris, "History of Lesbian, Gay, Bisexual and Transgender Social Movements," American Psychological Association, 2009, https://www.apa.org/pi/lgbt/resources/history.

139 **Being married doesn't necessarily guarantee:** "Being Married Doesn't Necessarily Make You Happier Than Staying Single, Finds New Study," *Malay Mail*, July 28, 2020, https://www.malaymail.com/news/life/2020/07/28/being-married-doesnt-necessarily-make-you-happier-than-staying-single-finds/1888670.

139 **"Vinegar Valentines":** Natalie Zarrelli, "The Rude, Cruel, and Insulting 'Vinegar Valentines' of the Victorian Era," *Atlas Obscura*, February 13, 2020, https://www.atlasobscura.com/articles/vinegar-valentines-victorian.

139 **Fathers-to-be sometimes go through hormonal:** Shereen Lehman, "Fathers to-Be May Have Hormonal Changes Too," *Scientific American*, January 8, 2015, https://www.nhs.uk/news/mental-health/fathers-to-be-experience-hormone-changes/.

139 **Kiss their wives in the morning:** Linda and Charlie Bloom, "Kissing Adds Years to Your Life . . . and Life to Your Years," *Psychology Today*, July 16, 2019, https://www.psychologytoday.com/us/blog/stronger-the-broken-places/201907/kissing-adds-years-your-life.

139 **Separate beds:** Ryan W. Miller, "Why So Many Married Couples Are Sleeping in Separate Beds," *USA Today*, February 9, 2020, https://www.usatoday.com/story/news/nation/2020/02/09/separate-beds-married-couples-can-help-relationship-experts-say/4657215002/.

139 **Cuffing season:** Kristine Fellizar, "The Science Behind 'Cuffing Season' Is Actually Not as Romantic as It Seems," *Bustle*, October 16, 2017, https://www.bustle.com/p/is-cuffing-season-real-heres-why-people-crave-relationships-in-the-colder-months-according-to-science-2478180.

139 **Early stages of romantic:** Nicole Natale, "7 Physical and Psychological Changes that Happen When We Fall in Love," *Business Insider*, July 11, 2018, https://www.businessinsider.com/falling-in-love-changes-your-body-and-brain-2018-7.

140 **Sex can alleviate headaches:** Adrienne Santos-Longhurst, "Does Sex Really Help Relieve Migraine?," Healthline, March 31, 2020, https://www.healthline.com/health/healthy-sex/does-sex-help-migraines.

140 **Romantic partners tend to rate us as:** Madeleine A. Fugère, "3 Reasons Why You Look Better Than You Think You Do," *Psychology Today*, January 13, 2018,

https://www.psychologytoday.com/us/blog/dating-and-mating/201801/3-reasons-why-you-look-better-you-think-you-do.

140 **Single women would put an apple slice:** Desmond Morris, *The Naked Woman: A Study of the Female Body* (New York: St. Martin's Press, 2004), 120.

140 **Scent women find most arousing:** "Scent of a Woman—or a Whiff of Good & Plenty," *Chicago Tribune*, January 29, 2006, https://www.chicagotribune.com/news/ct-xpm-2006-01-29-0601290367-story.html.

140 **Mickey and Minnie were married:** Michael Cavna, "She Was the Voice of Minnie Mouse. He Was the Voice of Mickey Mouse. That's How Their Romance Began," *The Washington Post*, July 30, 2019, https://www.washingtonpost.com/arts-entertainment/2019/07/30/she-was-voice-minnie-mouse-he-was-voice-mickey-mouse-thats-how-their-romance-began/.

140 **Emojis while flirting:** Justin J. Lehmiller, PhD, "People Who Use More Emojis Have More Sex and Get More Dates," *Psychology Today*, August 16, 2019, https://www.psychologytoday.com/us/blog/the-myths-sex/201908/people-who-use-more-emojis-have-more-sex-and-get-more-dates.

140 **Netherlands became the first country:** "The Dutch Went First in 2001; Who Has Same-Sex Marriage Now?" Associated Press, April 1, 2021, https://www.usnews.com/news/world/articles/2021-04-01/the-dutch-went-first-in-2001-who-has-same-sex-marriage-now.

140 **Dating app users who have the same initials:** Hayley MacMillen, "The 6 Signs That You're Compatible With An Online Match," *Refinery29*, March 9, 2016, https://www.refinery29.com/en-us/2016/03/105242/dating-statistics#slide-5.

140 **Heart as the symbol of love:** Marilyn Yalom, "The Mysterious Origins of the Enduring Heart Symbol," *The Wall Street Journal*, January 26, 2018, https://www.wsj.com/articles/the-mysterious-origins-of-the-enduring-heart-symbol-1516984378.

141 **53.3 million Americans:** "Number of Online Dating Users in the United States from 2017 to 2024," Statista, March 2021, https://www.statista.com/statistics/417654/us-online-dating-user-numbers/.

141 **Juliet, Verona:** The Juliet Club, 2021, http://www.julietclub.com/en/su-di-noi/.

Life Hacks from Science & Psychology

144 **Make time for art:** Maria Cramer, "Another Benefit to Going to Museums? You May Live Longer," *The New York Times*, December 22, 2019, https://www.nytimes.com/2019/12/22/us/arts-health-effects-ucl-study.html.

144 **To-do list before you go to bed:** Amanda Macmillan, "Do This One Simple Thing to Fall Asleep Faster," *Time*, January 12, 2018, https://time.com/5097840/how-to-fall-asleep-faster/.

144   **Eye contact with a person makes them:** University of Tampere, "Eye Contact Reduces Lying," Medical Xpress, November 12, 2018, https://medicalxpress .com/news/2018-11-eye-contact-lying.html.

144   **Gum stuck in your hair:** "Tips for Removing Gum Without Cutting Hair," American Academy of Dermatology Association, https://www.aad.org/public/every day-care/hair-scalp-care/hair/removing-gum.

144   **Busy people are happier:** Polly Campbell, "Get Busy, Be Happy," *Psychology Today*, August 16, 2010, https://www.psychologytoday.com/us/blog/imper fect-spirituality/201008/get-busy-be-happy.

145   **Ice cubes in a hot dryer:** Loukia Papadopoulos, "9 Engineering and Science Life Hacks to Save Your Day," Interesting Engineering, March 5, 2019, https:// interestingengineering.com/9-engineering-and-science-life-hacks-to-save -your-day.

145   **Rinsing out your recyclables:** Nina Shen Rastogi, "The Environmental Pros and Cons of Washing Out Your Recyclables," *Slate*, February 3, 2009, https://slate .com/technology/2009/02/is-it-worth-it-to-wash-out-your-recyclables.html.

145   **Coffee gets bitter if left out:** Alison Spiegel, "Coffee Crimes: Reheating Coffee," Tasting Table, January 25, 2016, https://www.tastingtable.com/cook/na tional/reheat-coffee-microwave-leftover-lacolombe-Caribou.

145   **Adding a pinch of salt:** Nik Sharma, "Could Salt Make Coffee Taste Better?," Food52, August 16, 2020, https://food52.com/blog/25513-putting-salt-in -coffee.

145   **Sharing a goal:** Cory Stieg, "How to Stay Committed to Your Goals: Tell Someone More Successful Than You, Says New Study," CNBC, September 5, 2019, https://www.cnbc.com/2019/09/05/why-sharing-goals-with-someone-helps -you-achieve-them.html.

145   **Wind turbine blades black decreases:** David Nield, "Making One Simple Change to Wind Turbines Could Cut Bird Deaths by 70 Percent," Science Alert, August 27, 2020, https://www.sciencealert.com/a-simple-wind-turbine-paint -job-has-cut-bird-deaths-by-70-percent.

145   **Prices but no dollar sign:** Richard Gray, "The Secret Tricks Hidden Inside Restaurant Menus," BBC, July 31, 2020, https://www.bbc.com/future/article /20171120-the-secret-tricks-hidden-inside-restaurant-menus.

145   **Cheat days have more self-control:** Olga Khazan, "The Glory of the Cheat Day," *The Atlantic*, April 20, 2016, https://www.theatlantic.com/health/ar chive/2016/04/its-my-cheat-day/478881/.

146   **Sleeping on your left side:** Jennifer Chesak, "How These 3 Sleep Positions Affect Your Gut Health," Healthline, June 29, 2018, https://www.healthline.com /health/healthy-sleep/sleep-effects-digestion#back-sleeping.

146   **Plan B makes Plan A:** Suzanne Degges-White, "Does Having a Plan B Sabotage Your Plan A?," *Psychology Today*, July 29, 2016, https://www.psychologytoday

.com/us/blog/lifetime-connections/201607/does-having-plan-b-sabotage
-your-plan.

146 **"Backchannel" feedback:** Julie Beck, "The Secret Life of 'Um,'" *The Atlantic*,
December 10, 2017, https://www.theatlantic.com/science/archive/2017/12/the
-secret-life-of-um/547961/.

146 **Humidifier in your room reduces:** E. E. Kane, "5 Benefits and Drawbacks of
Air Humidifiers," Everyday Health, updated November 15, 2017, https://www
.everydayhealth.com/healthy-living/healthy-home/5-benefits-drawbacks-air
-humidifiers/.

146 **Strengthen your immune system:** Kylie Gilbert, "The Awesome Way Tattoos
Boost Your Health," *Shape*, March 10, 2016, https://www.shape.com/lifestyle
/mind-and-body/tattoos-may-boost-your-health.

146 **Part of a bigger picture:** Thomas H. Lee and Angela L. Duckworth, "Organiza-
tional Grit," *Harvard Business Review*, September–October 2018, https://hbr
.org/2018/09/organizational-grit.

146 **Changing up your routine:** Nancy Schimelpfening, "Changes to Your Daily Routine During COVID-19 Can Make You Happier," Healthline, May 21, 2020, https://
www.healthline.com/health-news/humans-thrive-on-new-and-diverse
-experiences-how-to-make-that-work-under-lockdown.

146 **Mosquito lands on you:** JoAnna Klein, "Swatting at Mosquitoes May Help You
Avoid Bites, Even If You Miss," *The New York Times*, January 25, 2018, https://
www.nytimes.com/2018/01/25/science/swatting-mosquitoes.html.

147 **Rub cooking oil on it:** Coryanne Ettiene and Jan Soults Walker, "How to Remove Sticker Residue Quickly and Effectively," *Better Homes & Gardens*, updated
August 3, 2020, https://www.bhg.com/homekeeping/house-cleaning/tips
/how-to-remove-sticker-residue-281474979530492/.

147 **Workouts, such as hiking, tennis, and running:** "Osteoporosis Exercise for
Strong Bones," National Osteoporosis Foundation, https://www.nof.org/pa
tients/treatment/exercisesafe-movement/osteoporosis-exercise-for-strong
-bones/.

147 **It's easier to listen to your body when:** Howard LeWine, "Distracted Eating
May Add to Weight Gain," Harvard Health Publishing, March 29, 2013, https://
www.health.harvard.edu/blog/distracted-eating-may-add-to-weight-gain
-201303296037.

147 **Ask people out on a sunny day:** Taylor & Francis, "Feeling Flirty? Wait for the
Sun to Shine," ScienceDaily, January 28, 2013, https://www.sciencedaily.com
/releases/2013/01/130128081950.htm.

147 **Reducing your consumption:** University of Arizona, "Buying Less Is Better
Than Buying 'Green'—for the Planet and Your Happiness," ScienceDaily, October 8, 2019, https://www.sciencedaily.com/releases/2019/10/191008155716
.htm.

147 **Watching nature documentaries:** "Watching Nature Programmes Makes You Happier, New Research Reveals," BBC, March 8, 2017, https://www.bbc.co.uk/mediacentre/worldwide/2017/rhp.

147 **Mayonaise into a wood surface:** Lindsey Mather, "5 Ways to Remove Water Stains from Wood," *Architectural Digest*, July 4, 2017, https://www.architectural digest.com/story/ways-to-remove-water-stains-from-wood.

147 *Hair of the dog:* Shaughnessy Bishop-Stall, "Who First Plucked the Hair of the Dog?," *Slate*, November 20, 2018, https://slate.com/human-interest/2018/11/hair-of-the-dog-history-hangover-cure.html.

148 **"Beer before liquor":** David Reid, "Liquor Before Beer? You Will Still Feel Terrible, New Study Says," CNBC, February 8, 2019, https://www.cnbc.com/2019/02/08/liquor-before-beer-you-will-still-feel-terrible-new-study-says.html.

148 **See the ocean from your home:** Christina Heiser, "What the Beach Does to Your Brain," NBC News, July 29, 2017, updated July 16, 2018, https://www.nbc news.com/better/health/what-beach-does-your-brain-ncna787231.

148 **Calling someone on the phone:** Billy Gates, "Phone Calls Form Stronger Bonds Than Text Messages, Research Shows," KXAN, September 15, 2020, updated September 25, 2020, https://www.kxan.com/news/local/austin/phone-calls-form-stronger-bonds-than-text-messages-research-shows/.

148 **Pain tolerance increases:** Ian Mason, "Laughing Away Pain," Medical News Today, October 15, 2013, https://www.medicalnewstoday.com/articles/267434.

148 **Hugging lowers stress:** Vivian Manning-Schaffel, "The Health Benefits of Hugging," NBC News, October 25, 2018, https://www.nbcnews.com/better/pop-culture/health-benefits-hugging-ncna920751.

148 **Rounded fonts with sweet taste:** Richard Gray, "The Secret Tricks Hidden Inside Restaurant Menus," BBC, July 31, 2020, https://www.bbc.com/future/article/20171120-the-secret-tricks-hidden-inside-restaurant-menus.

149 **"Toilet plume":** Caroline Picard, "Please, for the Love of God, Close the Toilet Lid When You Flush," *Good Housekeeping*, August 20, 2018, https://www.good housekeeping.com/health/a22777060/close-the-toilet-seat/.

149 **Take notes by hand:** Cindi May, "A Learning Secret: Don't Take Notes with a Laptop," *Scientific American*, June 3, 2014, https://www.scientificamerican.com/article/a-learning-secret-don-t-take-notes-with-a-laptop/.

149 **Looking at a photo of a loved one:** "Soothing Snaps: Looking at a Photo of a Loved One 'Reduces Pain By 44%,'" *Daily Mail*, updated February 24, 2011, https://www.dailymail.co.uk/sciencetech/article-1360227/Looking-photo-loved-reduces-pain-44.html.

149 **Debate and constructive critiques:** Rochelle Bailis, "Brainstorming Doesn't Work—Do This Instead," *Forbes*, October 8, 2014, https://www.forbes.com/sites/rochellebailis/2014/10/08/brainstorming-doesnt-work-do-this-instead/#1d1b1da65228.

149   **Choose a pumpkin with a green stem:** Dennis Patton, "Picking the Perfect Pumpkin," *The Kansas City Star*, September 30, 2016, https://www.kansascity .com/living/home-garden/article104279061.html.

149   **Walking at least two thousand steps:** Seth J. Gillihan, "Want to Sleep Better? Go for a Walk," *Psychology Today*, October 14, 2019, https://www.psychology today.com/us/blog/think-act-be/201910/want-sleep-better-go-walk.

149   **Wake up at the same time:** Brandon Peters, "First Step to Better Sleep: Wake Up at the Same Time Every Day," Verywell Health, May 13, 2020, https://www .verywellhealth.com/30-days-to-better-sleep-3973920.

149   **Label has a difficult-to-read font:** Richard Gray, "The Secret Tricks Hidden Inside Restaurant Menus," BBC, July 31, 2020, https://www.bbc.com/future /article/20171120-the-secret-tricks-hidden-inside-restaurant-menus.

149   **Predicting obstacles:** Jennice Vilhauer, "How to Overcome the Obstacles to Your Success," *Psychology Today*, March 11, 2019, https://www.psychologyto day.com /us/blog/living-forward/201903/how-overcome-the-obstacles-your-success.

150   **When you get in your car on a summer day:** Meghan Overdeep, "Here's What the Air Recirculation Button in Your Car Actually Does," *Southern Living*, July 13, 2019, https://www.southernliving.com/news/car-air-recirculation-button.

150   **Do not idle your car:** Matt Keegan, "Do You Need to Warm Your Car Up?," Carfax.com, February 3, 2015, https://www.carfax.com/blog/do-you-need-to -warm-your-car-up.

150   **We like seeing people's hands:** Joe Navarro, *What Every Body Is Saying: An Ex-FBI Agent's Guide to Speed-Reading People* (New York: HarperCollins, 2008), 133–64.

150   **Taking work breaks:** Rebecca Greenfield, "Keep Wasting Time Online at Work: It's Better for Productivity," *The Atlantic*, August 22, 2011, https://www.the atlantic.com/technology/archive/2011/08/keep-wasting-time-online-work-its -better-productivity/354398/.

150   **Most efficient way to wipe:** "Should You Fold or Wad Toilet Paper? A Physicist Settles the Debate for Good," *Mel Magazine*, https://melmagazine.com/en-us /story/fold-or-wad-toilet-paper-physics.

150   **"Quiet wakefulness":** Cassie Shortsleeve, "Can't Sleep? Try 'Quiet Wakefulness' Instead," Elemental Medium, December 27, 2019, https://elemental.medium .com/cant-sleep-try-quiet-wakefulness-instead-2b106e5b8e3c.

150   **Gratitude journal:** Maanvi Singh, "If You Feel Thankful, Write It Down. It's Good for Your Health," *Morning Edition*, NPR, December 24, 2018, https:// www.npr.org/sections/health-shots/2018/12/24/678232331/if-you-feel -thankful-write-it-down-its-good-for-your-health.

150   **Drinking pickle juice:** Megan Gambino, "A Spoonful of Pickle Juice . . . Helps Muscle Cramps Go Down," *Smithsonian Magazine*, June 16, 2010, https://www .smithsonianmag.com/science-nature/a-spoonful-of-pickle-juicehelps-muscle -cramps-go-down-30137937/.

151 **You cannot sink in quicksand:** Nicholas Bakalar, "Quicksand Science: Why It Traps, How to Escape," *National Geographic*, September 28, 2005, https://www.nationalgeographic.com/news/2005/9/quicksand-science-why-it-traps-how-to-escape/.

151 **Freezing your jeans:** Sarah Zielinski, "The Myth of the Frozen Jeans," *Smithsonian Magazine*, November 7, 2011, https://www.smithsonianmag.com/science-nature/the-myth-of-the-frozen-jeans-129092730/.

151 **When we have an article of our partner's worn clothing:** University of British Columbia, "Smelling Your Lover's Shirt Could Improve Your Sleep," ScienceDaily, February 13, 2020, https://www.sciencedaily.com/releases/2020/02/200213091723.htm.

151 **Word-guess game of Spaceman:** Brandon Specktor, "Here Is the Hardest Word to Guess in Hangman, According to Science," *Reader's Digest*, updated April 25, 2019, https://www.rd.com/article/hardest-word-guess-hangman/.

151 **Get sad after achieving a large goal:** Wanda Thibodeaux, "Why You Might Feel Empty After Reaching a Huge Goal (and How to Move On)," *Inc.*, March 26, 2018, https://www.inc.com/wanda-thibodeaux/why-you-might-feel-empty-after-reaching-huge-goal-and-how-to-move-on.html.

151 **Multiple strong friendships:** Tara Parker-Pope, "What Are Friends For? A Longer Life," *The New York Times*, April 20, 2009, https://www.nytimes.com/2009/04/21/health/21well.html.

151 **Breaks every ninety minutes:** Thibodeaux, "Why Working in 90-Minute Intervals Is Powerful for Your Body and Job, According to Science."

151 **Easiest passwords to crack:** Tomáš Foltýn, "The Worst Passwords of 2019: Did Yours Make the List?," We Live Security, December 16, 2019, https://www.welivesecurity.com/2019/12/16/worst-passwords-2019-did-yours-make-list/.

151 **Sans serif fonts have liberal connotations:** Lilly Smith, "The Real Politics of Type," *Fast Company*, February 5, 2020, https://www.fastcompany.com/90458816/the-real-politics-of-type.

151 **Writing about a traumatic event:** "Writing About Emotions May Ease Stress and Trauma," Harvard Health Publishing, October 2011, https://www.health.harvard.edu/healthbeat/writing-about-emotions-may-ease-stress-and-trauma.

151 **Wrapping your headphones:** Craig Lloyd, "The Definitive Guide to Wrapping Your Headphones Without Losing Your Mind," Lifehacker, August 14, 2012, https://lifehacker.com/the-definitive-guide-to-wrapping-your-headphones-withou-5930624.

151 **Five-cent fees for plastic bags:** Tatiana A. Homonoff, "Can Small Incentives Have Large Effects? The Impact of Taxes versus Bonuses on Disposable Bag Use," *American Economic Journal*: Economic Policy, 2018, https://are.berkeley.edu/SGDC/07_POL20150261_104.pdf.

151 **Napping is good for your heart:** Jamie Ducharme, "Go Ahead, Take a Nap. A New Study Says They May Be Good for Your Heart," *Time*, September 9, 2019, https://time.com/5672111/naps-heart-health-study/.

151 **Turning off push notifications:** Steve Glaveski, "Stop Letting Push Notifications Ruin Your Productivity," *Harvard Business Review*, March 18, 2019, https://hbr.org/2019/03/stop-letting-push-notifications-ruin-your-productivity.

151 **Forgiving others can reduce your stress:** "Forgiveness: Your Health Depends on It," Johns Hopkins Medicine, https://www.hopkinsmedicine.org/health/wellness-and-prevention/forgiveness-your-health-depends-on-it.

151 **Take a photo of it first:** The Conversation, "Taking Photos of Stuff Helps You Get Rid of It More Easily," Fatherly, July 17, 2017, https://www.fatherly.com/health-science/taking-photos-of-stuff-helps-you-get-rid-of-it/.

151 **Singing can reduce anxiety:** "The Health Benefits of Singing a Tune," *Chicago Tribune*, March 15, 2018, https://www.chicagotribune.com/suburbs/advertising/todayshealthywoman/ct-ss-thw-health-benefits-of-singing-a-tune-20180314dto-story.html.

151 **Ten to twenty minutes of direct sunlight:** Temma Ehrenfeld, "If Sun Makes You Happier, Think about Your Vitamin D Level," *Psychology Today*, July 31, 2017, https://www.psychologytoday.com/us/blog/open-gently/201707/if-sun-makes-you-happier-think-about-your-vitamin-d-level.

152 **Positive goal-setting:** Ryan R. Bailey, "Goal Setting and Action Planning for Health Behavior Change," *American Journal of Lifestyle Medicine*, November–December 2009, published online by National Institutes of Health, U.S. National Library of Medicine, September 13, 2017, https://www.ncbi.nlm.nih.gov/pmc/articles/PMC6796229/.

152 **People's biggest regrets:** Jeff Haden, "New Research Reveals What People Regret Most of All: 5 Ways to Make Sure You Never Do," *Inc.*, June 4, 2018, https://www.inc.com/jeff-haden/new-research-reveals-what-people-regret-most-of-all-ways-to-make-sure-you-never-do.html.

All Around the World

156 **La Tomatina:** "La Tomatina Information, Accommodation & Tickets," La Tomatina Tours, https://www.latomatinatours.com.

156 **Central Park is bigger than the country of Monaco:** "Infographic: Central Park Is Bigger Than Monaco," *Metro*, August 7, 2015, https://www.metro.us/infographic-central-park-is-bigger-than-monaco/.

156 **Penguin poo contains loads of the chemical:** Shivali Best, "Scientists Studying Penguins Accidentally Get High Off Fumes from the Birds' Poo," *Mirror*, May 20, 2020, https://www.mirror.co.uk/science/scientists-studying-penguins-accidentally-high-22057110.

157   **Alabama is the only state that has an alcoholic beverage:** Jennifer, "Here Are 12 Things They Don't Teach You About Alabama in School," Only in Your State, March 9, 2016, https://www.onlyinyourstate.com/alabama/facts-about-al/.

157   **Sumo wrestler makes your baby cry:** "Sumo Wrestlers Try to Make Babies Cry on Purpose in Unusual Japanese Tradition," *Business Insider*, September 22, 2014, https://www.businessinsider.com/afp-having-a-bawl-japans-sumo-wrestlers -grapple-with-cry-babies-2014-9.

157   **Our planet is 5 percent greener:** "Human Activity in China and India Domi- nates the Greening of Earth, NASA Study Shows," NASA, February 11, 2009, https://www.nasa.gov/feature/ames/human-activity-in-china-and-india -dominates-the-greening-of-earth-nasa-study-shows.

157   **Lightning can shoot out of an erupting volcano:** "Volcanic Lightning," *Na- tional Geographic*, https://www.nationalgeographic.org/media/volcanic-lightn ing-wbt/.

157   ***Titanic* will disintegrate:** Gina Martinez, "Divers Visited the Titanic's Wreck for the First Time in Over a Decade. Here's Why They Were Shocked by the Ship's Condition," *Time*, August 22, 2019, https://time.com/5658903/titanic-wreck -deteriorating/.

157   **Rate of twin births is four times higher:** "The Land of Twins," BBC World Service, June 7, 2001, https://www.bbc.co.uk/worldservice/people/highlights /010607_twins.shtml.

157   **There are more than 1,200 plants in Hawaii:** "Rare Plant Program," Native Ecosystems Protection & Management, State of Hawaii, Division of Forestry and Wildlife, https://dlnr.hawaii.gov/ecosystems/rare-plants/.

158   **Center of the United States:** Dan Barry, "In the Middle of Nowhere, a Nation's Center," *The New York Times*, June 2, 2008, https://www.nytimes.com/2008 /06/02/us/02land.html.

158   **Ball-pit bars:** "The Famous Ball Pit Cocktail Bar," Ballie Ballerson, https://www .ballieballerson.com.

158   **24 Hours of Lemons:** "Everything You Wanted to Know About Car Racing on a Budget," 24 Hours of Lemons, https://24hoursoflemons.com/wtf/.

158   **Cooper's Hill Cheese-Rolling:** Melissa Locker, "Video Shows Extreme Cheese Fans Rolling Down a Dangerous Hill for a Lot of Cheese," *Time*, May 30, 2018, https://time.com/5294136/gloucestershire-cheese-roll-2018/.

158   **Women in China were illiterate:** C. Textor, "Adult Literacy Rate in China from 1982 to 2015," Statista, May 26, 2020, https://www.statista.com/statistics /271336/literacy-in-china/; Parul Sehgal, "First Comes Love, Then Comes What Exactly?," *The New York Times*, February 13, 2018, https://www.nytimes.com /2018/02/13/books/review-heart-shifting-sea-elizabeth-flock-leftover-in-china -roseann-lake.html.

158   **New Zealand, birth certificate registration officials:** Barbara McMahon, "Parents Lose Custody of Girl for Naming Her Talula Does the Hula from Hawaii,"

The Guardian, July 24, 2008, https://www.theguardian.com/lifeandstyle/2008/jul/24/familyandrelationships.newzealand.

158 **Trees in Berlin:** Dan Fesperman, "In Berlin, Even the Trees Have Numbers. Pulp Nonfiction: Trees Are a Passionate Concern for Berliners, an Attitude That Was Heightened by the Cold War When West Berlin Was Cut Off from Surrounding Forests. Berlin's Tree Bureaucrats Are True Fanatics," *The Baltimore Sun*, April 26, 1996, https://www.baltimoresun.com/news/bs-xpm-1996-04-26-1996117052-story.html.

158 **Thirty-five years, creating a thriving forest:** "This Indian Man Planted a Tree Every Day for 35 Years. The Result Is Unbelievable," *India Today*, August 9, 2018, https://www.indiatoday.in/lifestyle/what-s-hot/story/this-indian-man-planted-a-tree-every-day-for-35-years-the-result-is-unbelievable-1309563-2018-08-09.

159 **"Green roofs":** Chiara Giordano, "Holland Covers Hundreds of Bus Stops with Plants as Gift to Honeybees," *The Independent*, July 11, 2019, https://www.independent.co.uk/news/world/europe/bus-stop-plants-green-roof-bees-holland-utrecht-a8997581.html.

159 **Minnesota is called the Land of 10,000 Lakes:** Jason Daley, "Minnesota and Wisconsin Are Beefing About Who Has More Lakes," *Smithsonian Magazine*, July 19, 2019, https://www.smithsonianmag.com/smart-news/minnesota-and-wisconsin-are-beefing-about-who-has-more-lakes-180972697/.

159 **Common American street name:** "Most Common U.S. Street Names," National League of Cities, October 21, 2016, https://www.nlc.org/most-common-us-street-names.

159 **You get a text message every time your blood:** Jon Stone, "Blood Donors in Sweden Get a Text Message Whenever Their Blood Saves Someone's Life," *The Independent*, June 10, 2015, https://www.independent.co.uk/news/world/europe/blood-donors-sweden-get-text-message-whenever-someone-helped-their-blood-10310101.html.

159 **Mammoth Cave:** "Mammoth Cave: Explore the World's Longest Cave," U.S. Department of the Interior, June 29, 2017, https://www.doi.gov/blog/mammoth-cave-explore-worlds-longest-cave.

159 **Longest life expectancy:** "Life Expectancy of the World Population," Worldometer, https://www.worldometers.info/demographics/life-expectancy/.

159 **Mini-castles in central Turkey:** Bethan McKernan, "Fate of Castles in the Air in Turkey's £151m Ghost Town," *The Guardian*, January 28, 2019, https://www.theguardian.com/world/2019/jan/28/fate-of-castles-in-the-air-in-turkeys-151m-ghost-town.

160 **LarvalBot:** Denise Chow, "This Undersea Robot Just Delivered 100,000 Baby Corals to the Great Barrier Reef," BBC News, December 22, 2018, https://www.nbcnews.com/mach/science/undersea-robot-just-delivered-100-000-baby-corals-great-barrier-ncna950821.

160 **Caga Tió:** Lindsay Patterson, "A Catalan Log That Poops Nougats at Christmas," NPR, December 22, 2017, https://www.npr.org/sections/thesalt/2017/12/22/572569325/caga-ti-a-catalan-log-that-poops-nougats-at-christmas.

160 **Cardinal is the most popular state bird:** "Illinois: Northern Cardinal," *Insider*, https://www.insider.com/every-states-official-state-bird-2018-12#illinois-northern-cardinal-14.

160 **Brazilians speak Portuguese:** Y. Yates, "How Many People Speak Portuguese, and Where Is It Spoken?," *Babbel*, August 9, 2017, https://www.babbel.com/en/magazine/how-many-people-speak-portuguese-and-where-is-it-spoken.

160 **Oldest living tree:** Umeå University, "World's Oldest Living Tree—9550 Years Old—Discovered in Sweden," ScienceDaily, April 16, 2008, https://www.sciencedaily.com/releases/2008/04/080416104320.htm.

160 **Battle of the Oranges:** "Battle of the Oranges," *Atlas Obscura*, https://www.atlasobscura.com/places/battle-of-the-oranges.

160 **Shanghai, China, is roughly equivalent:** abs, "03 Dec Shanghai Has as Many People as the Entire Population of Australia," Absolute Internship, https://absoluteinternship.com/blog/shanghai-has-many-people-as-the-entire-population-of-australia/.

160 **Longest zipline:** "World's Longest Zip Wire Opens in the UAE," BBC News, February 1, 2018, https://www.bbc.com/news/av/world-middle-east-42911788.

160 **Hell was hit by:** Benedict Brook, "Town of Hell, Michigan Freezes Over as Vicious Polar Vortex Envelopes Much of the US," News.com, January 31, 2019, https://www.news.com.au/technology/environment/town-of-hell-michigan-freezes-over-as-vicious-polar-vortex-envelopes-much-of-the-us/news-story/5baece59856982a660d04c133748d368.

161 **Los Angeles:** "Los Angeles," History.com, February 28, 2019, https://www.history.com/topics/us-states/los-angeles-california.

161 **"Cat Islands":** Angel Wu, "Top 3 Cat Islands in Japan," Hisgo, https://www.hisgo.com/us/destination-japan/blog/top_3_cat_islands_in_japan.html.

161 **Statue of Liberty:** "Lady Liberty: 10 Fascinating Facts," The Battery, February 22, 2018, http://thebattery.org/lady-liberty-10-fascinating-facts/.

161 **In Denmark, if you're unmarried:** Lindsay Dodgson, "Why Singles in Denmark Get Covered in Cinnamon," *Business Insider*, February 16, 2018, https://www.businessinsider.com/why-singles-in-denmark-get-covered-in-cinnamon-2018-2.

161 **"The Big Apple":** Victor Mather, "We Use Sports Terms All the Time. But Where Do They Come From?," *The New York Times*, August 6, 2018, https://www.nytimes.com/2018/08/06/sports/sports-cliches-metaphors.html.

161 **Three-ton ice block:** Kaushik Patowary, "The Ice Block Expedition of 1959," Amusing Planet, May 13, 2019, https://www.amusingplanet.com/2019/05/the-ice-block-expedition-of-1959.html.

161 **Mail is still delivered by mule:** Michele Lent Hirsch, "Visit the Only Village Inside the Grand Canyon," *Smithsonian Magazine*, November 19, 2015, https://

www.smithsonianmag.com/travel/visit-only-village-inside-grand-canyonso -remote-its-mail-delivered-mule-180955582/.

162 **Eeyore's birthday:** Jessica Pino, "Everything You Need to Know About Eeyore's Birthday Bash," The Austinot, April 22, 2016, https://austinot.com/eeyores -birthday-austin.

162 **Tokyo is the most populous:** "The 10 Most Populous Cities in the World for 2019," Travel Channel, https://www.travelchannel.com/interests/travels-best /photos/2019s-most-populous-cities-in-the-world.

162 **Kentucky has more barrels of bourbon:** Caitlin Dickson, "There's More Bour-bon Than People in Kentucky," *The Atlantic*, June 22, 2011, https://www.the atlantic.com/business/archive/2011/06/theres-more-bourbon-people-kentucky /352057/.

162 **Named after Martin Luther King Jr.:** The Conversation, "Naming a Street After MLK Is Easier Said Than Done," *U.S. News & World Report*, January 20, 2020, https://www.usnews.com/news/cities/articles/2020-01-20/for-many-us-towns -and-cities-naming-a-street-after-martin-luther-king-jr-reflects-his-unfinished-work.

162 **Independence days to honor their liberation from Great Britain:** "Most Countries to Have Gained Independence from the Same Country," Guinness World Records, https://www.guinnessworldrecords.com/world-records/most -countries-to-have-gained-independence-from-the-same-country/.

162 **Unclaimed Baggage:** "Welcome to Unclaimed Baggage," Unclaimed Baggage, https://www.unclaimedbaggage.com.

162 **Chicago River:** Jen Jennings, "The Chicago River Actually Flows Backwards," *Condé Nast Traveler*, October 8, 2018, https://www.cntraveler.com/story /the-chicago-river-actually-flows-backwards.

162 **Baggage fees:** "Man Wears 70 Items of Clothing to Avoid Baggage Fees," News .com, December 19, 2012, https://www.news.com.au/travel/travel-updates /man-wears-70-items-of-clothing-to-avoid-baggage-fees/news-story /7fc73f81cc8a1fa25a9068d949d9bafa.

162 **Ethiopian calendar:** Panchali Dey, "Ethiopia, the Country That Follows a 13-Month Calendar, and Is 7 Years Behind the Rest of the World!," *The Times of India*, July 26, 2019, https://timesofindia.indiatimes.com/travel/destinations /ethiopia-the-country-that-follows-a-13-month-calendar-and-is-7-years-behind -the-rest-of-the-world/as70396809.cms.

162 **3 million shipwrecks:** "Underwater Cultural Heritage," United Nations Educa-tional, Scientific, and Cultural Organization, http://www.unesco.org/new/en /culture/themes/underwater-cultural-heritage/underwater-cultural-heritage /wrecks/.

163 **There's a London Bridge in Arizona:** Evan Andrews, "How London Bridge Ended Up in Arizona," History.com, October 7, 2016, updated August 31, 2018, https://www.history.com/news/how-london-bridge-ended-up-in-arizona.

163 **Zozobra:** Tripp Stelnicki, "Organizer Claims Record Zozobra Attendance," *Santa Fe New Mexican*, September 2, 2017, updated September 3, 2017, https://www.santafenewmexican.com/news/local_news/organizer-claims-record-zozobra-attendance/article_6d4342fa-4827-526b-a2d8-21613c0cce72.html.

163 **Monkey Buffet:** "Monkey Buffet Festival," *Atlas Obscura*, https://www.atlasobscura.com/foods/monkey-buffet-festival.

164 **World Toe Wrestling:** "World Toe Wrestling Championships 2019," HUTC Archive, YouTube, June 4, 2019, https://www.youtube.com/watch?v=tuJXX3al8CQ.

164 **Mount Rushmore:** Jonathan Glancey, "Mount Rushmore at 75: How Did It Come to Be?," BBC, July 4, 2016, https://www.bbc.com/culture/article/20160704-mount-rushmore-at-75-how-did-it-come-to-be.

164 **Hawaii is moving:** "Your Place in the World," *EarthDate*, https://www.earthdate.org/your-place-in-the-world.

164 **All-water mail route:** Marty Roney, "In Alabama Town, Snail Mail Comes by Boat," *USA Today*, December 7, 2013, https://www.usatoday.com/story/news/nation/2013/12/07/mail-by-boat/3896137/.

164 **You can cash in thirty plastic bottles:** Melissa Locker, "In Rome, You Can Swap 30 Plastic Bottles for a Subway Ride," *Fast Company*, August 6, 2019, https://www.fastcompany.com/90386534/in-rome-you-can-swap-30-plastic-bottles-for-subway-ride.

164 **Princess Kay of the Milky Way:** Michael Levenson, "Finally, Some Good News (Carved from 90 Pounds of Butter)," *The New York Times*, July 16, 2020, https://www.nytimes.com/2020/07/16/us/minnesota-state-fair-butter-sculpture.html.

165 **Frankland:** Evan Andrews, "5 Would-Be U.S. States," History.com, August 28, 2012, updated August 22, 2018, https://www.history.com/news/5-would-be-u-s-states.

165 **Kennedy Space Center:** "3-2-1, Call Cape Canaveral," *The New York Times*, November 23, 1999, https://www.nytimes.com/1999/11/23/science/3-2-1-call-cape-canaveral.html.

165 **It was illegal to get a tattoo:** "State Last to Legalize Tattoo Artists, Parlors," *Chicago Tribune*, May 11, 2006, https://www.chicagotribune.com/news/ct-xpm-2006-05-11-0605110139-story.html.

165 **Red Bull has paid out more than $13 million:** K. Thor Jensen, "Red Bull Paying Out to Customers Who Thought Energy Drink Would Actually Give Them Wings," *Newsweek*, August 22, 2019, https://www.newsweek.com/red-bull-lawsuit-canada-1455780.

165 **You can't force a monkey to smoke:** Larry Holzwarth, "These Are Some of the Craziest Laws in the United States, as Well as Some That Were Totally Made Up," History Collection, February 17, 2019, https://historycollection.com/these-are-some-of-the-craziest-laws-in-the-united-states-and-some-that-were-totally-made-up/6/.

165 **Cap'n Crunch because there were no berries:** "Woman Sues Cap'n Crunch Because 'Crunchberries' Are Not Fruit," Legal Info, August 11, 2009, http://www.legalinfo.com/legal-news/woman-sues-capn-crunch-because-crunch berries-are-not-fruit.html.

165 **Sharing your Netflix password is illegal:** Suzanne Choney, "Share Netflix in Tennessee, Go to Jail," *Today*, June 2, 2011, https://www.today.com/money /share-netflix-tennessee-go-jail-1C8368478.

165 **God cannot hold copyrights:** Matthew Sparkes, "Monkeys, Ghosts and Gods 'Cannot Own Copyright' Says US," *The Telegraph*, August 2014, https://www .telegraph.co.uk/technology/news/11048695/Monkeys-ghosts-and-gods -cannot-own-copyright-says-US.html.

165 **It's illegal to frown at a cop:** Kris Seals, "Weird Laws," NJ.com, November 15, 2010, updated January 18, 2019, https://www.nj.com/newark/krisseals/2010 /11/weird_laws.html.

165 **In Gainesville, Georgia, it's illegal to eat:** Jessica Jordan, "Visitor Arrested for Eating Chicken with Fork," *The Gainesville Times*, updated July 20, 2009, https:// www.gainesvilletimes.com/news/visitor-arrested-for-eating-chicken-with -fork/.

165 **Dominoes on Sundays:** Yehuda Berlinger, "The Truth About Dominoes on Sunday in Alabama," Purple Pawn, July 28, 2020, http://www.purplepawn.com /2008/07/the-truth-about-dominoes-on-sunday-in-alabama/.

165 **Everyone take a bath:** "Criminal Justice Resources: The Top 50 Strangest Laws," Criminal Justice Degree Schools, October 14, 2020, https://www.criminaljustice degreeschools.com/criminal-justice-resources/criminal-justice-resources-the-top -50-strangest-laws/.

Crazy but True

167 **Birthday Paradox:** Science Buddies, "Probability and the Birthday Paradox," *Scientific American*, March 29, 2012, https://www.scientificamerican.com/arti cle/bring-science-home-probability-birthday-paradox/.

168 **It likely rains diamonds:** James Morgan, "'Diamond Rain' Falls on Saturn and Jupiter," BBC News, October 14, 2013, https://www.bbc.com/news/science -environment-24477667.

168 **Lost her wedding ring:** "Woman Finds Long-Lost Diamond Ring on Carrot in Garden," BBC News, August 16, 2017, https://www.bbc.com/news/world-us -canada-40956139.

168 **293 ways to make change for a dollar:** "Frank Morgan's Math Chat—293 Ways to Make Change for a Dollar," Mathematical Association of America, April 19, 2001, https://www.maa.org/frank-morgans-math-chat-293-ways-to-make -change-for-a-dollar.

168   **The 9 Nanas:** Olivia Fleming, "'Not Even Our Husbands Knew!' The Women Who Have Been Secretly Delivering Cakes to Underprivileged Families for over 30 Years," *Daily Mail*, June 22, 2012, updated June 25, 2012, https://www.daily mail.co.uk/femail/article-2162905/West-Tennessee-women-secretly-delivering -cakes-underprivileged-families-30-YEARS.html.

168   **Banana trees aren't trees:** Andrew Mach and Carey Reed, "8 Things You Didn't Know About Bananas," PBS.org, January 24, 2016, https://www.pbs.org/news hour/nation/8-things-you-didnt-know-about-bananas.

168   **Spanish Flu of 1918:** Bradford Betz, "NJ Woman, 107, Has Survived Coronavirus and Spanish Flu in Her Lifetime: Report," Fox News, August 11, 2020, https:// www.foxnews.com/us/nj-woman-107-survived-coronavirus-spanish-flu.

168   **Pandora opens a jar:** Stefan Andrews, "Evil Emerged from Pandora's Jar, Not Box as We've Believed, And It Might Be the Fault of Erasmus," *The Vintage News*, January 23, 2018, https://www.thevintagenews.com/2018/01/23/pandoras-box/.

168   **No woman has ever walked:** Paul Rincon, "Nasa Outlines Plan for First Woman on Moon by 2024," BBC News, September 22, 2020, https://www.bbc.com/news /science-environment-54246485.

168   **Don't use the metric system:** Katharina Buchholz, "Only Three Countries in the World (Officially) Still Use the Imperial System," Statista, June 6, 2019, https://www.statista.com/chart/18300/countries-using-the-metric-or-the -imperial-system/.

168   **"There is no news":** "'There Is No News': What a Change from 1930 to Today," BBC News, April 18, 2017, https://www.bbc.com/news/entertainment-arts-39633603.

169   **Stressing about your student loans:** Terrell Jermaine Starr, "Obama: Michelle and I Just Paid Off Our Student Loans 8 Years Ago," NewsOne, April 25, 2012, https://newsone.com/2004456/obama-student-loans/.

169   **Universe was created in a three-minute span:** Bryson, *A Short History of Nearly Everything*.

169   **Pepto-Bismol:** Anne Helmenstine, "How to Extract Bismuth from Pepto Bismol," Science Notes, May 14, 2020, updated August 1, 2020, https://science notes.org/how-to-extract-bismuth-from-pepto-bismol.

169   **Before bumper stickers:** Sean Winters, "Fun Facts about Bumper Stickers on Cars," Prime Insurance, https://www.primeins.com/insurance-news/fun-facts -about-bumper-stickers-on-cars.

169   **John Wilkes Booth's brother:** "Robert Lincoln's Life Saved by Edwin Booth," *The New York Times*, April 11, 1937, https://www.nytimes.com/1937/04/11 /archives/robert-lincolns-life-saved-by-edwin-booth.html.

169   **Fold American paper currency:** Cindy Perman, "10 Things You Probably Don't Know About Money," CNBC, February 1, 2011, updated September 13, 2013, https://www.cnbc.com/2011/02/01/10-Things-You-Probably-Dont-Know -About-Money.html.

169 **Pulverize a sea sponge:** "Sponge Reaggregation," Evopalaeo, YouTube, https://www.youtube.com/watch?v=N462jZFr13k.

169 **His mental illness disappeared:** "Brain Wound Eliminates Man's Mental Illness," *The New York Times*, February 25, 1988, https://www.nytimes.com/1988/02/25/us/brain-wound-eliminates-man-s-mental-illness.html.

169 **Great pyramids of Giza:** Chris Baraniuk, "Why Do We Still Not Know What's Inside the Pyramids?," BBC, November 13, 2015, https://www.bbc.com/future/article/20151113-why-do-we-still-not-know-whats-inside-the-pyramids.

169 **Life insurance from vending machines:** Jill Gregorie, "A Look Back: Whatever Happened to Airport Insurance Vending Machines?," Insurance Business America, May 27, 2015, https://www.insurancebusinessmag.com/us/news/breaking-news/a-look-back-whatever-happened-to-airport-insurance-vending-machines-22593.aspx.

169 **Fidget spinner was patented:** "Fidget Spinners Were Invented to Bring Peace to Middle East but Haven't Made Their Creator a Penny," *The Independent*, June 27, 2017, https://www.independent.co.uk/news/world/middle-east/fidget-spinners-middle-east-peace-inventor-creator-name-profit-craze-trend-novelty-a7810516.html.

170 **Metal is odorless:** Philip Ball, "A 'Metallic' Smell Is Just Body Odour," *Nature*, October 25, 2006, https://www.nature.com/news/2006/061023/full/061023-7.html.

170 **Neil Armstrong:** James R. Hansen, *First Man: The Life of Neil A. Armstrong* (New York: Simon & Schuster, 2005).

170 **Man in Nepal:** "Man in Nepal Can Lick His Own Forehead," *New York Post*, December 3, 2018, https://nypost.com/video/man-in-nepal-can-lick-his-own-forehead/.

170 **Retrieved during a colonoscopy:** Anne Thomas, "Woman Swallows $5,000 Diamond: Has Colonoscopy to Recover Precious Rock (VIDEO)," *The Christian Post*, April 25, 2013, https://www.christianpost.com/trends/woman-swallows-5000-diamond-has-colonoscopy-to-recover-precious-rock-video.html.

170 **"Buttload" is a real weight unit:** "How Much Is a Buttload of Wine?," Ever Wonder Wine, October 6, 2017, https://www.everwonderwine.com/blog/2017/10/6/how-much-is-a-buttload-of-wine.

170 **Cricket chirps in fifteen seconds:** Catherine Boeckmann, "Predict the Temperature with Cricket Chirps," The Old Farmer's Almanac, July 15, 2020, https://www.almanac.com/content/predict-temperature-cricket-chirps.

170 **Struck by a meteorite:** Chelsea Gohd, "How a Meteorite Ruined an Alabama Woman's Afternoon 65 Years Ago," Space.com, November 30, 2019, https://www.space.com/meteorite-hit-alabama-woman-65-years-ago.html.

170 **"Zombie preparedness":** "Zombie Preparedness," Centers for Disease Control and Prevention, https://www.cdc.gov/cpr/zombie/index.htm.

170 **Carl Sagan said marijuana inspired:** Achenbach, "Why Carl Sagan Is Truly Irreplaceable."

171 **Mars, sunsets are blue:** "What Makes Skies Blue . . . or Red?," NBC News, February 8, 2005, http://www.nbcnews.com/id/3077395/ns/technology _and_science-science/t/what-makes-skies-blue-or-red/#.X4BZry9h10s.

171 **Carrots into wet cement:** Joe Quirke, "Carrots Make Concrete Stronger, Study Finds," *Global Construction Review*, July 25, 2018, https://www.globalconstruc tionreview.com/news/carrots-make-concrete-stronger-study-finds/.

171 **Play-Doh:** Curiosity, "Play-Doh Was Originally Supposed to Clean Your Walls," *Chicago Tribune*, December 31, 2015, https://www.chicagotribune.com/redeye /redeye-the-surprising-history-of-playdoh-20151231-story.html.

171 **Velma Thomas:** Gigi Stone et al., "Doctor Calls Near-Death Experience a 'Mira-cle,'" ABC News, April 15, 2009, https://abcnews.go.com/GMA/story?id=4923 465&page=1.

171 **Viruses can catch other viruses:** Jason Socrates Bardi, "Even Viruses Catch Viruses," Live Science, September 28, 2008, https://www.livescience.com/2908 -viruses-catch-viruses.html.

171 *La Bougie du Sapeur:* Eleanor Beardsley, "For Leap Day Only, a Rare Newspaper Goes to Print," *Morning Edition*, NPR, February 29, 2012, https://www.npr.org /2012/02/29/147572689/for-leap-day-only-a-rare-newspaper-goes-to-print.

171 **IKEA bed:** Dino Grandoni, "One in Ten Europeans Were Conceived in IKEA Beds," *The Atlantic*, September 27, 2011, https://www.theatlantic.com/interna tional/archive/2011/09/one-ten-europeans-were-conceived-ikea-beds/33 7380/.

171 **550 people have traveled to space:** Oliver Holmes, "Space: How Far Have We Gone—and Where Are We Going?," *The Guardian*, November 19, 2018, https:// www.theguardian.com/science/2018/nov/19/space-how-far-have-we-gone-and -where-are-we-going.

171 **Buzz Aldrin's mom's last name:** "Buzz Aldrin Biography (1930–)," Biography, April 11, 2018, updated November 12, 2019, https://www.biography.com/astro naut/buzz-aldrin.

171 **Their wings became interlocked:** Martin Chalakoski, "In 1940 Two Twin-Engine Airplanes Collided Mid-Air–Interlocked, They Flew for Five Miles and Landed Safely," *The Vintage News*, May 18, 2018, https://www.thevintagenews .com/2018/05/18/1940-brocklesby-mid-air-collision/.

171 **Blow bubbles when it's below 32 degrees:** "Blowing Frozen Bubbles— Minnesota Cold (Part 4)," Minnesota Cold, YouTube, https://www.youtube .com/watch?v=OM9WXrGftXE.

172 **Mel Blanc:** Paul Feldman, "From the Archives: Mel Blanc Dies; Gave Voice to Cartoon World," *Los Angeles Times*, July 11, 1989, https://www.latimes.com /local/obituaries/archives/la-me-mel-blanc-19890711-20160706-snap-story .html.

172   **Raindrops aren't tear-shaped:** "Are Raindrops Shaped Like Teardrops?," U.S. Department of the Interior, USGS.gov, https://www.usgs.gov/special-topic /water-science-school/science/are-raindrops-shaped-teardrops?qt-science_cen ter_objects=0#qt-science_center_objects.

172   **Explored only about 5 percent of the world's oceans:** Sarah Emerson, "Why Haven't We Explored the Ocean Like Outer Space?," *Vice*, June 18, 2016, https:// www.vice.com/en_us/article/pgk3z9/why-havent-we-explored-the-ocean -like-outer-space.

172   **Sixty-nine babies:** Adam Hadhazy, "Did One Woman Really Give Birth to 69 Children?," BBC, October 20, 2015, https://www.bbc.com/future/article/2015 1020-did-one-woman-really-give-birth-to-69-children.

172   **Opera house on the U.S.-Canada border:** "Did You Know There's an Opera House Where the Stage and Audience Are in Different Nations?," World Atlas, https://www.worldatlas.com/articles/did-you-know-there-s-an-opera-house -where-the-stage-and-audience-are-in-different-nations.html.

172   **Teleportation exists:** Kenneth Chang, "Scientists Teleport Not Kirk, but an Atom," *The New York Times*, June 17, 2004, https://www.nytimes.com/2004 /06/17/us/scientists-teleport-not-kirk-but-an-atom.html.

172   **UPS trucks don't make left-hand turns:** Joel Lovell, "Left-Hand-Turn Elimina- tion," *The New York Times Magazine*, December 9, 2007, https://www.nytimes .com/2007/12/09/magazine/09left-handturn.html.

172   **Hiccups for sixty-eight years:** "In Pictures: Guinness Medical Record Break- ers," BBC News, http://news.bbc.co.uk/2/shared/spl/hi/pop_ups/05/health _guinness_medical_record_breakers/html/2.stm.

172   **Fire hydrant patent:** "Who Invented the Fire Hydrant?," World Atlas, https:// www.worldatlas.com/articles/who-invented-the-fire-hydrant.html.

172   **Twenty-one seconds:** Patricia J. Yang et al., "Duration of Urination Does Not Change with Body Size," Proceedings of the National Academy of Sciences of the United States of America, June 26, 2014, reprinted by PNAS, August 19, 2014, https://www.pnas.org/content/111/33/11932.

172   **Family in Italy that doesn't feel pain:** Matthew Shaer, "The Family That Feels Almost No Pain," *Smithsonian Magazine*, May 2019, https://www.smithsonian mag.com/science-nature/family-feels-almost-no-pain-180971915/.

173   **We don't actually swallow eight spiders:** Annie Sneed, "Fact or Fiction?: People Swallow 8 Spiders a Year While They Sleep," *Scientific American*, April 15, 2014, https://www.scientificamerican.com/article/fact-or-fiction-people-swallow -8-spiders-a-year-while-they-sleep1/.

173   **Nixon's signature is on a plaque:** Robert Z. Pearlman, "Richard Nixon's Apollo 11 Artifacts on Display at Presidential Library," Space.com, May 6, 2019, https:// www.space.com/apollo-11-artifacts-nixon-presidential-library.html.

173   **Wedding veil that was more than sixty-three football fields long:** Connie Suggitt, "Bride's Dream Comes True with Wedding Veil That's Longer Than 63

Football Fields," Guinness World Records, February 11, 2019, https://www.guin
nessworldrecords.com/news/2019/2/brides-dreams-comes-true-with
-wedding-veil-thats-longer-than-63-football-fields/.

173 **You're as old as the universe:** Peter Tyson, "The Star in You," *NOVA*, PBS.org,
December 2, 2010, https://www.pbs.org/wgbh/nova/article/star-in-you/.

173 **If the sun exploded:** Neel V. Patel, "If the Sun Explodes, We'll Have Just Enough
Time to Scream," *Inverse*, October 28, 2016, https://www.inverse.com/article
/22816-if-the-sun-exploded-would-we-see-it-supernova-apocalypse.

173 **Black boxes:** Daniel Engber, "Who Made That Black Box?," *The New York Times
Magazine*, April 4, 2014, https://www.nytimes.com/2014/04/06/magazine
/who-made-that-black-box.html.

173 **Twins do not have matching fingerprints:** Anahad O'Connor, "The Claim:
Identical Twins Have Identical Fingerprints," *The New York Times*, November 2,
2004, https://www.nytimes.com/2004/11/02/health/the-claim-identical
-twins-have-identical-fingerprints.html.

173 **Thirteen astrological signs:** Gina Vivinetto, "Your Life Is a Lie: The Zodiac Has
Changed—Here's Your (New?) Sign," *Today*, September 26, 2016, https://www
.today.com/popculture/your-life-lie-zodiac-has-changed-here-s-your-new
-t103295.

174 **Astronauts are 3 percent taller:** "Station Spinal Ultrasounds Seeking Why
Astronauts Grow Taller in Space," NASA, January 2, 2013, https://www.nasa
.gov/mission_pages/station/research/news/spinal_ultrasound.html.

174 **The biggest snowflake ever:** William J. Broad, "Snowflakes as Big as Frisbees?,"
The New York Times, March 20, 2007, https://www.nytimes.com/2007/03/20
/science/20snow.html?pagewanted=all.

174 **Monopoly money:** Cindy Perman, "10 Things You Probably Don't Know About
Money," CNBC, February 1 2011, updated September 13 2013, https://www
.cnbc.com/2011/02/01/10-Things-You-Probably-Dont-Know-About-Money
.html.

174 **Portuguese artistocrat who didn't have family:** Patrick Jackson, "Where
There's a Will There's a Whim," BBC News, January 17, 2007, http://news.bbc
.co.uk/2/hi/europe/6268015.stm.

174 **No one knows who named Earth:** Rachael Bletchly, "63 QI Facts to Stop You
in Your Tracks—from the New Book by Hit BBC Trivia Team," *Mirror*, October 18,
2018, https://www.mirror.co.uk/news/weird-news/63-qi-facts-stop-you-13
435563.

ABOUT THE AUTHOR

Emily Winter is a comedian from Chicago who's written for the NPR trivia/comedy show *Ask Me Another*, *The New Yorker*, *The New York Times*, Nickelodeon, TV Land, Fusion TV, *The Barnes & Noble Review*, and *Glamour* and is a former editorial director of SparkNotes.com. Her stand-up comedy plays on SiriusXM, and she hosts the podcast *Comedians with Ghost Stories*. She lives for beach volleyball, karaoke, and eating cheese in the great state of Wisconsin. Is this starting to sound like a dating profile? Oh well. Emily resides in Brooklyn with her husband, Chris, and dog, Bingo. She can be found on Twitter and Instagram @EmilyMcWinter.